Thank You

Always Know Where You're At

180 Degrees from Prison to Hope

Hamin H. Rashada

The opinions expressed in this manuscript are solely the opinions of the author and do not represent the opinions or thoughts of the publisher. The author has represented and warranted full ownership and/or legal right to publish all the materials in this book.

Always Know Where You're At
180 Degrees from Prison to Hope
All Rights Reserved.
Copyright © 2012 Hamin H. Rashada
v2.0

Cover Photo © 2012 JupiterImages Corporation. All rights reserved - used with permission.

This book may not be reproduced, transmitted, or stored in whole or in part by any means, including graphic, electronic, or mechanical without the express written consent of the publisher except in the case of brief quotations embodied in critical articles and reviews.

Outskirts Press, Inc.
http://www.outskirtspress.com

ISBN: 978-1-4787-2078-2

Outskirts Press and the "OP" logo are trademarks belonging to Outskirts Press, Inc.

PRINTED IN THE UNITED STATES OF AMERICA

Dedication

I would like to dedicate this work to my mom, my wife, and my sons. They all did more than they'll ever know to help me through what was probably the most difficult period of my life. My mom made a journey with me that few, if any, will ever understand! Even when life itself seemed to have turned its back on me, she was there! It was her mother who told me that it is alright not to know because one day I'll understand; and man ole days how right she was! As for my wife, I'll tell no one that I made things easy for her! She held on to promises and dreams when obstacles seemed insurmountable; but she held on! She could have chosen to run, but she stood. I am afraid of where life would have taken me had she not been there; had she not chosen to hold on to the dignity of marriage. In her strength, there is softness about her. It might be a man thing, being difficult to admit, but for the record, I'm very proud and appreciative of my wife. Where might I be were it not for her dedication? We have many years together; she's my shining star! When it comes to my sons, they went through many changes as kids. To say they had it easy would be a wrong conclusion on my part. In spite of it all, they grew, and life unfolded for them. Each with different personalities, they stumbled and struggled, showing and teaching me much. They each had a way about them; handling feelings, some good, some bad; my love for them is as such that I find it hard to explain. I'll just say I wish I could have done more of what fathers who really understand do!

Table of Contents

Introduction vii
Chapter 1 The Worst Day of My Life 1
Chapter 2 The Ultimatum 4
Chapter 3 Initiation Layover 15
Chapter 4 The Last Stronghold 34
Chapter 5 Blood and Agony 58
Chapter 6 Unexpected Destination on D Block 69
Chapter 7 Nurse Johnston is No Lightweight 98
Chapter 8 How Long Will This Keep Going On? 118
Chapter 9 The Home Plate Umpire 152
Chapter 10 Transferred and a Return to a Calling 194
Afterword 238

Introduction

AMERICA, LAND OF the free! New York, however international, is like yet unlike any place in the world. Crime with stories; criminals with history! It's Baby-face Nelson, it's Al Capone, Fat Cats, it's Jr. Lamb with his flesh-rotted-maggot infested arm; and the medical association offering to pay him for the rights to bring medical minds together to explain how this rotten medical mystery could possibly be alive, and still of (seemingly) sound mind!

MURDER is a crime with a story, with a history so thorough, so complete, that it takes you all the way back to its etymology! Humanity's first crime! Its first criminal! Humanity's first victim! How many people know or even care to know the name of the first murderer of a man, and that a bird showed the murderer what to do with his victim? Cain killed Abel in a plot of envy! Two sons of Adam and Eve, and a crime, a history, a BIBLE story to be read and taken for all time!!

This writing, "Always Know Where You're At", and the story of Cain and Abel have something in common; neither would be, were it not for a choice made by homo sapiens (a thinking mind), a human being! The self interest of Cain resulted in the murder of his brother! The self interest of a chief of police and a Yonkers Police Department resulted in the crucifixion of the past, of a young man and his mother; A crucifixion that has continued its agonizing anguish forty years later, and will continue for many years into the future. Since the very first criminal (a murderer); since the first crime (murder); criminals have come and gone. But since times beginning, has anyone ever told about the making of a criminal? Has an indictment ever been put against a chief of police and/or the police department of a city, and placed before the world to read? I will take you on a journey upon which few human beings have ever gone; or will ever go! What makes this book all the more gripping, breathtaking is that it's true. I'm telling you the truth; and nothing but the truth! I will take you where the writer of "NEW JACK" was probably unable to take you. Being a Correctional Officer is different than being a PRISONER in every sense of the word! The New York State Department of Correctional Services is arguably the most involved, most in depth Prison System in America and possibly across the globe! By the time I left NYSDOCS on parole in 1982, and went back into the same NYSDOCS, "employed" as a Chaplain in 1996", it had increased by another forty prisons or more. What one manages to learn about life while graduating from one of the world's most famous universities, has a lot to do with whether or not he lives through it! Having been there, done that, "nobody" would have ever made me believe I'd meet state employees more devious, cut-throat and hypocritical, than most of the prisoners I'd encountered as a prisoner myself!

1

The Worst Day of My Life

I HAD GONE to the store on Ashburton Ave, in Yonkers, to get something for my mother's lunch. Just as I crossed the street from the store, a police car passed. Like numerous other times, the car would screech to a stop; the police car backed up, and the police jumped out after me! This night, one of the policemen called my last name and yelled halt! halt! as I ran across a lot, then to the stairs leading to the aqueduct! I dropped the bag with my mom's lunch as I ran down the stairs! The aqueduct was pitch dark; making it almost impossible to see! I'd gone up and down those stairs numerous times. I'd walked the aqueduct for years. I had no problem with the dark. As I ran, suddenly I heard shots ring out; pow, pow, pow; Stop or I'll shoot! Being shot at so-many times in the pitch darkness, I wondered how many more times was this cop going to miss me!? I let out a sound (uuuhhh) like I'd been shot, just as I heard the second of three shots! It worked, the shooting stopped! But, there should be an obvious and immediate question! Why were shots being fired? Had the cop firing the shots, taken a different course related to firing his pistol? Shoot first, mention stop later. I wasn't threatening and had no weapon of any kind! I was trying to make it to the safety of home before I got shot to death!

Just as I made it to the front porch, a police car ran onto the sidewalk, blocking the steps! The alley way leading to the back porch was my only option. I ran into the alley and up the first steps, when I heard: "Take another step, nigger, I'll blow your fucking brains out!" As I turned to come off of the porch, the cop tripped me, causing me to fall to the ground. By that time there were six policemen in the backyard, stomping and kicking, kicking and stomping me! Being in the backyard of an apartment building of five other families, I started screaming for help! Maaaaa! Bunny (my sister) help! Mr. Williams, Mr. Jackson, Mrs. Smith help! Maaaaa help! Bunny, help me! Bunny help! Help! Lights came on, and along with my mom and sister, all the other tenants stood looking on as the police dogs (policemen/cops) became all the more brazen! I heard my sister scream out, "Maaaa they're gonna kill him!" They're trying to kill my brother! My sister ran down the stairs and into some of the policemen; trying to do something to help me! She was knocked to the ground by at least one cop who looked at her, called her a bitch, and threatened to split her fucking skull if she put her hands on him again! The only other voice I really heard was that of our mother's. She was standing helplessly on the 2nd floor of a back porch looking at her two children being bludgeoned, stomped, and kicked! It must be assumed that at some point these sadistic minded police dogs eventually paid attention to all of the possible witnesses standing on the porch; they stopped! The police dragged me down the alley and to one of about half a dozen police cars, and threw me into the back seat! With one of my legs still dangling out of the car, one of the cops slammed the car door on it three times before he pushed my leg into the car! I had been beaten so badly that the police had no choice but to take me to the emergency room!

Having had a number of x-rays taken, I was lying there with my mother standing by the examination table with me; one of the cops walks into the examining room. That animal steps over to the bed; opens his right hand; in it were six spent shells! What this cop would say next, no sound minded human being would guess! He looks at me; whom he and his fellow cops had almost beaten to death; He says: "You see these, you black bastard, pointing at the shell casings, I have to pay for these, but, if I were standing over your stinking body, I wouldn't mind having to pay for them!" My mother was standing there; she let out an unusual gasping sound and collapsed to the floor! For years there was S.S., a black detective who'd played a major role in the crucifixion of my mother and me! Just as the cop holding the shell casings made the last part of his cold, calloused hearted comment, S.S. was standing there. S.S. was picking my mother up off of the floor when he said to the cop: "If you don't get your pale-white ass out of here I will break this size 14 off in your ass up to my fucking knee! What the fuck is wrong with you, huh? Are you trying to kill this woman?" That night, my mother was being resuscitated and given oxygen in one room; and I in another room was awaiting x-ray results before being taken to jail "again" like many times before!

2 | The Ultimatum

"**MRS. TARVER, YOU'RE** going to be sorry you wouldn't let your son cooperate with us!" This statement began the threat made by the illustrious police chief of the City of Yonkers. It began early one morning on a day that for most young men marks a high point in life; but for me, it would prove to be anything but that; it would prove to be the beginning of my real education...

I was sixteen years old, and ending a summer in which I'd worked, doing home improving with a friend of my mother. There were days when I'd work from 7:00 in the morning to 7:00 in the evening, doing everything from demolition to painting houses. The work was dirty and hard, but paid $350.00 per week. With no bills to pay it was great! My mother didn't ask me for anything, so my money was just that, my money. For 2 ½ months I slaved and saved so I'd be able to get myself ready for school (my first day of high school). Back then, there was a fashion that had been created by black, street youth. Oooohh man, you should have seen the wardrobe I'd put together! I'm talking about this naive kid who'd only six months ago managed to get his first pair of CONVERSE SNEAKERS! I bought Italian knit shirts ($45.00 to $75.00), Alpaca Shirts ($150.00), tailor made pants ($60.00 to $90.00), snake, lizard, alligator, turtle shoes

($95.00 to $135.00) per pair. When the sun rose on my first day of high school, I was ready! Trying this, that and the other thing on, I'd spent hours the night before, mixing and matching, styling and profiling! Since my mom was working nights at Cabrini Nursing Home, I got myself up and got ready for my first day of new hallways, stairs, students, teachers, etc. My mom and I lived in a railroad apartment. You could stand in the kitchen, and see straight through to the living room. As always, I took the dogs (two mean dogs) down and chained them up in the back yard for them to go to do whatever they had to do. Before leaving for the day, I would always bring one of them back inside. But this particular morning, I had other things on my mind; my first day of high school! I went off to school and did not bring one of the dogs (Prince or King), inside.

When I returned home from school, I tried to unlock the door, but it swung open. I dismissed it saying to myself, wow, my mom must've really been tired when she came in! I entered, closing the door behind me; going on to my bedroom which was the first room after the kitchen. I took off my Italian knit shirt to hang it in my closet; but, when I opened the door my closet was empty! I mean every Italian knit, Alpaca, every pair of pants, every pair of shoes (some costing as much as ($135.00), all gone! The only clothes I had to show for 2 ½ months of sweating and working harder than I had ever worked in my life was what I'd worn to school that day. More than $3000.00 worth of clothing gone! My mom and I didn't have anything else of any value in the house. My mom had never even brought anything fancy. She simply worked to make life comfortable; worked to make sure life would simply be day to day for herself and her son; I was so proud of her for that! As far back as I could remember she'd done that. God willing, I will share my childhood, my growing up, with you some day. But for now, I'll just say when I was growing up she'd tell everybody: "My two kids, I've always put them right here (gesturing to her bosom), here I can keep the cold world away from them!" After the painful reality of what had actually happened set in, I went and set on the front porch steps. When my mother came, I got up to give her a hug and a smile, but she pulled back and looked at me. Back then she called me Anton. For a few seconds, she looked at me then said; Anton, what's wrong! I don't remember answering; just hunched my shoulders and tried to smile. When we got upstairs, I showed her my closet. She stood for a moment, then turned and looked at me. Anton, Anton, where are your clothes! What happened to your clothes Anton?! What did you do with all of your clothes?! I looked at her and hunched my shoulders, but my mom still didn't seem to understand. As she looked at me for a few seconds, the empty expression on my face, things must've become clear. As she stepped towards me, she whispered; Oh Anton! Oh Anton, mommy's sorry, mommy's so sorry!

   I can remember my mother very clearly in my life since age four, and I can't remember seeing her look so helpless! Like I said, she'd proudly tell anyone; my children, I put them right here (gesturing to her bosom) to protect them from hurt, I put them right here! But, something had happened that she could not absorb for me! After asking me the normal questions such as, who do you think it was; how did they know I wasn't home? Do you think it was so and so, etc; we sat and talked about what we should do. There my mom and I sat, having made a decision to do something for a reason few other than black people in our neighborhood ever have to consider! My mom was calling the police to tell them her residence had been burglarized! My mother had made a decision to do what thousands upon thousands of people do every hour of every day of the year. My mother called the police! See, you could do such a thing in this country because this is America. You could call the police in this country and not fear it! Before she called the police, I looked under my bed and got the box with the receipts for all the clothes taken by whoever had broken in. We didn't know whether to show the police all or just a few of the receipts, so we left the box on the table for them to see whatever they wanted. It seemed like my mom had just called them, but they were already knocking on the door.

Though we were sitting at the kitchen table waiting for the police to come, when they knocked at the door my mom and I just sat there and looked at each other. Who is it? Officer so and so and officer so and so; did you call about a burglary? I opened the door and they came in; but there was an attitude, a manner, even a body language about them! As they came in, my mother was sitting at the kitchen table. One of them kept walking on into my bedroom; the other stopped and stood in the kitchen saying nothing. The one who'd walked on into my bedroom stopped just between my bedroom and my mother's. No questions had been asked about anything, but like I'd said, one of the policemen was now standing in the doorway to my mother's bedroom. Why? It wasn't until my mother spoke up and asked whether anyone wanted to know what had happened, what had been taken that it was asked; Mrs. Tarver, what, if anything was taken? The manner of the question made my mother angry, which I'm certain could be heard in her voice. The first policeman came out of the bedroom, and asked if I could give a description of some of the items taken. As I did so, I began handing them different receipts for clothing items being named. The looks they gave as they looked at the receipts, then back and forth at each other, had nothing to do with concern for the burglary itself, I don't think! After a few moments of looking at the receipts, passing them back and forth, one of the officers excused himself stating he had to contact headquarters. In a few moments, he returned, whispered something to the other officer, picked up some of the receipts and began looking at them again. During this time, they seemed to be taking notes about the receipts; but they never asked any questions; none!

About fifteen minutes after returning from contacting headquarters, there was a knock on the door. The knock was more like a banging; it actually caused my mother to jump; the knock on the door was just that aggressive! Before my mother or I could respond, the officer who'd gone down to the patrol car opened the door. Standing there were four men in suits (two detectives, a Lt, and a Chief of Police)! Without saying a word, the Police Chief, the Lt, and the two detectives enter. My mother and I seldom experienced calling the police to report being victims of a burglary; so having half the police department responding to our call didn't seem strange. It wasn't long before we found out what it was that warranted such a heavy response. Never introducing himself, the police chief asked: What's this about clothes being stolen? No televisions, stereo units, silver, gold, china, diamonds, furs; nothing like that? Somebody just broke into this, broke in here and took (pause) clothes?! The officer who'd gone out earlier to make a call (obviously this call) said; Sir, here are a few of the receipts that I...The chief interrupts and says something to the effect, oh so you make a habit of keeping your clothes receipts! I doubt it; but perhaps it's fear of this type of treatment which had us (African Americans) unwilling to call the police. By this time, my mother was annoyed! I called you people because somebody broke-in and took my son's clothes; you haven't asked a single question about them yet!

At that point, the chief took the receipts from the officer; looking at the receipts, he did a double take! Why in the hell would you buy clothes like this living here?! How can you explain being able to pay what these clothes cost?! What kind of work could you possibly be doing to afford these prices? Let me rephrase that: There's only one thing you could be doing to afford these prices! He looks around the kitchen, looking at the other officers; what kind of work do you think he's doing to afford Italian knit shirts, $150.00 alpaca sweaters, alligator skin, snake skin, lizard skin or turtle shell shoes, et cetera? Take one guess; I'll give you one guess! Shit, Frank Sinatra can't afford these prices!! My mother spoke up and said; he worked this summer and saved his money because he knew I wouldn't be able to afford what he wanted! I'm proud of him, I'm really proud of him! Like I said, Frank Sinatra can't afford these prices! What are you doing huh, selling dope!? Huh, is that what you people call work?! He reaches into his inside jacket pocket takes out an envelope and tosses it on the table. Know anyone in any of these pictures? Not even taking a look at the pictures, I said no. The chief gestured to the detective who stepped to the table, picked up the envelope, and spread the pictures out in front of me. He began pointing at one picture, then another; who's this; how bout this guy? Who do we have here (pointing at me in one of the pictures)? It was a picture of me standing in Doyle Park with a few guys I'd play basketball with! One of the pictures showed me either taking or giving something to someone, another one was similar but I was putting something in my pocket! There was nothing illegal being done at all! Across the street from the park, there was a little candy store run by an old man (everyone called him pop). He didn't sell much of anything other than soda, candy, hard ice cream (sold by the scoop, in cups), news papers, chips, cigarettes, et cetera. Summer time, having just played two full court games of ball, everyone was thirsty; one of the brothers opted to buy soda for everyone; so he gave me the money. When I returned there was change, so I returned it. Returning the change meant I had to put my hand into my pocket, take the change out and hand it to the person who'd given money to me. That adage: a picture is worth a thousand words may be true, but nobody has ever said anything about two very important points; those words depend on who it is looking at the picture, and how it's looked at; both have to do with what's said! Case in point, the pictures on my mother's kitchen table; and yes, the C-Cipher-Power (COP) looking at them! They also had pictures of me walking with different individuals of the group they were watching! In all of those pictures, I was shown either carrying my basketball or bouncing it. Who is this person? Who is this?! How about these individuals, and this one, huh?! Oh, I know, I know; I'm just playing basketball with them, right? Right, just playing ball huh?! You might tell her that shit (pointing at my mother) but I'm not stupid; you're not paying my rent!

My mother was shaking badly! She stood up, pushed the Lt. and one of the detectives out of the way and shouted, get the hell out of my house you dirty bastards! If I were a white mother alone and calling you about being burglarized, you white bastards would be trying to move heaven and earth to find out what happened! None of them moved, so she grabbed the chief by the jacket and began screaming. Get out! I said get out! Get the hell out, now! They all stepped out into the hall, as the chief stepped aside, just outside the door; my mother tried to close it; but the Chief of Police put his foot in the doorway! Look, we'll be back, we'll be back, you can count on it! My mother was so stressed after they left her nose began to bleed! I was told later that her nose bleed might have saved her from a stroke (the stress resulting from the police visit must have caused her blood pressure to rise dangerously high)! We talked the next day about what, if anything, we might be able to do; who we might be able to call about what the police department had subjected us to. But everything happened so unexpectedly, neither of us even got a name, a precinct, nothing; we had no information about them at all! Other than we called the police, shortly thereafter two police came and later the Police Chief, a Lt. and two detectives showed up at our door; we knew nothing!

As for the threat made by the chief of police, what were we to make of that!? What was their coming back going to bring? If we tried to tell it, who'd believe it?! By 1:00 pm the afternoon following the burglary and the police visit, my mother was still badly shaken; she called her doctor who told her to come to his office immediately! He did an EKG; whatever the results were, he tried to admit her into St. Josephs Hospital but she wasn't having that, not her. So, he sent her home for bed rest, since she was not going to cooperate with being admitted, unfortunately, what the doctor ordered wasn't going to happen. Those last words by the Chief of Police proved to be more than an empty threat! That night, at around 8:00pm, my mother and I were in the living room watching Mod Squad (It was like I watched this program religiously). Suddenly there was the sound of people coming up the hall stairs, almost like stomping. It was quiet for a few seconds, then, suddenly boom, boom, boom, boom! We looked at each other, but didn't say anything; then my mother said to me, who'd be banging on someone's door like that? Then again, boom, boom, boom, boom, boom, boom! Tarver, open the door; it's the police!

It was no longer a threat, just as he stated before leaving a little more than twenty four hours ago (look, we'll be back), the Chief of Police and the same detectives were once again at our door! Before my mother could say anything, the Police Chief starts by asking if they could please come in for a moment. Mrs. Tarver, what happened to you and your son happened for a reason; we really need to talk to you and your son. This is my first Lt. and two of my primary detectives heading up this assignment; can we come in? That purring like a kitten didn't last but a moment; but he knew it would be necessary to present an affront of humility if he were going to be allowed in again! It worked just long enough to get him in the door, because just as my mother asked what they intended to do about my clothes, wham! One of the detectives presents those same pictures and put them on the table. Mrs. Tarver, we know you're doing the best you can as a single parent trying to raise a son. You can't control everything he does, who he hangs out with! We know you want to believe what he tells you about where he gets all that money he had to have to pay for the clothes that he had receipts for, but Mrs. Tarver look at these pictures; do you know these individuals? We do and so does your son; we want to help your son, but he has to help us! He looks at me and says; don't stand there like you don't know what I'm talking about! What are you doing in this picture and in this one?! Where are you and so and so coming from on this day? Do you think we don't know that you're about the drugs this bunch is selling? When we bust you, and you can bet your life on it we are going to bust mommy's good, hard working son! You can stand there now and lie, but we're right on your ass! Your son is going to go down with the rest of these low life bastards Mrs. Tarver, but he doesn't have to. Are you going to help us or what? Are you going to cooperate with us now while you can or wait until it's too late?

My mother sat there rocking back and forth…What they'd said was actually said in a few minutes. It came across as somewhat of a surprise after hearing the way the chief presented himself when asking if they could come in for a few moments to talk to us. My mother says: My son isn't getting involved in any of your mess, now or later! As calm as one could be she says to the chief: correct me if I'm wrong, you're the Chief of Police? Amuse me for a moment if you can! Picture this being Scarsdale, New York; your precinct receives a call; Hello, I'm calling from Scarsdale; someone has broken into my home… You tell me if that mother would be going through what you've put me through? Cowards, you're cowards! You people make me sick! By now, I bet you would know how many shirts, pants, and everything else the stores have sold like those taken if we were calling you from some rich, white neighborhood! But here it is two days, and you bastards haven't asked a single question yet about my son's things! Instead, you almost send me to the hospital by talking to us like we're dirt; like my rent is being paid by my son selling drugs! When is the last time, no, when is the first time you remember ever acting this way at the door of a white burglary victim? I've always been proud of my mother, but that evening, I was "proud" of my mom! It was that evening I started referring to her as my mama/dad! She got up from the kitchen chair, calmly stepped to the door; opening it she says; not now, but right now get the hell out of my home! Get the hell out now!

That night, that moment, a statement was made by the "Chief of Police," which would attach itself to my existence like a leech! For more years than I care to remember, those words would slowly drain the health, the life out of my mother! One mini undetected stroke at a time would take its toll; a massive stroke would cause her to lie down to never rise to speak, or even smile again! It's almost as though I could say: A more accurate statement has rarely been uttered than the threat made that evening by that police chief of the city of Yonkers; "Mrs. Tarver, you're going to be sorry you wouldn't let your son cooperate with us, because anything that happens in the outlines of Yonkers, from Central Avenue to Warburton Avenue, we're going to pin it on him, unless he in bed sleeping; and he'd better not be sleeping by himself, he'd better be sleeping under you!!

Should a mother or son have had any reason to believe that deciding to call and report the burglary of their residence would cause them to dread another day, or wonder whether or not they'd even see each other alive another evening? Not even their worst nightmare should've caused them to see themselves being the prey of such a predator! After-all, when has America ever been known for such gross injustice meted out against a mother and a son reaching out for help, as victims of a crime have always been able to do? If coming home and finding their residence having been burglarized, and calling their local police department were criminal acts, then yes, we were guilty! But, you know, we know, everyone across the globe knows, that in our land of the free you can search the annals of our great judicial system's history, but will come up empty! No case file, not even in the dead letter/cold case files can be found the crucifixion and castigation of a single mother and a fatherless child! The mother referred to in this travesty of justice, returned to God taking the scars of her crucifixion to her grave! If one wished, and if one were able to resurrect the hospital records of this poor mother, whose only crime was not having a father in the house (if such is a crime), would not find it much of a surprise that her numerous ambulance trips and hospital stays to save her life starting from 1966, coincide with the threat made by the Chief of Police! A threat given life when his police dogs (policemen), were sicced on her and her son! My mother and I had no way of beginning to realize that neither of us really knew what sorry would come to mean...I recall hearing that someone said; a little power corrupts, and absolute power corrupts absolutely! What my mother and I were subjected to at the hands of the Police Department in Yonkers, New York, convinced me that few if any power exist more absolute than the word of a cop!

3

Initiation Layover

COME, LET ME take you on a walk through years of hurt, pain, sorrow, fear, and rape; a walk which will take you into and through the covering up of death, dying and outright "murder"!!

To start our walk, we will go back in time to that threat made by the police chief in the City of Yonkers, N.Y. Neither, my mother nor I (at that time) had any experience with having been arrested; so who would have ever imagined that the words of a frustrated chief would lead me to Sing Sing Prison thirteen years later, the same place that housed individuals such as one convicted for allegedly "murdering Malcolm X" (El Hajj Malik Shabazz)! Know that there is no amount of money, no level of education which one can receive from the world's institutions of learning that could ever prepare one to enter the world of prison…

I was sentenced to 2 1/3 to 7 and 3 to 9 years which I was to serve in the New York State Department of Correctional Services; I was ultimately filtered into that multi-billion dollar business! Yes, Sing Sing initiated me. Sing Sing Prison was only a layover for me until the criminal processing charts showed that it was clear to transfer X number of bodies to Clinton Prison in Dannemora, N.Y. I was in Sing Sings F-Block for about two months. This was probably the most important two months of my entire prison stay, for I would be introduced to the realities of a system, a society of ethics, values, principles and laws all its' own! In spite of the frightening reality, I did not even qualify to be referred to as naive, but an embryo if anything!

My first day in prison would place two tender, young white boys, under my wing. Don't ask me how they got there, but there they were! I'd always taken issue with it being said that I was meant to be followed, and that I had a magnetic personality which seemed to attract people to me; that I was very likeable, et cetera. Whatever truth there may be, it would prove to be a good thing for them that I was there! It may be hard to understand how it was possible for me to take someone under my wing, being like I said, an embryo in the system myself. Perhaps it had something to do with the fact that I am a Muslim, and it was known! Maybe, just maybe, what I was able to get away with this particular day had something to do with the fact that I was a Muslim in a prison wherein one of the individuals convicted for allegedly murdering Malcolm X was doing time. There I was walking two tender looking, young white boys through two months in one of the "world's most infamously legendary prisons," Sing Sing! They had asked me if they could go out to the yard with me when I went. I must've said okay, because I found the three of us not only going to the yard together, but to the cat-walk showering area also. Truthfully speaking, I never gave it a thought; and the last thing on my mind was protecting them! One weekend one of them, Patrick, went on a visit while I was on the flats with another prisoner who'd confided in me about a marital problem he was having. The other young kid didn't know where I was, and managed to get tricked into going to the yard with a booty bandit. I don't know what sent me to the yard without going to look for Matty. In any case, I reached the yard about a minute before I saw him go into the shower area across the far end of the yard. Running across the yard was not allowed; any running in the yard was only allowed if we were running laps. Seeing Matty going into the toilet area is not what made me run across the yard; it was seeing who it was following behind him! He had no clue that he was, of his own free will, on his way to get raped; and probably repeatedly!! If I had to wager on it, I'd be ready to bet all or nothing on him being raped repeatedly! When I reached the area, there was a spot/interceptor at the entrance to the bathroom, and he wasn't going to let me go in. Just as I reached him I said; whas hapnin brother; slapped my right hand to his, put my left hand on his right shoulder like I was going to complete the greeting! Just as I did that, I was able to move him slightly to one side, and enter the toilet area! There were three black prisoners there with Matty. One of them had Matty in a headlock; one had a shank, while the third stood there with a tube of Vaseline, greased and ready to violate a young kid who was bent over with his pants around his ankles! Two of them were from F-Block; the one greased and ready was in population. I had never seen anything like this, though I'd heard tales about it! There I was, standing in the middle of something that shocked the hell out of me! My reaction expressed exactly what I felt; AAAH MAN! AAAHHH! Brothers, what are y'all doin? Yall don't know what y'all gettin ready to do man! Y'all don't wanna do this! The brother from population (prisoner doing his time in Sing Sing) said to me; get the fuck out of here! What the fuck do you care bout dis devil?! The white kid, still standing there with his pants down, didn't know what to do! He tried to say something, when the brother with the shank said; shut the fuck up, think I was playin wit you! I'll leave your white ass layin right here; I don't give a fuck about you or your fuckin life; say something else! I don't know who was more scared, Matty or me! I didn't know what to do, didn't know how something like this played out! For some reason, I said; check dis out, Abdul is waiting for dis kid,(I think I said calmly): You three do whatever you think you wanna answer for; because, dis young brother (referring to Matty) is already part of the Muslim community, under Abdul, because I already told Abdul, that wants him to give him, the Shahada! You understand what I'm sayin ta yall?! (Abdul is the individual who allegedly took part in murdering Malcolm-X)! Nothing was said for a few seconds, (during this time, the one who had the Vaseline, had pulled his pants up) he turns to the one with the shank, and yells at him; what the fuck is wrong with you, stupid mother fucker? All the punk-ass white boys in F-Block, you bring this mother fucker, this mother fucker! He slaps this dude; I mean, the sound might have been heard by the spotter outside the door! The one who'd, been slapped is looking at me; then at the one who'd slapped him! He steps toward the one who had slapped him, and says; you think you bad, huh mother fucker? You in this mother fucker for the same thing I'm in here for! I'ma give you dat one on me, but, (shaking his head from side to side) we ga have some drama up in nis mother fucker, if you ever even make me think you thinkin bout dissin (disrespecting) me again!

People in so-called free society, people who've never had the misfortune of a stay in prison, most likely don't understand one very important factor about prison; prison is also a society. Prison has its own laws, rules, regulations, ethics, morals, principles and values! However unpleasant it may be for our so-called free, hard working, tax-paying citizens to hear; everything witnessed in the convicted criminal society exists in the so called law abiding public; those exact same characteristics roam the streets everyday; reporting to work in every position of responsibility; from the corporate CEO, to the janitor; (law-abiding until they're caught)!

Now, there I was in the middle of a prison situation which

still had the potential of going wrong any second! A number of things had been presented to Matty and I both; what, if anything we extracted from them, were not going to be pointed out to us, as though we'd enrolled in some institution of higher learning in so-called free society! The prisoner from population told Matty; get the fuck out of here; you can thank brother Abdul, that I ain't make you my bitch! Before I could let out a sigh of relief, the one with the shank is still feeling like he needs to establish that he has some power in this situation; so he steps in front of Matty and says: I use to be with the Nation of Islam, and I know they don't accept white people! This stupid nigga might believe that bullshit about the brother waitin for you; but, I'm bustin that ass wide open when you get back to the block! He looks at the prisoner from population (the one who'd slapped him), and says: You ain't runnin a fuckin thing here with me, and I'm hopin ya feel like tryin your luck again! Seeing the one in population just turn and walk out, I didn't have a clue as to what had just happened. The one with the shank and the one who'd had Matty in a headlock, both left out, leaving Matty and I there alone...(Swwuuuhh)! I finally let it out; waiting to exhale is an understatement!!

To answer your question: Was Abdul really waiting to give the young white kid Matty his shahada (the Islamic declaration of faith)? No, it was a statement made in desperation! Walking across the yard, I saw Abdul sitting at his table. I had no idea whether that booty crew was still in the yard; or had gone to their blocks. It was my intention to go and sit with Abdul; so I asked Matty to come with me. In light of what he'd just escaped by a hair, he had no intention of going back to the block, without me. Just as we got (guessing) about five feet from the table area, a couple Muslim, (inmate security) for Abdul; stepped to us, stopping us from getting any closer to the table! One brother asked; what do you want? I responded with As Salaam

Alai- kum Ahki; Abdul acknowledged me, so I went on to the table; but, Matty was stopped and searched! Seeing that the brothers were not going to let him come to the table, I told Abdul that Matty wanted to come to Ju'mah this week to see what it was like. He nodded his head once; one of the brothers walked to the table with him, and stood over him the entire time! It was Ramadan (Islamic Month of Fasting); so, the conversation was about the meal we'd be having that day. Anyone observing would have had no clue, what was being discussed while sitting there. It was clear that he didn't want to have any problems coming in during this month (Ramadan); and he, not be informed! The brother over Muslim security says: It's only because our beloved Imam made arrangements for me to visit F-Block that I'm able to get your name! Do you even know who our beloved Imam is brother? Huh? Do you know who this is standing before you? Do you think the brothers all over the state eat like you've been eating? Oh yeah, they eat, but not like this; not during Ramadan! I'm going to ask you again brother, what's your problem?! The Imam didn't say a word the entire time. He just stood there with his back and one foot against the wall, with his arms folded! I looked at the Imam, then, at the wazir (head) of shurta (security); yes brother, I know who the Imam is, and I also know what he is. When I said that, the Imam stepped away from the wall; the wazir grabbed me and pushed me against the wall; what are you saying brother?!

    The Imam was standing in front of me, and for the first time, that calm, nothing bothers me facial expression was gone! You were asked a question brother, you heard it didn't you?! What do you mean; you also know what I am?! What am I brother?! I don't know what they thought I had on my mind, but I only acknowledged being a fool, not a damn fool! Imam, I've heard you say a few times since I've been here; brothers, I'm an American, my language is English; I'm not an Arab, and don't intend to act like I need to speak somebody else's language to be a Muslim; correct me if I'm wrong. No Imam, you don't have to speak Arabic to be a Muslim, but, we have to follow the traditions and practices of Prophet Muhammad, regardless of who we are! As for me knowing what you are, I know you're Muslim. Imam, I know I'm not telling you or the brother anything you don't know, but, sometimes we lose sight of things, because we're trying to take care of so-many things at the same time. Both of you, trying to stay on top of the activities for our holy month, it's easy to overlook something! Abdul smiled and said to me; take it easy ahki (my brother), what makes you think any of the other brothers are having any problems waiting a few more minutes, for me to get my dinner? What are you trying to prove? Brother, quite a few of the brothers have come to me about wanting to deal, hurt, or shut you up. There are brothers here with me who love me, and do not mind showing it; understand what I'm saying brother?! Leave things alone brother! I can tell certain hot headed brothers not to do anything to you, but, if you're going to keep making a scene, it's on you, brother! Believe me I heard very clearly what Abdul was saying! Imam, don't think I don't appreciate what you've done to get me down here. I don't know what it is, maybe it's all the papers you've written and teach on. Since I've been here, you've given us papers on Gant, Freud, Plato, Aristotle, etc; philosophers and philosophy. I just got here a couple weeks ago; maybe I'll understand things better after I'm here awhile. He put his hand out and greeted me (As-Salaam-Alaikum Ahki); we hugged, then he asked me if I wanted to stay in Sing Sing.

    I didn't know anything about transit, holdovers, movement and control, or anything else related to where I'd ultimately end up, and why. At most, my family would be forty minutes from me, if I am able to do my bid (time) in Sing Sing! After Ramadan ends, the NYSDOCS permits us (the Muslims) imprisoned in its system throughout the state, to further practice our religion, with the observance of Eid-ul-Fitr. This is a feast celebrating the end of the month of fasting (Ramadan), which is marked by the ninth month of the lunar calendar (when Prophet Muhammad began receiving the revelation of Qur'an from Allah! I must say, it seemed to be a more festive celebration, than on the outside! Then, a few weeks after the actual holiday celebration, the state extends a privilege date to us, for a family day event (Post Eid-ul-Fitr Family Day Event)! The Muslim prisoners are allowed to invite outside guest (family and friends); it was a day wherein you'd almost forget you were in prison! There were "special perks" enjoyed by those visited by their wives and/or female friends! During the course of the day, those who were made privy, to the slip away opportunity, were able to do just that; slip away! Such brothers could nonchalantly slip away with, his wife or girl friend; down to where the mosque was located. There was not even the slightest need to concern yourself with privacy, because, "shurta" (Muslim Security) was no joke! Remember, I'm talking about Sing Sing, one of the most renowned prisons in the history of America! Our (Muslim) security was posted in several locations in route to the mosque, with one of the top "Shurta" outside the immediate entrance to the mosque! Imam Abdul would ask me that following Friday after Ju'mah (congregational Prayer), if I'd taken advantage of the opportunity to enjoy some private time with my wife! I smile and told him my wife hadn't come alone; that our two sons had come with her. He smiles and says to me: Ahki (my brother), all you had to do was go to one of the brothers on shurta; they deal with all of that... To say Imam Abdul was set up in Sing Sing, would be like someone saying, Abdul was a lion, a king of the jungle, and all the other animals know it, without doubt! In the couple months in Sing Sing, I witnessed the clout that Abdul had, clout which almost made you tell yourself, he had his own keys... There was one sister, I can't say who she was, but saw him walking to and from with her like they were on a co-ed college campus or something! Oh No, she wasn't a counselor! The administration knew Abdul represented a group of prisoners (inmates) who would have had "no problem" stepping to and bringing closure to a situation! I'd find myself fortunate, to say the least, that such was true! If you were in the yard, in no time, you would notice something different about a particular area just off from the basketball court; there was one table not sat at by anyone. Did you ask why? The Imam was not supposed to have to wait! I don't think prisoners even realized how much they focused on him! There was an invisible barrier, a perimeter which the other prisoners stayed out of... Even though Imam Abdul was no light weight where "martial arts" were concerned; brothers would step to or stop anyone whom they thought might be approaching Imam Abdul too quickly, or if the prisoner was thought to be suspect!

About two weeks before I was shipped out to Clinton Prison, I went out to the yard (on a Sunday), Matty and Patrick had visits. I'd been sitting, looking through the chain link fence, down onto the Hudson River. I had taken a pen and pad with me so I could do some writing, should something come to mind. It was just one of those beautiful days; I'd had but a few since entering Sing Sing. All of us have probably had at least one day like I'm going to share; perhaps not consisting of similar incidents, yet the same. One moment, everything was quiet; sitting, thinking about some pleasantries of days gone by, of days yet to come; if in fact they were meant to be. One moment everything seeming like you don't have a worry, in the world; suddenly... I'd been sitting in the yard about an hour, behind me there were basketball games being played. I get up to get back to the block, but, stop for a moment to watch a few shots. The design for the poles holding the backboards and rims up were not given much thought, to say the least; an accident waiting to happen. It was like I'd thought the incident into reality, because, I'd been in the yard on other occasions and seen individuals either trip or stumble on the crossbar base! After one incident a few days prior, going back inside, I dropped a line to security, telling them that someone was going to break his neck, tripping over the cross bar on the base of the basketball pole in the yard! I went as far as to explain that I'd seen players stumble, trip, even fall when coming down after jumping for a rebound! I don't know, maybe I hadn't worded the concern properly, or sent it to the right person? [Oh well] One of the prisoners shot the ball but, missed; others jumped for a rebound and, aaaahhh! Aaaaahhh man! Aaaahhh man! One of the brothers came down with the ball, he comes down on this cross-bar support, with his foot; I'd never seen bones cut through the flesh, like that! His foot was at least two inches up on the bone where his ankle had snapped! My brother-in-law had afforded me many opportunities to hear a human being in agony; in the full definition of the word, he was probably one of the most sadistic of sadist!! Standing there looking at this prisoner, listening to a human being in a state of agony as such that, something said; right now I wander if he thinks he'd rather be dead! Besides the ankle break, he'd also snapped his shin bone! Had another prisoner tripped over and fallen on that shin bone, I don't know which would have been more severe; that or being shanked! Believe it or not, for a few seconds, the game actually went on; in games, players fall all the time. But, once what was wrong with the brother was seen; gasp in dismay, shock, et cetera could be heard! Suddenly I noticed something happening which struck me as strange! Not just one or two of the other prisoners began to move away from the brother in obvious agony; everyone moved away from him! I guess it was fortunate for me that I was on the other side of the court fence; because knowing me, I'd have been right there, "in a world of trouble"! It didn't take long for the police (CO) to come running! After seeing certain obvious signs, questions followed; questions of sorts which quickly made it clear for me, just why the brother was left lying there alone! What happened?! Who saw what happened?! Who was on the court with him?! Who saw who pushed him, stomped him?! You, come over here; (everybody began walking away quickly) Hey! Hey you, stop and come over here, right now! A couple prisoners turned around and went back! Where are you going?! Where were you going in such a hurry, huh?! Playin ball with this inmate, huh?! Must've been, sweatin' the way you're sweatin'! You do this, huh?! You had to see what happen, who did it?! (I'm standing there shocked; I mean, I couldn't believe what was happening)! Where do you lock?! You, where do you lock?! Another CO takes their cards and orders them to stand right there!

In prison, it's like I said; you might not get a second chance to learn a life saving lesson from any given incident, at any given time! Again, in this university (prison); few of the learning sessions are formal! As I stood there taking it all in; unbeknown to me, I was in fact being blessed to ingest, digest and store; ingest, digest and store information; an unbelievable world of information! But, more importantly than this, I was interpreting it correctly into knowledge which would in turn, become something priceless! Let me go on so that you might understand… I'd seen what had happened to cause that brother to be lying there in the condition he was in! The questions being put before other prisoners, the accusations being made; I could have easily spoken up and cleared things up! Humph, is that so? Think about what I have shared with you related to the behavior, the attitude, the response of not just one or two of the prisoners; but like connected to a common nervous system, they all stepped away; nobody uttered a word, not a single word! I hadn't been there (Sing Sing) long enough to be a part of that system, but, I'd been born with faculties of hearing and sight, which at any given moment can bring forth reasoning. Watching that incident unfold, because of something within, it all was becoming clear; Anthony, when in Rome, do as the Romans do; keep your mouth shut! Before long, a lieutenant showed up and began accusing one then the other of the two inmates standing there! You saw, you did, you know who did; you know why one of the other inmates (prisoners) stomped this inmate, don't you?! We don't care which of you we get it from; but, one of you are going to tell us the truth or take responsibility for it! One of them finally says; the brother fell on that fuckin thing ner! Ain't nobody push, no fuckin body! We was playin ball, he went up forda rebound, an came down on nat fuckin pipe! The lieutenant looks at the other prisoner; is that what happened? He says, I ain't see nuffin, nuffin! The lieutenant drilled and drilled and threatened the other brother, until the brother finally says; what the fuck, lock me the fuck up again then shit! What the fuck, all I got is time, lock me the fuck up, I ain't no fuckin punk! If you know me, if I did dis shit, I'd tell ya; do what da fuck you goa doda me; do it! He told them to box him; and, from what I heard; the other one was locked later! He was questioned and questioned for days! The brother who'd fallen and messed his leg up, his family put in a big lawsuit! It was also said that all the prisoners who'd been playing ball with him that day, were unexplainably transferred to prisons throughout the NYSDOCS!! I don't even want to imagine me opening my mouth and offering what I saw happen! In our so-called free society, the same is true; crap rolls down hill.

    After standing there a few more minutes while the brother was put on a stretcher and taken inside; I headed back to my block. It's a long walk up this long hall; pass the auditorium where a movie was presently being shown. To get back to F-Block, I had to walk up that hall to the end and turn right. Coming down the hall were two faggots; one huge six foot eight inch called (of all things), Tiny; the other (you guessed it) a five foot-eight or so), called sweets! The furthest thing from my mind was what happened next! I'm walking on the right side of the hall, they're on the left. We're about ten feet from each other when, Tiny steps over, walks up in front of me, says to Sweets: Look at this one, don't he look like he probably taste, sweet?! Whatcha think? This faggot grabbed me by my shoulder blade; the grip was like a vice! Carrying a Bic Pen in one hand, my note book in the other, I lunged upward, sticking him in the neck, just under the right side of his chin!!! He let out a squeal like a stuck pig (Sweeeeets, Sweeeeets), he stuck me Sweets! The bastard stuck me Sweets, help me Sweets! Sweets, says to Tiny as I'm walking away; Oh God; Tiny you're bleedun! Jesus Tiny, your neck is bleedun bad! Like it was nothing, I'd walked around somebody who I'd just stuck in the neck with a pen! Walked away from it, on back to my block, like it was nothing! In little more than a month, there I was acting and reacting like a seasoned, well experienced convict, who knew what it was going to take to survive in this "daughter of Babylon!" There was no doubt about it, "Sing Sing was a haven for anything foul and/or filthy!"

    I sat in my cell for a few minutes, thinking about what had just happened, what I'd just done. In a span of time as short as six weeks, I was able to stick another human being in the neck, step around him and walk away, like I'd just taken out the trash! I sat in my cell, on my bed and thought about how I came in, washed my hands, got rid of the pen, and for a moment or two, laughed about it, as I sat there questioning myself/my future! What was it that I'd found humorous?! How could I have found anything humorous!? The humor was short-lived, as I found myself asking myself a seriously disturbing question;

had six weeks in prison actually made me capable of such behavior? If the answer to that question was yes, then, there was another even more disturbing question of which I could not turn my back on; what was the full run of my bid (sentence) going to have on me?! Something said; wait a moment Anthony, wake the hell up, what's wrong with you?! Have you forgotten where you are, what you just did?! You just stuck some big three pound prisoner here in Sing Sing; (one of the most infamous prisons in the world) faggot, gay, homo-sexual or not! How do you plan to handle this reality here and now?! Never mind what affects the rest of your bid (prison sentence) is going to have on you. What are you going to do to keep from being shanked before the week is out?! Little did I know that I was about to find out the truth about one of the unspoken laws in my new society (prison). Of course there is the exception to any societal law; here, it's the occasional snitch/rat/stooge! But, all in all, the "turn-key, the COs, the police, the brass, the administration represent the same system!" Like that saying; what happens in Vegas, stays in Vegas; whatever happens amongst prisoners, we have our own code of ethics, our own system of justice; we handle it ourselves! All that having been said, the administration is well aware of it!

The rest of the day went with no security cell sweeps or lock downs. Lock-in was called, lights out announced, with nothing happening to indicate that what I'd done, wasn't a dead issue as far as it related to security! A few days would pass before I found out that the qualified to be (left-tackle) football player was in the infirmary, and was going to be keep-locked! That only meant one thing; Tiny had refused to, tell security who'd stabbed him! For security, not knowing who committed the assault meant there were three or four things they didn't know! When was Tiny going to retaliate? Where was this retaliation going to take place? Who was the prisoner going to be? One prisoner seeking revenge on another prisoner is a problem for security and the prison administration, but, was this revenge/retaliation going to end up in the death of one or both of those involved? Putting Tiny in the box (solitary confinement) or under keep-lock wasn't going to keep anything from happening. The communication system between prisoners throughout the system is most of the time, more reliable/dependable than that of the administration! The truth, regardless of how much it's disliked, makes it no less true! Who the filthy, foul, corrupt, low life correction officers are, is something residing in prison, makes you privy to! For the right price, you can get the right one(s) from amongst NYSDOCS, to either take or bring you almost anything you want as a prisoner/inmate! There's more "money" inside the walls of NYSDOCS than you'd ever imagine, much less believe possible! Having said that, it shouldn't be hard to understand how a prisoner in the box (solitary confinement) is able to get messages (whatever they may be) out into the prison population! Depending on the extent of what one wants done, determines how involved (dirty) our CO/corruption officer gets! How was this going to play out for me? Tiny was in the box, for a week, to no avail, administration got nothing!

It was and is still unbelievable, how much I learnt about doing time and surviving, in such a short amount of time. Taking a shower might have cost me my life, were it not for intuition! I'd gone to take a shower; down the middle of two long rows of showers, is a cat-walk for COs (prison guards) to walk; two other prisoners walked into the area, right after me. At first I hadn't noticed whether or not they were carrying shower slippers, a towel, etc. It was only after they walked back pass my shower that I noticed, but, I made nothing of it. Like anywhere, I adjusted the water before getting into the shower. The first thing I've always done was wash my hair, but, something said; don't, don't wash your hair! A minute or so later, those same two brothers walked pass me, then back again. It was unusual that I hadn't started washing my hair, but, something kept telling me not to! A third time the two brothers walked pass my shower; but, this time they'd stop at the shower next to me, and began talking like they were arguing. Believe me when I tell you, it couldn't have been but a few seconds later; "four Muslim (shurta) fell on them, like a fishnet! Ahki! Ahki (my brother, my brother); are you alright?! Are you ok ahk (brother)?! The brothers had those two pushed into the shower next to mine! One of the brothers said to them: "Imam Abdul told us to tell you to tell Tree: the next visit will be to his (Tree's) house! One of the brothers from shurta, pushes one of the guys back into the shower and says to him; "repeat what the Imam said, ain't gonna be no excuses, and we won't be doing nonna dis"! I said to one of the brothers; ahki, let me get dressed, then I'm willing to give them a chance, one at a time, to see what they can do; since they came to jump me! One of the brothers from shurta says to me, in a teaching sort of way: Ahki, what are you talking about, do you think these kufar (unbelievers) were just hanging around here, waiting for a chance to beat you up?! The other three shurta laughed, while the brother who'd asked the question, started searching the two! On one of them, he found a tooth brush sharpened to a point on one end; on the other, he found a thick, clear piece of plastic, (looked like plexi-glass) about an inch and a half wide, eighth inch thick, seven/eight inches long shank, with a taped handle! I went to swing at the one closest to me, but was grabbed and held back! Tree had put the word out on me because of what I'd done to his prostitute! Tiny was out of business for at least a week, costing Tree at least seventy five dollars in commissary, money or the two combined! Throughout the rest of that day, I stayed in the block, and for the most part, on my tier (2nd tier) reflecting on the state of life I could be in had it not been for some brothers stepping to concerns for which I was too prison new, to know I should've had! That night, after lock-in, I laid on my bed thinking about the damage done to me in 1972, when I was stabbed once with a pin knife! My next book will make you smile, it will make you laugh, it, will make you cry... Though I walked to and from, remembering that I had concerns, the message must have been delivered to Tree, and obviously understood; because my health never became a reason for my Muslim brothers to pay his house a visit!

Before I left Sing Sing, I'd hear one inmate threaten another for snoring! The tiers in Sing Sing are long, but the walls between each cell, are very thin! There was a prisoner who had one of the worse, if not the worse snoring problem I'd ever heard! He was threatened by the inmate/prisoner who locked next to him, on the flats. Earlier in the evening the one told the other; hear me well motherfucker; and I suggest you believe me homeboy; if you keep me up tonight, snoring, when they pop the cells in the morning, I'm going to cut your fucking throat; so, you better be awake homeboy! He said it while we were having night rec. on the flats; playing cards (spades blackjack, etc)! He was so calm about it, to the point that everybody laughed! Maybe it was my imagination; but, that night it sounded like the snoring was louder than ever; I mean like a lion roaring! I don't believe anyone really took the brother seriously; but, I was unable to sleep that night; so, I was wide awake! When the cells popped, I would've sworn I heard something which sounded like gurgling! When my cell gate popped, I was out of my cell, down the tier and around the corner on the flats! A voice was saying, just as calmly, not even the slightest sound of anger in his voice: You thought I was playing with you! Everybody in the block has to lay wake all night, looking at the dark; because you're making all that fucking noise all night!!! Anyone else have problem snoring, come see me if you need treatment! What the fuck, all this fucking time I've got; the only thing I have to look forward to all day, is night time! (stress in his voice, but no anger; he continues): The only thing I have that they haven't taken from me, is my sleep at night! I'm going to let some mother fucker with a skid bid (1-3 yrs 2-4 yrs 2 1/2-5 yrs et cetera to serve) , just say, fuck you; after I told him he's keeping me up all night! (All this time talking, he's sounded fairly correct in his diction, etc; suddenly, I think he lost his temper; because he starts: I just did whaddal yall punk ass niggas ain't hadda heart ta do; doe yall'd talk shit all day bout it!

It was something; the CO didn't have a clue of what had happened! After popping the cells on my side, he went to pop the cells on the other side of the block! I'd made it to the flats to see the brother who'd just had his cut throat; as well as the brother who'd done it! The one inmate/prisoner slept with his head toward the front of the cell; so the other just had to step inside the cell and serve him! I don't think the one prisoner even woke up; after-all, how many, if anyone thought that he, this other prisoner would carry out the threat he'd made!! I don't know what was more insane; the act itself, or the prisoner who'd done it not even trying to do anything to hide what he'd done! When the CO came back a short while later, he found the one, just washing his hands! It was outright crazy; for snoring, the brother got his throat cut; the brother who'd done the cutting was not even trying to hide what he'd done; the entire thing was insane! It was only after the police came back, was the throat cutter trying to wash his hands! Tree was after me for doing something crazy, and had put a hit on me for it; [I'd stuck Tiny in the neck]; something which someone who'd been in prison for some time might have done! I was so-naive that I was ready to get dressed and fight the one brother, straight-up! It took a reality check; a small dose of prison reality to bring me down to earth! I mean the [6 inch] piece of plexi-glass taken from one brother, and the tooth brush shank taken from the other guy! They were not there to talk to me; they'd come to help me take my shower! There was only one thing left out; they'd be the only two leaving on their own free-will, had they had things their way; had the brothers from shurta [Muslim Security] not showed up! After a few words with the two hit-men, everyone went his own way! Tree got over his so-called commissary loss; Tiny was back in business for Tree; Shurta was back to its' regular; and I was on the draft to the Last Strong Hold [Clinton]!

4

The Last Stronghold

MATTY, PATRICK, AND I were transferred out a few days later, on our way to Clinton correctional Facility. I guess one might see Sing Sing as a sort of boot camp for what I'd find myself having to deal with in the "Last Strong Hold"! As for Imam (A) asking me about wanting to stay in Sing Sing, I don't know what happened with that, but, I was definitely on my way to Dannemora, New York! The few months of Ju'mah (Friday Prayer), Ramadan (Muslim Fast), and the Family Day Event had done a lot for me; though I was unaware of it! The Imam was definitely one with whom I had issues; he and I didn't see eye to eye on a number of things he did; but, he was the Imam; he was also falsely accused; so, he was in Sing Sing for a crime he hadn't committed; that alone should have meant volumes to me; but, I was still in a growing phase! I was still growing, I had not yet arrived! It was like I'd stated earlier; Sing Sing was like a "boot camp," preparing me for the days and times yet to come; those times, such as I'd need to pull on; fall back on myself!

The trip to Clinton was set-up as such that you were able to get attached to each other like you would have never imagined! Besides being handcuffed and shackled together for more than eight hours, a bus has a way of showing you just who your friends are… Follow me in this scenario; I'm going to let you enjoy coming up with what you think the final picture will look like…Lunch time is no problem, though you're cuffed through a waist chain; I don't care how much time someone does, there are certain little harmless details, even the prisoner with his masters degree in convicted convict, over looks; using the toilet!! This is one of the times, if you've never been, you hope you are, constipated; you and your travel buddy! Yes, I was in prison, this was a bus ride; but, I was in the middle of a whole lot more!! We'd been on the road, for a few hours, when we began noticing helicopters over head!

The escort police laughed and said; I can't run around the bus twice; and, this is a long ride; some of you might get tired of riding, and decide running is better! I'm not sure, but I think this is the most years, I've ever rode shotgun for; almost a thousand years amongst you! One of the prisoners said; damn, a thousand joints! For awhile, the prisoners went back and forth commenting on bids they'd done. As I'd stated above, I was amidst much more than prisoners, and/or a bus ride; I represented a percentage of almost a thousand years of life which would be slowed down! Sitting there listening, something more complexly profound was revealing itself in front of me! At the time, I didn't have the slightest clue that what was trying to reveal itself, was in fact trying to let me see such a troubling truth! When I later lay it out for you, hopefully you'll see its painfully disturbing reality, for what it is…! Listening to the different conversations, it began to sound like nothing more than a cacophony. I don't know just how long we'd been riding, but, eventually I became oblivious of what was nothing more than noise to me; I drifted off into my own world for awhile, just thinking. Suddenly I noticed it was quiet; nobody was talking! I looked to my left and down the bus, in front of me; quiet! Then! Wha! Wha hew say?! I doe even know hew! How much time I got! How much fuckin time I got! Why?! (pause) Why, hew gou do it fa'me?! Wanna knoda fuckin truth blood? Nona ya biniz! Less you gonna become somebody's bitch; ouh payda fuck up fasum rec, don't be axin nobody bout dae fuckin time! But, forda record, I got more jail-time, (time in jail, before sentenced) din you got time to do. (hahahahaha) he laughs... The conversations on the bus went back to the low-keyed tone, between transport buddies for the most part. The bus rolled on, the day went on, I continued listening to some of the passengers reflecting, as they tried to outdo each other, boasting about what they had, what they'd done; who this, that, or the other thing was done to, and why! About five hours into the ride, the one thing I'd been looking forward to, happened. It wasn't a thing of which I was preoccupied thinking about; in fact, I can't even say it crossed my mind again after the escort CO said; I got two things to tell you convicts, but only once: I won't tolerate any bullshit; and if you have take a shit; you'd better have a real friend... (ha ha ha)

The two prisoners must have been talking between themselves before anyone knew what was happening, because suddenly; I can't help you homeboy; come on man, what am I suppose to do man, I gotta shit! Hey CO! Hey CO, you gotta unlock me so I can take a shit; this brother said he don't wipe his wife's' ass, what the fuck he look like wiping mine! You could hear comments like: Don't even think about it homes; I can feel for ya, but I cain't reacha; dam, dats fucked up, dats fucked up man! While the prisoner's trying to get the officer to unshackle him, to no avail, another situation presents itself. There's another prisoner who has to urinate, this should have been no problem whatsoever! I should have said, having to urinate should have been no problem, unless you happen to be one of those idiots caught-up in the vanity of your reputation! There wasn't anything to really try and suggest to the prisoners in the bowel movement dilemma; but the other, either could relieve himself regardless of which seat he was in. As a Muslim, males just as do females; they sit to urinate; this prevents the urine from splashing up onto our clothing! So, after listening to the nonsense, I suggested: Brothers, check this out; if you have to take a piss, why don't you just go inside, shut the door as much as you can, pull your pants down and sit? If someone had promised me immediate release, if I were able to say what would happen next, I never would have been able to tell them! You would have thought I'd called the brother a faggot or a punk, whatever! Go on, take a guess or two or a dozen or two; believe me, if what I tell you transpired as a result of an innocent suggestion, was something even in the back of your mind, WOW!! The brother didn't comment, but, he and his riding partner got up and started towards the back! On the way, one of them asked who had the idea about being able to piss! I thought nothing of it, so, me being me, I acknowledged it! I was sitting in an isle seat not that I think it would have made a difference. The prisoner who had to use the toilet, his seat was by the window; so, coming down the isle, he followed the other prisoner. Just as he passed the back of my seat, he swung around and tried to chain choke me! Had it not been for his waist chain being the length it was, restricting how high his hands could be raised, he'd have tried to chock me out! I leaned forward, the other prisoner shackled to him, pulled towards the toilet, preventing this fool from reaching me! The commotion got the attention of the CO still behind the gate. He stood and asked what was going on! Before I could say anything, the one who'd tried to choke me (angrily) says; this punk mother fucker must think he sees bitch in me! Is dat what it is homeboy, you see bitch in me?! You think I'm bout bein a bitch homeboy?! This knucklehead was about to get both of us into a world of trouble! Still, before I could comment, the brother chained to me spoke-up and says: officer, my partner here has long legs; if you remember, we asked if you would switch us around before we started, because his knees would be against the back of the seat, the entire ride! Remember asking the police? Unintentional, yes unintentionally, one of the brothers tripped on their way pass, to the toilet; that's all, ain't nothin! The CO says; Ok, but the one place you don't want to start no shit, is while being shipped, in transit! While all of that is being said, this stupid nigger (I don't make it a habit of calling a black person such), instead of trying to blend in with the nonexistent incident, he's whispering to me: you want me to sit and piss for you, huh homeboy?! I ain't never had no problem pissin like a man! When we git where we goin, I'ma give you ya chance to prove you man' na'nuff to make me sit and piss like your bitch homeboy! Don't sleep on me homeboy! You should'a found somebody else ta git ya rec off! I'm sitting there; (to say I was perplexed would be an understatement) the brother next to me is (believe it or not) squeezing my thigh! I could only assume that such was telling me not to say anything, I didn't! After all of that, the killer didn't use the toilet, but, went back and sat down! I would learn later, that had an altercation taken place during transit, I would have been looking forward to: any amount of time in the box (solitary lockup), or additional time, or both; for attempt escape or attempt to aide in such!

 The brother chained to me, hadn't said two words to me the entire ride; finally says: My last bid, there was a father, in everybody's business, trying to help everybody! I didn't think he was ever going to learn to mind his own damn business; regardless of how many times different prisoners were taking his commissary, claiming something he'd done, got them in trouble! Whatever it was, he stopped trying! Maybe it had something to do with him having to be put into pc (protective custody)! Just as he opened up and started talking, he shut back down! After going through what I'd just gone through, I wasn't sure whether to say something or not, so, I thought I'd take the low road, and keep my mouth shut! Though I didn't say anything for the duration of the trip, I couldn't help thinking about whether or not anything was going to become of the ranting directed at me by a fool in doubt of his masculinity! I sat there thinking; damn, I haven't even made it to Clinton, and it seems like I'm going to have a grudge to worry about! It was absurd to the point that I sat there trying to convince myself that that guy couldn't have been serious!

The helicopters mentioned early in the ride, had disappeared hours ago, but, suddenly there was one hovering over head. Shortly after finding out about the helicopter, the bus made a stop off in a lot. We sat there for about ten minutes; then a garage truck and three police cars showed up! The bus was running hot, and, it was going to be dark soon! I could only imagine that the last thing they wanted was a crippled bus, with almost a thousand years prison time between the prisoners, on it! After having the bus sit there, and the two CO (bus driver and escort officer) talking with the area police, getting them situated; we were taken out of the bus a couple at a time and directed! When I got off the bus, one of the first things I noticed were the policemen situated, with shotguns! We'd been told, the policemen have been told about some of the criminal minds being transported, as well the fact that we're transporting almost ten centuries of sentenced time amongst you all! There was not the least doubt in my mind that those police wouldn't hesitate for a second to take as many of us down as necessary, to bring things under their control! You could see in their eyes, they were there to do whatever had to be done! I remember standing there praying that no one would sneeze with exaggeration, or start acting antsy! Whatever had to be done was done, and we were seated back onto the bus, and on our way. The helicopter stayed with us until we got back onto the highway; it got dark shortly after. The next time we stopped, I knew we'd arrived at Clinton, because the CO riding shotgun left the bus and could be heard talking to someone he referred to as Sgt.

Being inside the gate, the Sgt; enters the bus and gives us the once over; tells us to get off the bus, and line up beside it. The Sgt; was handed different folders, one at a time. As he looks through them, I noticed him looking up at different prisoners! He steps in front of the line of prisoners still hand cuffed and shackled, standing side by side, facing him! He walks down the line, stopping in the face of this one, that one, and the other one! Not a single word has he said to any of us, not even to the prisoners he'd singled out. Suddenly: "You're in Clinton now!" This is 'The Last Strong Hold!' When they can't control you in Attica; when they can't control you in Great Meadow; when they can't control you in Green Haven; when they can't control you in Napanach; when you animals can't be controlled no-where else, 'The Last Strong Hold!' Give us a problem; please give us a problem; ain't a plane get cha mama here fast enough to save ya!" Please give us a problem! We would find out almost immediately that his definition of problem wasn't what you'd find in the dictionary, because there was a brother who'd when nervous, he'd channel his nervousness by laughing! As fate would have it, the Sgt; got nose-to-nose in the face of this same individual, and shouts: "You look like you don't understand what I just said; give us a problem, when we get finish witcha, your soul, will understand!" Just as the Sgt. turned to walk away, the brother snickered... This was one of those times in which I'm not sure whether one or all three of the following are correct; (i.e.) tell me, I might remember; show me, I might forget; involve me, I'll understand! It was made clear to me, though I'd left Sing Sing, I'd only changed rooms in Sodom and Gomorrah!! At first it seemed that the brother was going to get away with the snicker, because the cuffs and shackles had been removed, and we were told to line up, walk to and through the door, to the end of the hall and stop. Three COs walked pass us, and were standing midway in the hall. Suddenly it was like all hell broke loose; the snicker hadn't been over-looked after all! Unfortunately for the prisoner with the nervous laugh, he became the introductory reference point for the rest of us. I don't know which was the bigger mistake, the snicker or the fact that the prisoner saw one of the COs swing his stick, and he (the prisoner) blocked it with his arm! The Sgt; says, "We don't only have a nigger who likes to laugh, but, this nigger doesn't know how to keep his hands where they belong!" All you heard after that were thumping sounds, and moaning sounds; and more thumping and moaning! They were stomping and beating this brother, like we weren't there; they knew we were seeing what they were doing, but, they didn't care! In fact, one of the COs involved in the beating, stops and shouts; "what are ya'll looking at; turn around unless ya think ya seen something; less ya wanna be a witness!"

Matty, Patrick, and I were towards the back of the line, so we were able to see this prisoner get beat down; lying there; no movement at all; lying on the floor with a gash in his head! One of his eyes swollen shut, the size of a small plum, blood coming from it! Then there was his right arm, looked like it was broken about the forearm, the way it was bent, it had to be broken! All that time, we stood in the hall, allowed to witness a beating; like they didn't have a concern in the world! In fact, before we were told by the Sgt; to turn the corner; we were asked to explain what we'd just seen! Do I have to tell you that no one saw anything; that in fact, no one even said anything when asked! We made the turn and walked down that hall in which we were told to open the door and continue up the stairs (four flights), to the second tier. Having been on the road all day, I was tired, hungry, and in possession of some crash course wisdom in a subject of disturbingly vivid memory; "The Last Strong Hold;" CLINTON CORRECTIONAL FACILITY! If I didn't understand before, I now had both an understanding and an appreciation for the saying: "You only get one chance to make a first impression!"

Whatever time of morning it was, we were finally taken to our hotel suites; mine was (H-2-21)! Before I knew it, I, was being awaken from the peaceful escape of sleep, for the body count. Little did I know that counting bodies would be something I'd find myself doing; literally keeping a body count, for myself! Only a few short hours ago, a number of us had been marched single file past the body of a prisoner who lay motionless! I did not know what his lying there motionless meant; was he unconscious or was he…? In any case, sooner than later, I'd start my personal body count of prisoners who'd meet death for one of three reasons; i.e., Natural death, another inmate, facility neglect; least of three reasons for prisoners meeting the inevitable would be "natural death!!!" On that note, I began to wonder whether or not Clinton had a meaning; like Alcatraz, though known as "The Rock!" It's unnerving to the point of sleeplessness, realizing that "natural death" would be the literal meaning in, "Strange Pelican Bird!" I would soon come to know that "Clinton Prison" (The Last Strong Hold) was notorious for "prisoners dying, prisoners disappearing!" For the briefness of a moment, I went on a motionless journey, thinking about the possibility of Clinton having some diabolical meaning! Did Clinton literally mean: "DEATH IS INEVITABLE?" It was the unfortunate prisoner who was not fore-warned, or if fore-warned, did not heed the warning! Like "Death Valley", its conditions give rise to rules which are unspoken! Again, like "Death Valley", knowing about the end result of unfortunate others, should be example enough for you not to follow! To the best of my knowledge, those of us who'd arrived at Clinton only a few hours ago, we were there to go through testing for "classification", and be placed throughout NYSDOCS according to our classification status. I don't think most of us had any idea that some of us would end up staying there.

As I'd began to write about, a few paragraphs ago; I was awaken for a body count. As the officer was going pass my cell, I tried to get his attention, but, he didn't stop. He went to the end of the tier and came back pass. A few minutes later, my cell gate opened and I heard; (21 cell) front of the tier. I peeked out, and must have been seen, because the CO says, "front of the tier, now!" I went to the front of the tier, that's both the control area, as well as entrance to my cell area. The CO says to me in a firm voice; "what's wrong with you, are you stupid or what?! Don't you ever say anything to a CO when the count is being done! Understand?" Understand? I answered yes. He asked; "What did you want that couldn't wait until I was done doing the count? I was a little nervous, but I managed to tell him I was use to working, and would really appreciate it if he'd consider me, if there was a need for a porter or something. He didn't say anything, just stood there looking at me! I didn't mean anything by looking him directly in the eyes, just as he was looking at me. Believe me, I wasn't trying to be brave or anything like that; it was just something my grandmother had said to me one night when she and I were sitting on the front porch in the little country like place (Laudge) in Pennsylvania. She never spoke much about things, and whenever she pointed something out to me, she'd only say; that is okay baby, one day, you will understand. Well, this particular night, she'd been sitting there humming and rocking; the notes in the humming seemed to mean something important to her, even at my age! Then, she turns my head to face her, and said what seemed to be the odd to me; every man baby, every man baby, the soul will see it. I sat there looking at my grandmother, thinking to myself, that she was crazy.

(I guess I was thinking to myself, but sometimes I wonder if she knew what I thought).

Anyway, this particular morning in Clinton, I guess you can say, I stared him down, he looked away for a second then looked at me again! We were looking each other in the eyes, but, there was something about it this time; I don't know, can't explain it… The CO having said nothing to me one way or the other, finally says; "attention (21) cell is the new tier boy, anyone give him a problem, has given me a problem; you don't wanna give me a problem!" Why I responded at all to what he'd just said, I won't even attempt to explain, so don't ask! I said: Excuse me CO but I assure you that as long as I'm here doing what you've given me the responsibility to do, you'll never see me behave like a boy! There was no puffed up sound of pride, haughtiness, et cetera in my voice; I wasn't even mindful of a motive! He stood there for a few seconds, him and me looking at each other, eye to eye! "Attention, attention, (21) cell is the new tier "man", anyone give him a problem, you've given me a problem, you don't want to give me a problem!" He went on to explain to me what all I'd have to do, and that my cell would be left open all day, allowing me to be out of my cell. My responsibilities for the first part of the morning; if you can imagine getting hot water for about (180) cell, as well as the disposable shaver, envelopes, writing paper, check for toilet paper, soap needs, et cetera, along with providing the broom and damp mop! After that, it was up to me to go up and down each tier, sweep the dust (whatever) from in front of each cell, then mop each tier! As if that wasn't enough, one day per week, the prisoners were to turn in a set of greens, as well as dirty under wear (in their net laundry bag); another week day, their linen sheets and pillow case are turned in to be washed and returned by noon! Now that I think about it, the shaving was funny, because hair on my face consisted of a mustache which looked like a dirt smudge over my lip.

Whether one had to or not, you were told to shave, guess what I did; exactly, I shaved to practice what I did. Exactly, I shaved, even if it was nothing but dead skin cells! That detail was great! The ability to come and go, when everyone else can't, and can do nothing about it, is really an amazing experience! The way it makes you feel! The way other prisoners respond when dealing with you, even though you're just another convict, you have something they don't have... When lights went out for the night, and the quiet bell rang, all cells had radio channeled to it, and you could lie there and listen to whatever. Clinton was not far from Canada, so one of the two channels, came in from, Canada: that was an experience.

We were in Clinton about a week, when one night, about fifteen minutes or so after the quiet bell, a loud voice was heard. No, not through the radio, not a CO, no one was calling for help or anything which would have possibly warranted it; the voice was coming from prisoner on tier three, the first cell! It was quiet for a few minutes, maybe that was the end of it; wishful thinking, because, there it was again! Allah-u-Akbar! Allah-u-Akbar! Allah-u-Akbar! Allah-u-Ak... (another voice says) what the fuck is wrong with you, huh? I gotcha fucking Aalay akber! I gotcha Aalay fuckin akber! If you don't shut the fuck up, nigger! Have you lost your fuckin mind nigger! Let me hear something else! If you fart, you better hope you're sittin on a pillow! He was a Muslim, and had come to Clinton on the same bus I'd come on! He stood in the same hall I'd stood in that night, and had seen...! What could have suddenly come over him to give him reason not to believe in that first impression! He had, just as I had; seen a sure truth! No thousand word picture would have stated with more clarity and less emotion: "We need no reason to introduce you to the "Destroyer of all Pleasures; Death!" Nothing short of a "death wish or a sentence longer than he wanted to do" could have made that brother become a lone rebel! Suddenly you'd hear him chant an absolute truth; he would chant what my heart tells me were his last words! Allah-u-Akbar! Allah-u-Akbar! Allah-u-Akbar! (God is, Great! God is, Great! God is, Great)! The next sound I heard was the sound heard when a cell is popped (gate opened at the control panel). That was followed by a weird thump-thump-thump sound; then an ear piercing scream, and another one! Again there was another thump, a pause, and then another thump and sounds of moaning followed by the sound of something hard, hitting the cell bars! Though it was not clearly audible, someone trying to say please, please, please, could be heard! Then very clearly someone shouted: Say Aalay akber (Thump... Thump)! comoe nigger, say Aalay akber (a mixed sound of a thump thump thump and something hard hitting the cell bars)! Aalay akber Aalay akber, comoohhh, (the person sounded like he was exerting himself, while saying comoohhh, there was a phhh phhh sound)! What's wrong nigger (phhhh, phhhh)! comoohhh (phhh, phhh)! Aalay ak (phhh) ber! This went on for what seemed like an eternity! But, something was missing in a short time; after the initial sound of pleading, nothing else! Finally it was quiet! I stood at the bars, listening with everything in me, trying to hear, hoping to hear a moan, a cough, something that would dispel the gut wrenching feeling that I had! My heart was beating fiercely! It was beating so hard that it was causing throbbing pains to run down my spine! I wasn't going to even try and kid myself, I knew one thing for sure; my brother (Muslim) was in a terribly bad condition, but how bad!

 Just as I stepped away from my cell gate to sit on my bed, my gate popped! I kid you not, it sounded like a 4th of July cherry bomb (BOOOMMM)! I fell back onto my bed, literally gasping, trying to catch my breath! I couldn't think of any reason why they'd be opening my cell at this time of night, except that they know I'm Muslim too! My cell was open, but nothing had been said, not a word! Suddenly; (21) cell (pause)! Couldn't move; tried moving my legs, I couldn't! I wasn't even able to acknowledge hearing the CO yell out my cell number; what did he pop my cell for; "(21) cell, front of the tier now!" (21) cell…I remember thinking: Oh Allah; just as I thought that, I said in a gasping voice; "I'm putting my boots on!" As I walked to the front of the tier, my imagination was running wild; the things I was imagining weren't even within the realm of the reality I was about to have placed before me! When I reach the front of the tier, the CO pops the gate to the slop-sink; get a mop, bucket, wringer, sponges, soap balls, and meet me upstairs. He was calm, like he didn't have a care in the world! I had to make more than one trip to take everything upstairs. When I had everything he'd told me to get, he took me to the cell wherein I believed the Muslim brother had just been beaten to death! What I saw on the floor outside the cell of the Muslim; what there was on the floor outside of the next two cells; what I saw up and down the bars outside the cell along the tier; what I finally saw inside the brother's cell shook my soul! Fighting to keep my wits about myself; struggling to keep my composure, I made several deep gulps then filled my jaws with air and slowly blew it out (exhaling)! OOOHH, you should have seen what I was looking at! From the cell floor to the cell ceiling, blood! All over the cell, the sink, toilet, walls, the sheets, pillow case, papers, all over his boots, sneakers; if it was in that cell, blood was on it! In case you didn't notice, there's one obvious omission, the prisoner, my Muslim brother! Where is his body?! The CO says to me; "clean this mess up, let me know when you think it'll pass my "white glove inspection." I don't like disappointments (21) cell, and I don't want any overtime! We understand each other, right?" Just as calmly, he says; "I know we understand each other!"

Nobody would ever believe what I saw, or the cleaning that

had taken me almost the entire night! I started, mopping so I wouldn't keep tracking the blood all over, every time I made a trip back down the stairs to empty the bucket into the slop-sink on tier two! After making trips up and down the stairs for an hour or more, I didn't understand why the CO didn't open the gate to the slop-sink on tier three, but I wasn't about to ask! I mopped and wiped, mopped and rang mops, wiped and sponged and mopped and rang mops, and emptied bucket after bucket after bucket of bloodied water! I told the officer I needed some rags; he told me to rip the sheets and use what I could from them for rags! As I was sliding a piece of rag between the cell gate and the opening (if you've ever used a cloth to shine shoes, you'll picture what I was doing), I pulled the rag like I was buffing a shoe; a patch of scalp and hair fell to the floor! At the time, I hadn't learnt the Arabic, so, I began repeating in English; from Allah we come, to Allah we return! From Allah we come, to Allah we return! The brother's blood had splattered onto the wall outside the tier, at least ten feet up and down that outer wall, onto the floor of the flats! Just when I thought I was about done, except for that splatter, the officer gives me a bonus! He comes and says, are you about finished, I said yes. He smiles and says; so you're saying that I'm going to be satisfied. So that means, I'm not going to have to worry bout getting no "dust" on my new "white gloves" when I follow-up, right? I didn't say anything! The CO says, okay, get your stuff and come with me Mr. Clean! I'd mopped outside the brother's cell (3rd floor), as well as the main area of tier three, so the blood spoke for itself! The blood showed me that the brother had been dragged across the floor and down the steps to the second floor. But, for some reason, even after making trip after trip up and down the steps, I never noticed the blood trail going around and down another flight of steps to the first floor! This meant at least another few hours for me before I was finished, or should I say, until this sick bastard was satisfied! I eventually cleaned up the crime scene where a murder had been committed, all the way to the flats! But, before I was finished, I'd also find a bloody broken front tooth! That morning, a hose was brought in and hooked up for me to sparingly spray water to remove blood splatter still noticeable on outer walls of the tiers; evidence still existing from the savage, sadistic murder of a prisoner, the night before!

Before that officer was relieved that morning, he came around with the relieve officer, and told each of us; your letters are not to be sealed if you want them mailed out! All of our visiting tables are equipped with state of the art listening devices; I wouldn't want to be you if the wrong things are heard being talked about! I'd strongly suggest you keep in mind what was said to you by the Sgt., during his welcoming speech! I'm sure you're convinced that there is not a plane to get your mama here fast enough to "save your life!" Oh, but that's if "you give us a problem!" He smiled and walked away! For the next few nights, things were quiet! I think just how quiet things were could not have been better described than it had been one day in the mess hall, during chow; One of the prisoners said; It's been so quiet that, you could hear a cat peeing on cotton! He was not saying what he had said the way he'd said it; trying to make anyone laugh! Things were very, very quiet; even the night fishing that went on to get things up and down the tier after lock in, ceased! That having been said, there was no reason within the realm of logic for anyone to have expected what happened next! One night on the flats to the right of me, two prisoners (we were being referred to as inmates) strike up a conversation. As if that wasn't bad enough, their conversation was of such content that hearing it, you'd come to only one conclusion; those having this conversation, must have a "death wish!" (I'll let you decide for yourself)! One inmate says: I don't even want to think about that faggot mother fucker popping my cell and coming in on me, without backup! I hear you man; that punk mother fucker knew that poor guy was scared; that's why he went in on him with no backup; punk ass faggot bitch! That's what he'd probably be in here, some- bodies bitch; gettin fucked and suckin people off! (They laughed between each other) Yoo, jus thinkin bout that bitch gives me a hard-on! I ain't about stickin nobody up the ass; but I'd make that motherfucker suck my cock; then I'd cum right in his fuckin face! I'm lying on my bed, just like everyone else must have been, because the quiet bell had rung and the lights were out! I'm saying to myself; do they realize how their voices are carrying; they can't know; they can't possibly know! None of the other inmates tried to get the attention of those two unfortunate inmates to try and warn them! How do you explain what was happening? Can it be explained? Whatever the reason was behind the ranting; they made a few more comments, and then... There I was lying with my head towards the sink in my cell, when I noticed the CO easing past my cell! It was the same CO who'd beaten the Muslim inmate to death only a week or so prior! As he tipped past the cells, he'd hold his finger up to his lips, gesturing for us to keep quiet! All the while, the two inmates were still running their mouths! As I listened to them ranting, I thought about the poem called Desiderata: "Go placidly amidst the noise and haste; and remember what peace there is in silence…" Shortly after passing my cell, he came back pass, making the same gesture with his finger! I assume he'd made the same finger gesture, the length of the tier. A short while later, another CO comes past my cell, in the same manner as the first one had; he came by just in time to hear the last comments which the two inmates were making! "I wish one of those red-neck, hillbilly motherfuckers would put his hands on me; know what I mean! Fuck all ofum; long as zay don't disrespect me, they ain't gonna have no problem outta me! Damn I'm hungry; cain't wait for chow;

see ya in the morning; Yeah!" The CO who'd passed my cell just long enough to hear the asininities, walked normally back down the tier, past my cell. Whoever they were on the flats, had to have heard the CO walking away from over them! All I could do was shake my head; because what was about to happen was no mystery to those of us who'd seen the officers ease past our cells while two inmates were signing their "death wish!" Though things were quiet, I don't think anyone doubted something was going to happen, but, when! Lying there listening to the radio, almost two hours had gone by with nothing happening! I think I'd dozed off when: OK, pop it, pop this tough guy's cell! The cell popped, you could hear some rumbling; the familiar (thump thump) sounds from about a week ago! Loud moaning, screaming, someone screaming for help! Then there was what sounded like people running to the back of the flats! After that, it was obvious what was happening! "Ok Mr. Tough Guy; make me suck you off!" (thump…thump thump…bumph bumph bumph…thump thump bumph bumph), along with screaming and the sound of something hard, hitting the bars! Unlike the first incident, there were a number of different voices and noises in the commotion! I'm really disappointed tough guy, I was looking forward to having you make these red-neck faggots suck you off! Ooohh, I understand, you're not the one who said that, huh?! Then another voice said; you called me over here for this, I thought I was gonna be somebody's bitch! All we have here is fuckin white trash, fuckin worthless white trash! Fuckin (bumph) white (bumph bumph) trash! What are we gonna do with this trash? Another voice says: what we always do with garbage…I kept saying to myself; something is missing, I'd only heard one cell pop. What did that mean? My question was answered with a double sound; there was a loud clack, then a pop! One cell had been shut, another opened! Your turn tough city boy; show us what you're gonna do with your hard-on. Come on and show everybody what you're gonna make a faggot do! (thump) There was a slight moan! Aaahh, come on, you don't want to be quiet now, do you? (thump, bumph, bumph) In between the moans and groans, the inmate could also be heard trying to say something, but what he was trying to say, did no good! (I'm sorry, please, it was just talk, I'm sorry)!! He didn't complete the last sentence; it was cut off by another one of those eerie sounds! It was a sound as such that I don't think can be made by anything other than a club ripping through flesh and bone of a human being! There was an expression of agony so intense, that I'm convinced; the pain caused by that last blow, must have touched the very soul of that inmate!!! One of the CO said; oh no, he's not going to get off that easy, get some water, throw some water on him, this is the punk with all the mouth! Give me the cup! I must assume the CO got water from the toilet, because, if you push the button to get water from the sink, it can be heard. Come on punk; show me what you had in mind to do with your cock! Thump, come on big mouth, shoot-off in my face, punk! Thump. One of the CO said something that I couldn't make out. Whatever it was, caused another CO to say; so what! I could hear their foot-steps as they walked back towards the front of the flats. A few minutes later, the gate slammed shut! It seemed like I was lying there for hours, looking at the darkness, wishing I could fall asleep! It was not going to happen, not this night! Just like a few nights ago, my cell gate opened, followed by; "(21) cell, front of the tier!" I put my pillow to my face and let out a deep sigh (haaawwhh)!

Something had told me to get dressed, maybe in anticipation of being called! I was at the front of the tier, in no time, this time! I just stood there, looking back down the tier. When the gate to the slop-sink popped, I jumped! The CO laughed, then, asked me if I was alright. Then he says, on second thought, use the stuff from the flats, I'll be down to open up in a minute. I went downstairs, but the gate to the slop-sink was locked like he'd said. I stood there for a few seconds; then, ran back upstairs. He hadn't told me to go downstairs, only that he'd be down in a minute to open up. He walked down the other side of my tier, and back; good, he looks at me, and says; good, tha's good; you waited for me to walk you down. Tha's good, otherwise it might have seemed like you were trying to do something before I tell you to! You know what's going on here, right? Yes sir. What did you say! Did you say you know what's going on here? Yes sir; this is reception, and we're here to get our medical evaluations, mental evaluations, et cetera, so that we can be classified and placed accordingly. The CO stood there for a second, the stiff look that came over his face disappeared; he smiled! You're one of those smart niggers, don't slip up; come with me! We went downstairs, he opened the slop-sink gate; everything you need is here, get busy! No, first come with me, you have to remove something from the cell before you can clean it up! I don't know whether the inmate in the next to the last cell was dead or not, but, he was swollen about the head and face and badly beaten; but who knows what all was broken under his clothing! At that moment I managed to kid myself about what I'd witnessed a few nights ago, though I saw no way my Muslim brother could possibly be alive, I did not know. My will to hold on was still there; maybe because I'd yet to see "death with my own eyes!" "POP", the CO pops the last cell and says: Clean this cell out, pull that (points to a big rolled up bundle) to the front, strip the bed, and pack up the personals into the pillow case! It was obvious that the bundle referred to by the CO was the body of an inmate; whether or not it was the one who'd been told; you're not getting off that easy; I can't say. I had never touched a body before! What was going to happen to me if I showed this guy that I wasn't as capable of standing up to this inhumanity as he was; as they were capable of bringing it about!? I stood there for a few seconds, thinking! The CO stood there looking at me, then he says; let's go, this better not take you all night! Why wouldn't this guy leave so I could try and settle my heart? It was pounding as such that I just knew he heard it! Then I asked the coif I could have another pair of gloves please. He actually had the ridiculous nerve to say; I gave you a pair of gloves, what did you do with them?! (He was referring to those he'd given me, the first time!) You told me to give them back to you after I finished what I was doing; so I made sure I cleaned them, walked up and handed them to you before I was locked in. As he turned to walk away he says, come with me. Asking for the gloves worked; the time it took for me to go with him for the gloves and return, I was somewhat settled, and he wasn't standing over me! Being alone gave me a chance to see the other cell; that inmate was lying there on top of his blanket, with his clothes on; wet from the water they'd thrown on him, to revive him for what… (so he wouldn't get off that easy!)

Through all this time, not a single inmate uttered a word; made a sound! By no means were they asleep; but, suffering from psychological blows to the brain! I ask you to put yourself (a prisoner/inmate) in one of those cells, listening to blow after blow being meted out against the body of another human being as vulnerable as you might prove to be next! Blow after blow, sounding like thunder in a valley; echoed by the almost equally disheartening sound of plea filled moans! Who could blame them for their atrophy?!! Who'd possibly doubt that they were suffering from and through one degree or another of aphasia?! Imagine being so induced with fear, that you're unable to speak; my God! My God! After all, the only thing that might possibly account for me being able to go on, had to be that I'd succumb to the psychological trauma myself and was suffering from apathy. I did things like I was unconcerned; dragged that "bundle" from the cell to the front of the flats, like I was pulling dirty laundry! You tell me, what was happening to me?! What was really happening to me, to my humanity? Had a few short months been like shots of procaine (Novocain) to my conscience, enabling me to take on the "three monkey, second nature?" No, it wasn't that, I would never relinquish my soul to the house of Sodom and Gomorrah! There was something bigger, something greater, something, more important to me than I could ever be to myself; my wife and my three little guys! When I was taken away from them, "everything making it appear as though I'd left them on their own;" it was an unyielding determination in every breath I took, to return home to them, with the same, no, an even stronger sense of provider, protector and maintainer than I was when taken! The one (God) with power over all things was going to walk me, the new kid on the block, through it all! He (Allah) was going to do this; because I'd already shown I didn't have a clue! Had me making it this far been contingent on any knowledge that I had, I would have already been food for the maggots; I would have never left Sing Sing alive!! For me to say the beating of the this inmate was not as severe as that of a few nights ago would be making light of it; so I'll just say, it wasn't as savagely, as sadistically bloody! The extra-curricular activities of the CO's this night, allowed me to go back to my cell before dawn! The other inmate who'd been beaten that night, I have no idea what became of him; he was gone by the time the cells popped for chow in the morning!

After that night, everything was calm, not peaceful, but calm; not even the sound of a CO raising his voice at an inmate! I remained tier man my entire stay in reception, but, I was amongst five or six others who were selected to take test for consideration to work in the prison hospital as aides! My score must have been good, because after my tier detail, they'd take me right to the hospital floor to work! It was great; I'd work the remainder of the day in the hospital clinic! It's amazing, how things happen in life; one thing leading to and preparing you for another! There'd been many things I'd done in my life; the kind of things that when taking place, didn't seem relevant to anything that could possibly be worth anything!! Such isn't true, because there I was learning in some of the most unbelievable and heart wrenching ways; that life is always unfolding as it should! In less than four months, I'd been walked through filth, evil and indecency, to the doors of a system possibly as wretched as the empire of ancient Babylon itself! Until arriving at "Clinton correctional Facility;" I had long been convinced that the evil wickedness of Nebuchadnezzar was unrivaled! But Clinton had established tolerance levels and rules, which had all been etched into the skulls, broken jaws, broken noses, teeth, broken arms, legs, ankles, backs, and shoulders, literally etched into the past existence of who knows how many prisoners/inmates!

A week or so had passed since I'd started working in the prison hospital clinic. I was really enjoying the opportunity. One morning, just as I got to the top of the stairs to the third floor of H-Block, there was a Christmas tree which wasn't there the evening before. I had seen trees with an angel, a star, cross, et cetera on top; but this was the first time I'd ever seen a tree topped off with a fully dressed Ku Klux Klan doll!! Prior to that moment, I didn't think there was anything else for me to witness in Clinton of which I thought could possibly add to the drama, but I was wrong. It was then that I realized there was actually a method to the madness! Yes, everything I witnessed since I had arrived at Clinton had taken place with an in-house understanding of immunity! Everything from the split skull, broken arm and busted eye in the first hallway, to that so-called bundle of stuff which I'd been told to drag from the cell on the flats to the front were done with the "confidence of belonging to a fraternity" possessing both the "power and authority" to govern and hold sway over all internal aspects of the laws dealing with and related to the New York State Department of Correctional Services (LAST STRONG HOLD)! In other words I'm saying; Clinton was a NYSDOCS Prison Fraternity of Ku Klux Klan being overseen by a sadistically deviant mind of their Grand Dragon (warden)!! In light of what I've told you to this point, what papers do you think left from behind the walls where "Death was Inevitable?" As I continue, it should become clear that this multi-billion-dollar "business" is corrupt to the core!

5

Blood and Agony

AS THE WEEKS passed, I saw many inmates die of "natural causes". It may sound cold, me saying I was actually glad; seeing those inmates dying the way they were dying! But past weeks and months had all but shown me the "castration and decapitation" of some of my fellow inmates; at the hands of "those very CO's who'd, arguably, completed the most thoroughly professional training available anywhere in the country; for anyone desiring a career as a correction officer! Yes, I was glad to finally see some inmates dying because they'd come to the end of their natural lives, rather than they'd been "murdered in cold blood" by members of a secret order, carrying out murder, with immunity from prosecution!

There was one inmate dying from colon cancer; (first time I'd ever heard of such) when I met him he didn't look sick at all. It was unbelievable what 17 days did to him! In less than a months; his eyes, cheeks, face were so distorted; that were it not for the fact that I'd seen him waste away, even I would not have recognized him! The day before he died, he had asked me if I would just sit and read to him for awhile! I spoke with the hospital sergeant, explaining what the inmate had asked of me; and that my heart was saying to me; he's not going to be here when you come back! I pleaded with him to let me; telling him I'd stay back and do what he'd asked. At first he told me no, so I repeated my appeal; saying to the sergeant; please sir, I believe he also knows this is it for him; I know you don't owe me anything, not even consideration; but, he's suffered like you and I will probably never understand; please don't let him die alone, please sir! He looked at me; smiled and said; for you, not for him; give me your card, you're gonna be staying here anyway! I didn't really know anything about colon cancer; what I did know I'd learned while covering this inmate; I'd never had an experience like this! It was obvious this inmate wasn't going to be alive much longer to suffer, so I took my Holy Qur'an from my net bag, to read to him as he'd asked. He was Christian, so I read to him from chapter (19) Mary! He was surprised to hear that Muslims believe in Maryam (Mary), Jesus, his return, et cetera. Then I talked to him for awhile about chapter Taubah (9) Repentance, went on reading it to him; explaining some of what was being said, why, etc! While I was reading to him, chow came. He had a soft and bland diet; and would only eat if I sat with him. The past two days I fed him lunch; his dinner would still be next to his bed when I arrive in the morning! This particular day, I went to get his dinner tray, when I came back he said he wanted to eat later and wanted to know if it was ok with me. I put the cover back over his food, and turned to walk away; he calls me back and asked me to give him a hug! I know I don't know what such would look like; but at that moment, that second; looking into his eyes was like, was like looking into his soul! I'd never given him a hug before, and he'd never asked! It was like he knew; because, he said thanks for being my friend; and turned himself towards the wall… "That was it, he died with a friend!" This/His death, the death of my friend, was more than the death of another inmate; more than the death of another human being; it became a point in my life, which gave me a different perspective about death and dying! This inmate was young, very young; he hadn't been on the planet three decades. As many times as I'd read in Qur'an; "death comes to all, and the term is fixed"; my perspective of death and dying had never been that such terms were inclusive of young people; the term being fixed and terminal illnesses took on different meaning! It was in that moment, what I knew about the inmate murdered in Clinton, felt like a weight had been lifted from the shoulders of my mind! There was also a hadith (saying of Prophet Muhammad) pbuh (peace be upon him) that also began to echo through my mind; "There are three things known by no individual; when he is going to die, where he is going to die, and how he's going to die! These are three things written when each individual "receives his/her soul while in the womb of his/her mother!" Prior to recalling those things, one might say my behavior was similar to being in a semi trance state of mind; enabling me to, as previously stated: "hear no evil, speak no evil, and see no evil (the three monkeys)!!!

When I arrived at the clinic the next morning, I was assigned to care for two old men. One was a cute little man who knew his condition was terminal, but, felt he'd lived life with the cards he'd dealt himself. In fact when I met him, he was playing cards by himself (solitaire). I'd heard W.D. Muhammad say; In order to reach a person, you have to reach him through his concerns. Since hearing that, I'd proven such to be true a number of times, and I saw this as an opportunity to put it to use again. I asked him what he was playing, how it was played, etc. With unexpected excitement, he went right into explaining the game, telling me how much he liked playing it and why! Young fellow, it took me a long time to appreciate this game; did it when I got bored with myself. (ha ha ha ha, ha ha ha ha) He didn't say anything for a few seconds; then he said: Can't believe it! Really can't believe it; what a lousy deck of cards can teach a fool! (I didn't comment). Pointing at the rows of cards, he says; see this and this, I can't win this. What I need is way up here; even if I keep moving on everything else, I won't be able to move this! Do you know what the whole point of playing is? (He asked me) I said; to see if you can win. He starts laughing hard, I mean really laughing; then he says; I don't care how many times I've asked that question, I get the same answer! See, that's a fool playing cards; if you get into anything, you're in it to win! You're in it to win; the point is to win! It don't take long at all to see "if" you can win; if that's what you want, you'd know when to quit, but the point is to win! See here, I can still complete this row and this row, but will I win or will I lose? Seeing what I already see, why waste time now? Before now, it wasn't a waste of time; you understand, do ya? (hahahahaha) I love this game! I love this game! After listening to him, I told him that I'd rather not answer him right now, but I would get back to him with one. They're waiting for me to do some other things; I only wanted to introduce myself, since I'll be looking after you while I'm here. We shake hands, and he says to me; the only thing he hopes he doesn't have to deal with is wasting away!

The other inmate had suffered a partial stroke while in his cell! According to him; had he not been put on aspirin, but given the blood pressure pills which they knew he needed when he told them his cell had been searched, and they'd confiscated his blood pressure pills at that time! He went on to say; now I'll be crippled for the rest of my life from a partial stroke! He went on to say: It's a fuckin shame; the fuckin CO lied and said they never took my pills! Then, then they wrote me up; put me on keep-lock (confined to your cell, no movement outside your cell) for two weeks though they'd never turned in the ticket (write-up)! I didn't get my name on the sick-call list for two weeks; though the CO kept telling me it was there; I didn't get called! He went on to tell me he'd give different inmates, notes to give the CO telling them he'd felt dizzy sitting on the toilet; that his speech sounded funny, his face was twisted a little, his right arm drawn-up and his fingers curled up almost like a fist!

That evening, back in my cell, I lay thinking about the difference in the attitude of the two inmates which I was assigned to in the clinic. Different as night and day, but I guess it was understandable. The old man who was terminal was a real eye opener to me; his introductory comments about the card game (solitaire), his ability/willingness to accept his circumstances, situation and condition being the result(s) of the hand he'd dealt to himself! The stroke victim inmate would end up being only one of many cases of inmates falling victim to medical neglect for one reason or another; but, to what extent I would ultimately become involved before leaving Clinton, I had no idea! As I thought about the willingness of the inmate with the stroke to be as openly vocal as he was; I could not help but tell myself he had to have the heads up on just how far to go with his comments; and to whom he should make them! Before my stay in reception would end, the cute little old man would take a turn for the worse, and become quite cynical and resentful! In spite of the fact that I was an inmate just as he was; to the best of my knowledge I gave him no reason to be the way he was. He openly began to express a real lack of trust in me! There were even a few times I over-heard him referring to me as that "nigger snitch;" when talking to different CO, it was obvious the CO knew I'd heard different comments he'd made; so I found myself wondering why they hadn't given him to someone else! Perhaps that hadn't been done because they knew the other inmate aides had heard some of his comments, and had expressed no tolerance for him. If not that, they were waiting for me to get fed-up with being called a nigger; and do something foolish to him! Little did they know that I'd "never considered myself a despicable, uncouth, low-life, person;" so the name supposedly being directed at me, didn't bother me at all! In fact, I found myself making excuses for and/or defending him! In fact, one afternoon after coming back from the cell count and lunch; I went to him, he was in bed; (myself speaking) need anything man? Check this out; I'm not going to try and ever tell you I know how you must feel, just to have something to say. There is one thing I want you to know though; I don't know how much longer I'll be here; but for however long it is, as often as you need to man; curse at me, yell and scream at me; if you start feeling like whatever it is that's wrong is just too unbearable for you man. Don't get yourself in any trouble man; lash out at me okay; take it out on me, okay? There is something I do know about your situation; about how you "must feel;" scared! I understand sir; I really do! I can't honestly say that I'd be as strong and as brave as you'd tried to be! I just want you to know I have a lot of respect for what you've tried to show me! I wish there was something I could have done to prevent what you didn't want to happen from happening; you said you didn't want to waste away! I've heard some of your comments, and perhaps the personality you've been manifesting is a result of what you were afraid of; wasting away! Maybe you were afraid you'd become ugly in character if dying became too painful for you; and you didn't want to be remembered that way! I don't know if what I've just said is correct at all; but I know it's possible! (While saying the latter, I thought about the word wasted) You know something; I don't see how you could ever feel that you've wasted away; when it's because of what I've seen you go through that has me able to understand now, that dying under any condition must not be easy! It's been because of the struggle you've put forward for all of us to see; that one who is dying should at least try and be pleasant for as long as you can! So people will try and understand if and/or when your, dying steals your pleasantness away; you tried your best to be strong! When something waste away, nothing good comes from it, nothing becomes of it! Sir, anyone with the will to think; can't help but remember to understand clearly what the "point" is for whatever they venture into! Man you don't hardly, have any more reason to feel that you just wasted away; if I can manage to do what I've seen you do in such a short amount of time, I know I wouldn't feel that way! Lying there the entire time, he didn't move; never said a word! As I turned to walk away I said; again, I don't know whether or not I could promise anyone that my disposition, if I was dying; would be pleasant! See you in the morning man. The inmate who had suffered a stroke was eventually returned to population; he improved much in three weeks. Would it surprise you if I said many of the beds were occupied like clockwork by prisoners/inmates who'd fallen victim to the Ku Klux Klan fraternity! It might sound strange but, I didn't see anything wrong with, nor did it bother me taking care of inmates in the hospital because of inmate on inmate violence; this was prison! For me to say I was waiting would be an understatement; but boy was I waiting to get the hell out of the 'Last Strong Hold!' Something had been said to me by one of the hospital clinic sergeants some time back (you're stayin here anyway); but I never paid any attention to it. Thinking back, that was said to me when I was pleading with the hospital sergeant to allow me to stay behind and read to an inmate dying from colon cancer! I'd only met him when I was given a work detail in the clinic; but, he came to see me as his friend; I'd like to think we'd become just that (friends).

Well, the words; you're stayin here anyway, didn't pass me by after the count early one morning. I was out on the tiers doing my tier detail like any other morning, when the CO calls out (2749) my Din number. He follows that up repeating my Din number, but this time I hear the unthinkable; (2749) pack up, you're going to "D-Block!" My heart fell to my boots, because that meant I was going to population; I would be staying in Clinton! Walking pass the cells of other inmates, I could hear expressions of shock and dismay, as well as a few comments from inmates saying; "hey H (Anthony), I'm not surprised man; look at all the things they had you doing; I knew it; I knew they were gonna keep you; oh shit H, etc; etc;!" Ok, I was now on my way to my main stay where I'd be doing the remainder of my prison time (possibly)! "Yes this move meant I'd be staying in the 'Last Strong Hold' (Clinton), but this move was telling something else; I now knew I'd been "classified Max A!" (Highest Level Maximum Security) THE LAST STRONG HOLD!! I went back to my cell and sat; thoughts running all over the place! How did it come to this? Man oh man, what do I do now?

As I sat there, I thought back to February 79 in the Westchester county Jail when a detainee David Brown had asked me what in the world I was doing in there! As I began to tell him and got to three sawed off shotgun robberies, he interrupted and said; a doctor, that was (D), he robbed them three times in one night; ooh shit T (David Brown knew me as T back then), he bragged aboudum! Ooohh shit T! You can't imagine how I felt at that time, you have no accurate idea of how I felt knowing that there was someone who actually knew I hadn't done what I was accused of, but also knew who had! I tried a few times to talk David Brown into telling the Warden what he knew, but he refused! I sent for the Warden myself; explaining that it was urgent that I speak to him; he came right up! (I knew all of the brass in both facilities, because I was the Imam for Westchester County as far back as that) When the Warden came up, I explained that what I needed to discuss with him was of an extremely sensitive nature and had to be kept confidential; instead of talking to me on the floor, he took me down to his office! You should have seen his face when I told him the above; he was very upset to say the least! I asked him if he would wait a day or two before calling David Brown, so other detainees might not suspect anything; he agreed! When he did call David and me down, David still refused, explaining that he was on his way back up north and there was no way he could snitch and "live" when word got out inside! I understood, so did Warden Jake; but the Warden expressed being more concerned about his Imam than, about somebody who deserved prison! Yes, the Warden knew about the so-called rap sheet of mine; but he'd come to see me for me! He threatened David Brown with keep lock, loss of commissary, as well as denying him visits for the remainder of his time in W.C.J. (until picked up by NYSDOCS)! David chose keep-lock et cetera, rather than taking a chance; after a few days, I asked to be taken down to see the Warden; I told the Warden I appreciated what he was trying to do; but that I believed I understood what David was worried about! The Warden told me he had no problem locking him for as long as he could, and sending an envelope along with him to NYSDOCS! I told the Warden it was really bothering me that I'd betrayed the trust that David Brown had in me, in order for him to even tell me he knew who it was; please let him out; he did! As for the other sentencing, I'll leave that to be read about in my next book.

For now, let's go on with my trip in and through, 'The Last Strong Hold! There I was; someone who'd never be the same! Oh yes, for those who are unfortunate enough not to understand how far removed the cover of the book can often be from its content; they'll see "what they see," haah (slight laugh)! On the other hand, I'm certain the same will prove to hold true for another aspect of society, capable of holding my future in the balance; they too will see what they see; true or not, they'll see! You may be saying to yourself; I don't understand why you're having a problem going into population, you've been in two prisons for awhile now; how different can it really be? I sat there, trying to psyche myself into that very frame of mind; prison is prison, but it wasn't working! Clinton had a reputation which preceded it; that reputation was the result of living and dying, life and death experiences! Yes, I'd been in two prisons in six short months; six months which were exactly as described, "short!" Early in my writing, I'd shared with you something which I'd heard W.D. Muhammad say: Anything that sends a message to the mind is a word; and words make people. A mere passing thought of that will not suffice if you are to appreciate the magnitude of what was said. That statement is like good food, just putting the food into your mouth and swallowing it, you'll miss all of the seasonings and spices unless you take time to chew!

In the short six months that I'd been in prison, messages almost without number had been sent to my mind, translating into volumes of words, doing what to me? Would I ever be the same again? There I was, someone who'd probably seen more death, more murder, more blood, in six months in prison; than many men had probably seen who'd survived Viet Nam! That's one hell of a comparison; seeing as how the blood and murders in particular; which I was referring to were the direct result of, and at the hands of CO/police for the NYSDOCS! Again, remember where I was; in a prison which was notorious throughout the state of New York, for its deaths at the hands of its corrections officers! This is where I was getting ready to enter into population, which held some of New York State's most violent; it held some of the most violent, most dangerous convicts not only in New York, but in the United States! It's hard to believe, with such being true, I'd not witnessed a single killing, a single murder by any of NYSDOCS Maximum-A Security inmates! It wouldn't be long before I would learn; before I would see that the "Clinton Fraternity had even deeper secrets;" but little did I know that I'd come to "play a more intricate part" in this "citadel;" under the watchful eye of its Grand Dragon!

6

Unexpected Destination on D Block

MY FIRST DAY in general population, I don't know whether to say I was happy or sad. The entire time in reception, I hadn't been out to the yard, that wasn't allowed for reception/classification; I was now an official top security convict, able to walk amongst the convicted mass population in the yard! I couldn't begin to imagine what to expect now, but one thing was certain; I was going to find out! While in reception, there was one afternoon out of the week; that I did have about two hours with certain inmates in population; that was on Fridays (Ju'mah). Friday was the day when those inmates of the Islamic faith observed their religious services. All Muslim inmates were brought together for congregational prayer in the school building; but, that gave me no idea how big Clinton was.

When I got to D-Block, it didn't take me but a few minutes to set my Hilton Towers Suite up; I took care of that, and was ready to mingle with some of the vacationers on the patio around the reserved cooking areas overlooking the handball courts, ball field, track, et cetera, et cetera! It didn't take long for the news to spread throughout the resort that a new high roller had just arrived (me 2749) hahahaha; just thought I'd mess with your head for a moment; back to what I had to do before I made it to the yard. There I was; all set to make my first trip to the yard when the CO who had brought me to D-Block yells out; "2749, 2749 let's go!" Surprised the hell out of me; he was calling me to take me to the hospital clinic, my detail! I'm going to leave it to you to express how you think I felt; what the look on my face must have looked like (smile)! Anyway, I went to work like nothing had changed; but believe me; things were falling into place faster than I could settle into them! Suddenly, the hospital sergeant: "2749 come with me, leave the inmate and come with me." As far as I knew, I hadn't done anything wrong; but this was Clinton, and I'd seen that wrong has a definition all its own! I had to ask: sergeant, is everything alright; I didn't get any bad news from home I hope; (that was my way of asking an innocent question)! Oh no, got some good news for ya; everybody's really pleased with ya! So, Mrs. Johnston asked me to bring you to see her; she wants to talk to you for a few minutes; that's all! We take the elevator to the next floor and walk around to a CO sitting at a desk outside a closed door (sick call). I have a seat for a few minutes; the two of them go into the sick call clinic; a few minutes later CO Travis comes out and tells me to go in. The nurse Mrs. Johnston, I notice is reading a file on me; while the sergeant and I stand there! She's actually reading and going through page after page after page; but of what? I obviously haven't caused any problems (I'm still breathing and healthy); so what is in that file, on me? I know I'd been told everything was alright, but I also knew where I was; I couldn't settle my nerves! Though I'd only been standing there fifteen minutes, it seemed like hours had passed! The nurse looks up at me and asked: Are you ok? I don't know, I can't help but feel like I've done something wrong; but I don't know what! She smiles and says take it easy; it's about a work detail in my clinic! Impressive;

your test scores are very impressive! Your behavior through reception has been noted! How did you like working in the hospital? Seems like you did quite well there; handled yourself well in stressful situations! I asked if I could ask a question; what kept me here, my test scores? "Your 3-11, reception officer spoke to the Warden about you!" I just stood there looking at her... The sergeant says; you're going to be working here in the hospital clinic with Mrs. Johnston, RN. I will start by telling you this detail calls for trust and confidentiality! Because of what you are going to have access to in the clinic; you can almost certainly look forward to other inmates "pushing up on you!" You might even find yourself thinking about taking advantage of opportunities; I'm sure you will have a lot of them! Hear me well; you better think "long and hard" about what you decide in any case! You will be Mrs. Johnston's clinic and sick call aide and make prison rounds with her as well; you will start tomorrow, a CO will pick you up!

The first CO I was introduced to, was CO Travis; his post, a desk was right outside the clinic; in fact he's the same CO that was there when I was brought up that day. He told me to have a seat; he went inside the clinic for about five minutes; when the door opens, the CO's standing there gesturing for me to come in. The nurse was not a young lady, but you were able to see that she had not just let herself go. Well! So you're my new aide, and from what I've read, you're going to do just fine! My name is Janet Johnston; what would you prefer, your first or last name? It, doesn't really matter, you can call me Anthony, if you want. She says; there are three things I want you to understand, clearly understand! Don't ever take it upon yourself to do anything on your own! Don't you ever answer any questions having to do with this clinic or anything having to do with another inmate or his file! Lastly, don't repeat anything you might see/hear pertaining to the clinic! Now, repeat what I just said... Sitting there, I began replaying what the nurse had said to me. I remember taking a deep breath then saying; there's no need. The CO was standing there and says; there's no need, what in the hell do you mean there's no need repeat what Mrs. Johnston told you to repeat! Repeat it right now! I said again, there's no need, I heard and understand what I was just told. Officer Travis, I'm not trying to be smart, but the last thing Mrs. Johnston said to me was don't ever repeat anything you might hear up here; Mrs. Johnston, I guess I'm going to have to put my trust in you helping me should I find myself confronted with something like this in the future! She asked; what do you mean? Mrs. Johnston, just as Officer Travis was insisting that I repeat something I'd just heard in here; it might happen that another officer confronts me for whatever reason, insisting that I tell him what was discussed whenever. I don't feel it should be on me to tell whoever it might be, about anything; I'm only going to say; the nurse Mrs. Johnston knows about that stuff; not me. What if it's thought that I'm trying to be smart? She looks at the CO then smiles at me and says; "Anthony, you don't have to worry about that; it's good you mentioned that to me. I'll deal with the possibility of that right now, believe me!" I'd made mention of how far removed the cover of the book can be from the contents; nothing about the appearance (cover) of Mrs. Johnston even began to suggest that she was a voice able to put a stop to anything that anyone might be doing/thinking about doing; if she wasn't in agreement with it! Keep reading, you'll see what I mean... You're going to do just fine; turning to the sergeant, she says; let everyone know Anthony is my clinic aide, and give them all of the "necessary information on him!" She thanked the sergeant; before leaving he says; I'm sure you'll call if you need me!!

Mrs. Johnston asked me if I had any question before we got

down to the business of the clinic. I said no, I'd wait until she had finished familiarizing me with what she felt I should know for now. She smiled and began familiarizing me with the cabinets, the equipment, the supplies, forms, labels, tags, utensils, filing procedures, et cetera! It was great! I was on the weekly "out count;" meaning I would not return to my suite (cell) until shortly after the CO shift change at 3:00 pm. I didn't go to the mess hall for chow (lunch), because there was a kitchen on the fifth floor of the hospital building. I was allowed to use the kitchen for lunch (Mon. – Fri.). When I say I was allowed to use the kitchen, this meant whatever the kitchen had been stocked with, was available to me. Fresh eggs, milk, ground beef, sodas, lettuce, tomato, pastries, fresh fruit, (vanilla, chocolate, strawberry) ice cream, wheat bread, cheese, et cetera; along with all the necessary kitchen appliances, including a juicer/blender; I had no problem at lunch time! Now that I think about it, my entire stay as the clinic and sick-call aide, I never had company for lunch! No, I hadn't just assumed that it was alright to make such use of the kitchen and what it had to offer, CO Travis had made it clear to me; Anthony, it's been made clear to us that you're "Mrs. Johnston's aide;" you're to help yourself; just don't abuse it by swaging (trying to sneak anything back from the kitchen)!!

We did Sick-Call rounds everyday to different cell blocks throughout the prison; I'd carry a basket containing the files of inmates to be seen; along with the sphygmomanometer (blood pressure cuff), stethoscope, and note pad used by me! It was my responsibility to go to the cells of those prisoners who were keep locked, and examine them! My examination of keep locked inmates, consisted primarily of checking their pulse, respiration, blood pressure and temperature, which I'd record in my note pad, and transfer them into their medical files after returning to the clinic. If there happened to be an individual in need of a bandage change, I'd take care of that as well. In case it's not understood, those inmates on sick-call but not keep locked would come to the front of his tier, and seen by the nurse. All in all, there was such a difference; being in general population rather than reception!

I'd made mention earlier that I'd been allowed to attend Ju'mah, the Friday prayer service for the inmates whose religion was Islam; so I'd met a hundred or more Muslims while in reception there in Clinton. If you recall, while in Sing Sing I was with one of the three individuals who'd been convicted for allegedly murdering Malcolm X; I would now find myself doing time here in the 'Last Strong Hold' with a second of the three convicted for allegedly murdering Malcolm! I would find them to be as different as day and night in their personality, manner and overall disposition! Inmate (I'll refer to him hence forth as Abdul) and I had some very interesting conversations; or would it be more correct to say my brother Abdul shared with me, some interesting facts! The inmate Imam (whom I'll refer to as Abd) was surprised when he heard that the prison had given me the work detail as clinic and sick-call aide. I can't help but play back the comment that had been made by an elderly black man one day while in the yard. He walked up to me and asked if it was true; I responded; is what true? I heard you were the clinic and sick-call aide. I acknowledged that it was true; he goes on to say: You know, when they brought me here, they brought me here in a horse and buggy; you're the first "nigger clinic and sick-call aide" in the history of this prison!

It was only my third time going to the yard, and my first time on the Muslim's cooking court. Every group had a cooking court located on the hillside in the yard. A couple of the brothers were cooking, making use of the accommodations of tree wood, half a steel drum and a pit. People on the outside think they can cook; if you want to see cooking, believe me, you haven't seen cooking until you see it done on one of the courts in Clinton's yard! I mean three course meals with deserts were cooked outside; even in the dead of bitter winter! It would be an absolute waste of my time, if I were to attempt to explain/describe the quality; the amazing quality of the meals! Perhaps it would give you a better sense of appreciation if you will realize that we're looking at decades of practice/schooling, just like individuals having attended chef school! In any case, there were inmates who'd endure the bitter cold to cook outside, instead of tolerating some of the mop water tasting meals in the mess hall! There were prisoners who actually had menu selections, and would take orders which included delivery right to your cell! I was surprised to see that the orders weren't skimpy; I laugh even now as I'm picturing how the different items were carefully arranged on the dish (cardboard wrapped with foil) with foil over the meal!

I remember being on the Muslim's cooking court one day; the weirdest thing happened. This guy comes across the yard, to the cooking court; he said Mr. Peterson told him to tell me to come to the weight court for a minute. So I got up and went to see what Mr. Peterson wanted. When I got to the weight court one of the guys stopped me. Mr. Peterson must have let him know it was okay for me to come on the court. The only thing Mr. Peterson said to me was: "always know where you're at"; and he went back to lifting weights! It was obvious that I was in Clinton; so what else did he mean?! I stood there for a few seconds thinking; then I smiled and walked away. What did Mr. Peterson mean; and why did he tell me that? When I got back to the cooking court I sat down, still thinking about what was said. Dang; what did that mean? I got up and went back inside. I could do that if I wanted to; after all, I worked for Mrs. Johnston! When I got to my cell, I kept thinking; "always know where you're at; always know where you're at"! What in the heck did he mean? Like I said, I knew I was in Clinton, how would I not always know that? Throughout the rest of the day I thought about what Mr. Peterson had said to me. I woke up thinking about it! Then it clicked. Anthony, always know who's around you; don't take where you are for granted; keep in mind that there are people who envy you your work detail; don't let yourself get comfortable in your detail! Brother, always remember you're in prison; always know where you're at! When I went to the yard that day, I went straight to see Mr. Peterson on the weight court. The same brother stopped me from coming onto the court; then let me on. I told Mr. Peterson what I thought he must have meant; he just looked at me and smiled; then went back to lifting weights! I smiled and walked the yard a few times; I kept saying to myself; always know where you're at Anthony!

I'd been in population about two months without incident, until one afternoon in the yard! It had snowed and the administration like always, had allowed a ski-jump to be made. Umph, traffic really picked up in the clinic during this time of year! The thrill of victory (a good jump)! The agony of defeat (let's call it a miscalculated jump)! Of the many things I learned while in prison, one of the most important of them was; there are prisoners who have mastered what should be called, the taking advantage of opportunity, art! Believe me, "New York State Department of Correctional Services Training Academy" beyond a practical degree, doesn't even begin to qualify its COs to do their job! The state can't have all of the right people as part of its training staff to help in the preparation of their CO. There are many things you can't learn from books; only with actual experience can many tools be passed on to those in the training academy classrooms! At the end of any shift wherein the prison population is up and about, the only reason the CO make it home is because the "prison population has chosen to be cooperative!" Anyone not in agreement with this is either a fool, blind, or lying to, himself. Which is the, more dangerous of the three!? In my opinion; a fool is a fool! Unbeknown to the general public, and perhaps even to the prison administration; the one thing which factors into the prison population cooperating is absolutely relevant to the Muslim population. In any of the maximum security prisons, nothing of consequence is going to jump off if we (the Muslim) object to it! What happened in Attica never would have happened, had Qur'an and Sunnah been factored into the equation and respected by the administration! The inmate Muslim population is not going to play into something which goes against the Holy Qur'an and the Sunnah of Prophet Muhammad (pbuh)! The inmate Imam holds sway over much of the prisons temperament; and is highly acknowledged by the remainder of the prison population! The State Senator should be ashamed of himself for using his position to undermine the Muslim Chaplain/Imam employed by the state! The general public doesn't have the first clue as to the truth pertaining to the vital role which these Muslim Chaplain/Imam play in keeping the thousands of inmate Muslim, sober minded while they (inmate Muslim) search for proper understanding of what they'd be left alone to interpret; were it not for the sober, balanced minded Muslim Chaplain/Imam!

Back to what I made mention of when I said one of the most important things I'd learned was; there were prisoners who'd mastered taking advantage of opportunity! Here's an example of what I mean; while the prisoners were doing their ski jumps, performing for both CO and prisoner, something was cooking on the cooking court...On one of the courts in the middle of the hill there were five prisoners; one sitting and four standing around laughing, or so it seemed. The appearance of laughter seemed normal, especially with the ski activities going on. But, an attentive look would reveal that one of the four inmates who'd been standing a few seconds ago was now sitting! His sitting would have been no problem had it not been that he was sitting on the lap of the first inmate seated! The up and down bouncing around movement made it clear what was happening! The, victim was pulled to a standing position, but only long enough for one of the other three to sit! I noticed what may have been one of the others putting something into the hand of the inmate who'd just sat! By his hand motion, I'd assume it was Vaseline! This inmate was sodomized again and again until the fourth one finished! Watching it happen, it was really amazing; how they'd perfected this rape method to the point that it literally looked like five inmates enjoying the skiing festivities and preparing food on their cooking court! I'd never have noticed it, had one of the brothers not helped me increase my education by asking me to look around the courts and tell him if I noticed anything crazy going on! He went to the point of directing me to the general location! I didn't notice a thing! Even after he directed my attention to that court, I still didn't notice anything at first! After he told me to keep looking did I notice the switch of the seats! It was funny, my reaction; because I had the nerve to say to the brother; brother, check that out; look at what they're doing man; like he hadn't been the one who'd shown me! That blew my mind! That blew my mind!! Reading this, you're probably asking yourself; how could this happen and nobody notice his pants were down?! To do what was done, and it goes unnoticed; they split the seam of his pants, through his underwear, with a razor! Let me share with you something more unbelievably amazing than that. What was being done to that kid was being watched across the yard; everybody on the hillside was aware of what was happening!

In fact, you can place a bet that there weren't more than a few inmates who weren't aware! I would have been amongst that few; not including the prison "guards!" It's a sad, pathetic shame; the fact that apart from a few new inmates, the only ones who didn't have a clue that an inmate under the watchful eyes of some of finest trained coin the country; were the correction officers themselves! Two days after the rape incident in the yard, an inmate is brought to the clinic, complaining of blood in his stool! Mrs. Johnston would examine him; only to find that he had a white sock stuffed with toilet paper in his briefs, trying to hide the bleeding; the padded sock was "soaked with blood!" The nurse knew immediately that he'd been raped (sodomized), but had no idea when; and that it was at the hands of four prisoners; one after the other! He denied being raped, but that it was due to being constipated!! The nurse wrote her report stating clearly that upon examination of inmate, evidence indicates that he'd been the victim of rape (sodomy); that the inmate is denying that anything of the kind happened! The prisoner is claiming that he's been constipated! In my opinion, there was something seriously wrong with that prisoner/inmate internally! I did the cleanup of the examination area after the nurse completed her examination of him; the padded sock, gauze, and padding were all indications of the amount of blood the prisoner/inmate must have loss! Had he been bleeding since the rape in the yard a couple days ago? Why he wasn't admitted into the hospital was not for me to question! Though everyone understood that I was Mrs. Johnston aide, I did not let whatever that meant fool me; I was still a prisoner/inmate, a prisoner! Instead of admitting him, he was given something that looked like milk to drink while there; and some to take back to his cell! He didn't come up to the clinic after that appointment and I didn't see him in the yard again; but I would see the four prisoners/inmates who'd violated him! He would end up being stabbed to death a few months later; word got around that he made an attempt to regain some sense of self worth! In the area just as you turn to exit the building, into the yard; he was waiting with a shank to stick the one who'd led the rape! Unfortunately, there was one thing the poor kid hadn't taken into consideration; when opportunity presented itself, was he going to be convict enough to kill!!! He was not in a convict preparatory course; wherein like martial arts, you're given sparing sessions! It was said that he stepped out talking about what he was going to do to the less than a dog that'd violated him so savagely! The true blooded convict saw the talking for what it was; cowardliness, fear; a punk giving a cold blooded convict another opportunity to establish his reputation! The kid was stabbed up; I'll leave it for your imagination to tell you whether or not the price he paid for peace was his only choice…!

Leaving the block one morning for the clinic, I saw someone; who for some reason I wasn't expecting to see again since I was now in population! Seeing him again really set me back! I would learn his nickname from prison population; and would also learn that he was notorious for his reputation (blue eyes)! Some of the things I heard about him didn't sound far-fetched at all in light of having witnessed the aftermath of some of his cold-blooded activities; his sadistic, heartless nature in reception! It was CO blue eyes who brought a halt to Allah-u-Akbar after the quiet bell one night! It was blue eyes who made my reception stay, a stay which I will remember for the rest of my life! Any prisoner having spent any amount of time in Clinton knows about and can probably tell you some blood curdling stories about blue eyes, the devil himself! It was no secret to the prison populations across the state back then; "death was inevitable for the prisoner who was unfortunate enough to get extra attention" from "blue eyes!" Only Allah/God, blue eyes, and the Grand Dragon "know how many prisoners vanished from Clinton" because of him (blue eyes)!! When I saw him, I know he recognized me, because he said; unfortunately, the nigger who replaced you in H-Block was a disappointment; I hear Officer Travis is pleased with you in the clinic! I didn't really know how to respond, so I didn't say anything; just stood there until he asked me what I was waiting for; if I was waiting for something! Then I said, I thought there was something you wanted me to do! He said no, and then told me to hurry and catch up with the rest of the hospital crew! All that day while working, I couldn't get him out of my mind! I was imagining all kinds of things; reasons for him being in my block! First of all, it was morning, not evening or night time; second, he'd made a comment about the prisoner/inmate (nigger) who'd taken my place, as being a disappointment; and another comment about Officer Travis being pleased with my work in the clinic! What was he up to? What did he have on his mind? This prison being a citadel in which he was "infamous," this was the deal; he was working his regular; a floater (a CO not assigned to any permanent post)! It seems he was covering for a CO when I was in reception; he's a general population CO regularly! As the weeks and months passed, old blue eyes, was acting like a CO on probation, though it wasn't the case! I can't say what was what at that time where it concerned him. Whatever it was, I was certain of one thing; there was no CO with those eyes; only blue eyes, was blue eyes! Once you came to know this guy, you'd know him regardless of behavior! A quarter century, and believe me, to date I've been around and in the immediate company of people from one corner of the globe to the other, every ethnicity; but it seemed like this leopard hadn't changed his spots!

In the meantime, I was still the clinic and sick call aide; and Clinton was still prison (The Last Strong Hold)! Not forgetting that I was in the only prison in the state, possibly in the country where "death was inevitable," most certainly kept me alive! I was and would continue to be privy to medical file cleaning such as following: It was just before the call to go back for the count and chow (dinner); The nurse, Mrs. Johnston had asked me to go to the prisoners medical file room for a file; as I get to the end of the hall, to your right was another hall with a prisoner's waiting room for inmates waiting to be seen by the dentist, talk, play cards, etc. As I look down the hall, I notice a weird scene; a head bobbing out and in, out and in the doorway; it was a faggot by the name of Shaky. It was obvious that the person was bending over, doing what he, it got paid to do! Yes, there was Shake-Shake; a five foot, six inch faggot; but was I right about who it was on the other end?! Having an idea, hoping with everything in me that I was wrong, I had to see; so I walked down the hall! Without realizing it, in a sort of gasp I said; aaahh Darryl! Aaahh Darryl! An individual who I might have been willing to stand back to back with, in this den of, in this den of iniquity; a father of three beautiful little daughters and an equally beautiful wife; had fallen victim to Shaky the faggot; and reduced to shame; at least in my eyes! Darryl had talked to and poured his soul out to me; he'd sat in either his cell or mine and cried real tears of regret! What can I say that might make you understand how I felt; was it hurt, was it sadness, was it disappointment, was it that I was afraid for him?! I stood there looking at and witnessing absolute shamelessness as he pushed and pulled, pushed and pulled! It must have been satisfying enough to such a degree that it made him oblivious, as he smiled and pulled away; spinning Shaky around; and without wiping himself, pushed the faggot to his knees to suck shit! I stood there and watched shit suck shit!! (Please excuse me for being so frank, so straightforward; but I want to present a reality of prison as such as you'll never have a chance to see;

even on a Hollywood screen!). One would think he couldn't possibly be brought any lower; but I haven't finished sharing with you all that I'd witnessed! Darryl, while being washed orally, was still smiling; he would now ask me to "keep check" (lookout, for him)! My response to Darryl was: Check this out Darryl, and hear me well; don't ever say anything else to me; I will never speak to you again about anything! Shaking my head, I turned and walked back down the hall to the file room! The faggot was suppose to be waiting to see the dentist; he was the first one upstairs for the dentist; but for a pint of ice cream, or sloppy rectum seconds, the inmate dental clerk would put your folder on bottom everyday of the week! While in the file room, I couldn't get what I had just witnessed out of my mind! It wasn't two weeks ago that Darryl had gone into a rage over an inmate who'd chosen to be emasculated, smiling at him! We were in the mess hall for breakfast one morning when this transvestite acknowledged Darryl, with a smile. Darryl went crazy; he was tight to the point that he had trouble eating! I tried to get his mind off of what he was feeling, but it was like he hadn't heard anything I had said! Sitting at our table he says to me; "Anthony, what do I look like, huh?! What do I look like to that sick, punk, freak mother fucker, huh?! See if sh'it (she/it) smiles when I get done! As we returned to the block, I tried talking to him; but he was only concerned about one thing; he was concerned about his image; what people would think about him; his reputation in the joint! As they say: If something is going to go wrong, it's going to go wrong! Just as we reach the block gate, another inmate says to Darryl; yo Darryl, if you ain't gonna tap dat ass, put dat word in fa me! I been tryin ta git dat attention since it came inna block; you know my lockas full, and I go toda store (commissary) every buy! This guy couldn't have had any idea of the state of mind Darryl was in, no idea at all! Darryl, turned like he was going to walk away, then spun back around, punched this guy in the face; grabbed him and pushed his face into the bars! Nigga, who are you talking to, huh?! You don't know me, nothing about me! A faggot is a faggot is a faggot! You're a faggot just like that castrated freak mother fucker down stairs; he takes it, you give it! If you ever dreama sayin something like dat ta me, you betta wake up apologizing ta me! He had this guys face into the bars the entire time; he then shoved him to the side and walked away! I decided to leave Darryl alone, because he wasn't thinking, and didn't seem to care! A minute or so later, I heard in a low but aggressive voice; "Smile now punk mother fucker; smile at me now!" Though it had been months ago, there were certain sounds which would forever be distinct to me! There they were again, those muffled ummph, ummph, ummph sounds were again in my ear; like ghost haunting me from H-Block! They were followed-up this time by apologies; I'm sorry! I'm sorry Darryl! I ran down to the transvestite's cell where I'd see Darryl stomping and kicking him/shit! (You may be asking yourself why I choose to refer to this individual as a transvestite instead of a faggot); he had made a decision to go through the procedure which would make him/shit what he/shit wants to be in his/shits heart; I'll not let myself put him/shit in the same category with that foul excuse for a human being, Shaky! It was puzzling me, I couldn't put it together; it wasn't making sense to me; so I asked Darryl the question; what's wrong with you man? What in the hell is wrong with you?! Why are you acting like you've lost your mind because this dude smiled at you man? Just as he gets ready to kick the guy again, I grabbed him; he looks at him/she-it and says; if you ever look at me again, even stand near me in a line, "I'll take you the fuck out (kill you)!" He breaks away from me and walks away saying; nobody in nis mother fucker better ever ged'it innair head that I'm soft! This is the same Darryl whom

I'd just seen aggressively involved both anally and orally with another male prisoner; what in the world was I missing here? Was Darryl trying to do something to put himself into a more masculine frame of mind, knowing he had tendencies which were as such that would bring him to what I saw? Was he trying to pull himself away from the direction he knew he was headed for? Both the inmates who'd been beaten up by Darryl were brought to the clinic the next morning and put in the box after they received medical attention; because they refused to give up the name of who'd beat them up! When the incident was finally written up, it was said the two had fought each other; reason or reasons, questionable!

I guess I'd taken longer than I should have to pull the file I'd been sent for; because the CO was sent to see where I was! When I took the file back to the nurse, I lied and told her that I'd been trying to get to the bathroom all morning; but because of the number of inmates scheduled for morning clinic, I'd held it until now! What I'd said about the number of inmates was true; that I'd waited to go to the bathroom was not true. We were still waiting on the escort officer to take us back for the count; so, by the time he arrived Mrs. Johnston was finished with the file and I had enough time to take it back to the file room! Still giving some thought to the madness I'd seen, I didn't pay any attention to the file until I was opening the drawer to the file cabinet. As I began to thumb through the alphabet location; it seemed that the file was lighter in content; I opened it to see if Mrs. Johnston had filed some medical up-dates; but the most recent medical update was awhile back! I dismissed it by telling myself that maybe she'd asked for the file because it was needed in order for her to do just that; check on whether or not it was time for him to get some follow-up medical exam of some kind, based on her desk calendar! I filed the folder and didn't think about it anymore!

Later that evening, I noticed Darryl had gone pass my cell to his a number of times over a short span of time! Finally he stops and tries to justify his sick act(s); I said to him: Darryl I told you not to ever say anything else to me! But I want to remind you of something; remember a week or so ago, how you went stark-raving-mad in the mess hall; simply because a transvestite smiled at you?! Let's not forget the guy who happened to come by at the wrong time and made the wrong comment(s) about that smile directed at you! Oh and there's the comment you made about a faggot is a faggot is a faggot; one takes it, one gives it! Check this out man; when your family comes to visit you this week end, and you know she's coming; because she doesn't miss a week; do you think you're any more in need of having your biological passions satisfied, than your wife is man? I'd really dread your wife finding out about your sick tail ride today man! Brother Anthony, I didn't mean for you to see that! I'm, sorry brother, I never would have wanted you to see me doing that! Listening to him, I had to tell him to stop; I'm the one you stood there; smiled at, then asked to keep check for you! But I can say one thing with no doubt at all; I don't have to live with it, you do! He was standing in the gate way of my cell; I said excuse me, walked passed him; and left him standing there! As I walked away, he says: "Ok Mr. I would never do that;" wait till you been down eight years, then come see me; come see me then! It was hard to believe, but it became a regular between the two of them; and he stayed away from my cell! In about six months, it would sometimes be heard; him being teased by certain inmates; they'd tease him with an expression which men direct towards men after they've been married awhile! Before the man got married, he was known to come and go and do whatever he wanted to do. But since getting married, you can't even get him to come play a game of ball; go out with the fellas for pizza, nothing;

unless the wife says it's alright After awhile, the other brothers will start saying; ooohh buddy, you're whipped, she got you… whipped! Well, that was what Darryl had become the joke; because of his manner when that faggot was around! It was sad, but I wasn't sorry for him!

There's something which I think must be worse than death that happens to two inmates when the facility catches them in a homosexual act! Well, what I'd said about Darryl; a husband and the father of three little heart stealing daughters; being reduced to shame, ultimately found its way home! They got caught by a CO in a homosexual act; they were written up and boxed (solitary confinement)! If the extent of the penalty had stopped there, it might not have been as shameful; but no, that's much too humane! The administration contacts the families of all parties involved; informing them that their husband, son, or nephew, has been caught being an active participant in an act of homo-sexuality! Having been found guilty, he's been placed in solitary confinement; and allowed no visits, et cetera, et cetera! One thing they don't tell the family is what his active part was; they leave that for the family member to further agonize over, as though the mere news of it isn't agonizing enough! It would have been one thing for his wife to learn about this heart breaking situation, by way of mail from the administration; but they didn't notify her in time; though he got caught on Monday! His wife came with the children to visit him, and was told in front of every other visitor within hearing range: Mrs. Johnson, you will not be allowed to have a visit with "your husband until further notice" because "your husband was caught engaging in an act of homosexuality;" and has been put in solitary confinement! One would think something as embarrassing and sensitive as that would warrant professionalism on the part of the employee breaking such news; but when had Clinton been known for professionalism!

On the other hand, if there'd been a book on methods and manners of presentation its table of contents would not have contained anything to deal with that situation. If the time ever comes for my wife to know that I'm having an affair, it won't be with another male; and I'll think of the best way to break the news. What was he going to do now? What could he possibly say? One would think eight years of prison would have helped him mature enough to know and understand that decisions leave one with consequences to deal with! There he was once again, left to deal with realities given birth by a choice he'd made! He was going to have to face something unlike anything he'd ever faced in his life! What he'd lusted for had taken on a different meaning because there were others now involved in giving definition to his acts! Darryl was a killer, a murderer in the full definition of the word! He'd kill a brick, and look for it to bleed; but, what now?? Week after week passed but he still hadn't come face to face with his wife! Forty-five days were over and he was brought back to the block. His spirit was gone; having known him to be more of a total person, that person was gone; nonexistent! Anyone who'd known him prior; would see without doubt that Darryl was no longer there! The rep; the image which he'd so concerned himself was gone; it wasn't even a matter of question, he was seen in a different light now! A couple weeks after being back in population, his wife came without the children to see him; as though he'd not put her through enough, he refused to go down for the visit! She was there the next day (Sunday) to visit him, so she must have stayed the night at Kay's (Hotel) across the street from the prison; again he didn't go down to see her! At first I'd told myself I wasn't going to allow myself to get caught-up in his situation, it was too deep! But, that wasn't me; though he had brought it on himself, he was going to have to face that long after prison; so I made a trip to his cell. He wouldn't face me;

in fact he didn't talk to me at all! I'd told myself that you can't go any lower in your marriage; but I guess I was wrong huh? You don't think you at least owe your wife an explanation man? In spite of being utterly humiliated and embarrassed; she still makes a trip through the night, to come here to visit you! Though you show her such absolute disregard by not going down to see her, she takes a chance and stays at Kay's; just to try and see you again! You've been here eight years, so you know better than I do about what has happened to female visitors who'd spent nights at Kay's! If you don't do anything else Darryl, go see your wife brother! I know she has to still be up here, because there's no ride back down state until after the visit is over today. If the Watch commander, lieutenant, or sergeant is on today, maybe I can tell the CO I have something important I've got to speak to him about, which I need to speak to him in confidence! (D) I have to know that you're going to agree to go down though, before I try and talk to the lieutenant! Your wife has probably gone back over to her room at Kay's; the Watch commander can call over there for her to come back over here. It was something after 9:00 am now, so Darryl still had plenty of time if he was going to go. He still hadn't said anything to me so I got frustrated and blurted out: This is exactly the reason you're in this predicament now; because you're a creep, an inconsiderate, selfish creep!

    I walked away from his cell. I was in my cell reading, hoping my wife and sons would be able to make it; though I would not have been disappointed. My wife was doing a fantastic job; struggling to keep life going for our family, while at the same time, going to college in the evening for an Associate Degree! The little change I managed to make for my clinic detail, I would fill out a disbursement form and send the money home monthly ($50.00 plus or minus). Occasionally I'd buy myself a jar of peanut butter and jelly; ice cream, cakes, soda etcetera,

Allah (God) had blessed me with a prison detail for which prisoners would kill, were that a way to possibly get that detail! Well, there I was reading something about Islam, when a shadow darkened my cell gate way; Darryl standing there, looking down says; Anthony, if you can do it, I'll go down! I could tell he was in serious need of someone whom he could feel was a friend, so I got up, stepped to him and gave him a hug likened to what Muslims give when greeting each other! He didn't say anything else, but he did look up at me; his eyes spoke the words which he was unable to speak! Wow, now what are you going to do, that kept ringing in my ears; a question that I asked myself. It will probably sound ridiculous to those of you who don't or haven't put trust in God, but turn a deaf ear to what Isa (Jesus) is reported to have said: I can of myself do nothing! I hadn't learned the Arabic yet, but I knew the English; O Allah, You have power over all things! Thinking about what I needed from my Lord, then I said O Allah, open the lieutenant's heart, please! I know you know what Darryl did; but for his family's sake O Allah! I went and found the CO told him what I told Darryl; the CO insisted that I tell him what was going on! But I told him it was something which I would only feel safe talking to the lieutenant about. I didn't know whether he'd call or not, but I'd called on my Lord, all I could do was wait, I went back to my cell. Time seemed like forever, I tried to read, but I couldn't put my mind on what I was trying to read. No, it wasn't a matter of doubt; it was a matter of Allah knowing what was best in and for this situation, and that possibly not being what I wanted it to be! Even if the CO called and the lieutenant came; that didn't necessarily mean he'd accept to do what I was going to ask of him! I take my wash cloth and put it over my eyes, lying there for awhile. I hear: "This better be an emergency Tarver; what is it?" I jumped and sat up; oh, thanks for coming lieutenant; I know you're going to think I've lost my mind or that I have gone too far; but I need help which I could only get from you sir! Look, you've been here long enough to know I'm busy, what's the problem; is another inmate after you or trying to get you to bring him something from the clinic? No sir, it is about another inmate, but it has nothing to do with me where anything like that's concerned. I can see that he's getting frustrated, so I start getting to what I called him for. Sir I'm sure you remember inmate so and so (Darryl) and inmate so and so (Shaky) caught involved in homosexual activity, well sir, he was in the one box forty-five days, and has been back in population two weeks! (He says; and what) Well sir, his wife hasn't sat with him to talk since before he was busted! She came up yesterday, so ashamed of himself, too ashamed to face her; knowing there's nothing he can possibly say to explain how he could possibly do this to his family, he wouldn't go down to see her! She stayed overnight to try and see him today; he wouldn't go down again today! (Thinking about they really enjoy stripping the inmate of whatever sense of choice they have, I thought I saw something in his face, so I acted on it). Lieutenant, this creep is a coward, and he's using the fact that he still has the freedom to do what he wants to do, where refusing to face his wife is concerned! Even if he's taken down there by an officer and made to look his wife in the eyes, so that he has to see her hurt, her embarrassment, her disappointment; it would show that faggot what he does and doesn't want to do, unless you allow it! He has three daughters, lieutenant; his wife wouldn't even bring them for him to see them again! I may be wrong, but I think she intends to tell him she's divorcing him; and he's too much of a coward to even face that. He does what he did to her, and as though that wasn't enough; he knows she travelled all night to get here, and that means nothing to him. He's able to hide in his cell, rather than face her; because, he knows nobody can tell him what to do in this, nobody! The lieutenant is standing there with a frown on his face; he turns to walk away and says; she's no reason to come back up here anymore; this way she knows it, unless she's just stupid! He left; and I went back to lie down! As for what I thought I saw, it seemed like I'd managed to push a button when I mentioned Darryl knowing he had the freedom to do whatever he wanted to do; so he could hide in his cell, because he was a coward; too ashamed to look his wife in the eyes! To hear me saying the inmate knew he had freedom to do what he wanted to seemed to be a no-no; because, they make it clear when you arrive; that you have no rights, no freedom to decide anything; so don't ever act like it! I was trying to use psychology, but it didn't seem to work… I didn't want to go right down and tell Darryl that it hadn't worked; I figured he'd assume such when he didn't get called. For some reason, that seemed to have taken a lot out of me; so I was hoping I'd be able to catch a short nap before chow. Suddenly (well after about forty minutes) I heard 72A1431, 72A1431 on the visit; 72A1431 visit! I jumped up and ran down to Darryl's cell; ok, Darryl, it's on you man! Then you hear; 1431, the lieutenant said to let you know that it's not a fucking option; it's a "direct order!" I smiled, because from the sound of things, it had worked; it had worked almost like clockwork! One element made all the difference in this incident; the right lieutenant was on; yes, but Allah/God has power over all things!

    He was back from the visit shortly after the count, that wasn't an indication that things had gone well! A few days passed before he said anything to me about the visit; even then he was vague; she cried a lot brother; kept asking me how I could shame myself; how I could introduce her to such shame and embarrassment! She never raised her voice even once, Anthony; what was I suppose to say? What was I suppose to say man?! I hope she don't come back up here; everybody's visit, looking and whispering; I hope she don't come no more!!

I felt strongly that I'd played a major part in him going down to see her, so I felt that it was necessary that I say something to him. Darryl, I hope you know it was something which you had to do; going down to see your wife. If nothing else, you owed her that; again, you would have been doing a greater wrong, not facing her, if it's possible for a greater wrong to be done! I'm sure she's coming again Darryl, even if she didn't say so; you know whether or not there was closure; you should know! If you know that there was no closure and don't want her to come back, get busy writing; not saying that's going to work! Darryl, I'm going to tell you this; not in an attempt to make you feel better about yourself; but to simply let you hopefully realize a little more about our strong sex drive as males! In Islam, the woman is required to cover herself, except for hands and face; one of the reasons Allah commands women to cover is because of our (man's) strong sexual desire; it's actually a weakness in the character/nature of the male; it is a mercy from Allah! In Islam, our sisters' covering; amongst other things, it is to help us as men!

My life didn't revolve around this dude, so I went on with doing my bid (time). There were the usual fights, shankings (stabbings), gang assaults, not to mention broken legs and arms, as well as concussions, et cetera, resulting from the ski jump set-up in the yard! An individual has to be a, Grade A; first class knucklehead to end up in the clinic; with his other leg broken! You might be saying; no, not necessarily; a person could trip and fall as a direct result of the initial broken leg! True, that's quite true, if that happened to be the cause of the other leg being broken. But what do you say about the knucklehead sitting in the clinic waiting area, with his other leg broken for the "exact same reason he'd broken the first leg!" He went to the yard, to the ski jump; cast, crutches and skis; everyone cheering him to victory because it all looked great until...! Notice that I said "until;" until he went up in the air at the bottom of the jump. Just like it's not jumping off of the roof that kills the person; but that landing, boy-oh-boy! He was the talk of the prison; just how long did it take the inmates at the bottom of the jump to get this second leg from around his neck (ha-ha)! Inmates were laughing about him being out of commission till next year, until I slipped up and said; since it was his other leg instead of an arm, he can still make it back to the top of the ski jump with two crutches and strong arms! The inmate heard me and got right into the spotlight, causing the Clinton bookies to take their pads out; ready for everyone bored enough to place bets on a fool in need of attention; and willing to do almost anything to get recognition! Out of sight, out of mind doesn't only hold true in so-called free society; the same can hold true in prison. With time passing, things behind Clinton's forty foot high wall returned to; it's prison; and shit happens! With that, Darryl seemed to be coming to grips with things, in light of it being a fact that homosexuality was as much a daily reality in prison as prostitution and homosexuality is in public society! The one thing which made such a bang with Darryl was that he got caught, along with the sad fact; his wife was in his corner, right there every week with their three beautiful (thank God) innocent minded daughters! A month or so had passed since his wife had come for that visit; had she gone on with her life? Whatever it was, he seemed to be coming around, though not as bold, not as vocal!

Surprise! Surprise! Surprise! Guess who got called for a visit?! 72A1431, 1431 on the visit! I had not spent any real time with or around him since that last visit, so I didn't make anything of this. Not hearing the CO announce his number again, I assumed he'd gone down for the visit this time. I hadn't thought about what time of day it was when he was called for the visit; it was after 2:00 in the afternoon when he was called; even if he took no time to dress, by the time he got to the visiting room, it would be 2:30 at least, leaving him no time for a visit! What had happened? At first I'd told myself that his wife must have driven or come by car and had not intended to have a long visit; but no, something must have happened to the bus because the CO had called other inmates before and after Darryl. There was a bad accident on the highway. Being too late for the visit, she decided to stay at Kay's Hotel as she'd done on her last visit. I recall when my wife decided to stay overnight at, in order to visit with me again the next day! When she told me what she had planned, I told her no way! I didn't tell her at that time about what was known about wives of a lot of inmates having been raped by Clinton COs, when they'd spent the night at Kay's! Years and years of inmates, wives having become rape victims at the hands of Clinton COs; sometimes raped multiple times in one night! Not a single investigation or complaint submitted, because the CO made it clear to the victim that it wouldn't be healthy for their husbands, boyfriends, et cetera! On the other hand, if and or when the inmate happened to find out; the CO rapist would play the other fear tactic hand. You know we'll see to it that you disappear, but we'll take good care of your wife, sister, and girlfriend on her next trip up here…! It wasn't even a matter of question as to whether or not the members of this Klan fraternity were capable of doing what they'd presented to the inmates because several of their loved ones had already been raped by Clinton COs! I relented when my wife managed to assure me that she'd be safe, after describing to me what all she would do to block the door to her room; that along with the fact that she'd come with another sister who would be sharing the room! I don't know if Darryl had ever told his wife about them rape stories. The next day, Darryl wasn't called for a visit; he said she must've changed her mind about staying and went back with the bus, since the bus had offered a free trip for anyone who wanted to come the following weekend. If only that was the case; if only that was what had happened! Monday would put another light on what actually happened to his visitor (wife)! With what his wife was already dealing with, who would have imagined that things could and would get worse for her! That Monday, word was already going through the facility that Darryl's wife had been raped! There's an old saying: what goes around, comes around! Well, Darryl's wife received the news about her husband, in the worse way, she didn't expect anything; it was just dropped in her lap! Now Darryl, not expecting anything that Monday morning, he was in fact, already out of the block. Though the rape of his wife was already in population, he may not find out about it; because this wasn't just any kind of news! On top of that, except for a hand full of prisoners/inmates who may have just recently arrived, general population knew about the incident involving Darryl and a faggot; so any prison wise inmate is going to stay away from this because…! Along with word of the sister being raped, it was also being said that she'd been taunted by somebody say stuff like: "You want a man, not a faggot"! I was in the clinic when one of the inmates who'd come up for an ear irrigation which I perform, asked me had I heard about what had happened at Kay's last night! I answered no; he hesitated for a few seconds, until I said; if somebody told you I was a mind reader, they told you a lie; What happened man!? Aaahh man; brother; hhsewww (deep sigh) "Word is in population that Darryl's wife got raped last night"! When he told me, I actually dropped the ear irrigation syringe on the floor! I started saying; naw, naw, naw man! Naw man! Mrs. Johnston heard me. I didn't realize I was that loud; Anthony are you alright? Is everything alright? I answered; yes Mrs. Johnston, the inmate was just telling me something; and it shocked me! Having dropped the syringe, I had to put that one in the pressure oven [Autoclave] to sterilize it; I got a different one. The inmate was behind a curtain, unable to see me; so, I went to the nurse and whispered to her; Mrs. Johnston, I have to talk to you, it's very important! Mrs. Johnston was not going to let anything happen to me; she really seemed to care about me! Anthony, is he after you or something? I smiled and said no, it's nothing like that at all Mrs. Johnston, he's ok; I'll do his ear first! I did his ear, gave him some drops to take with him, he left the clinic. She went to the door and told CO Travis to hold off sending the next inmate until she calls for him!

7

Nurse Johnston is No Lightweight

I TOLD HER what the inmate had told me, and explained that I was certain he didn't know what was circulating throughout population! She didn't understand at first; how or why it could be that he wouldn't know if the population had heard about it! So I explained what I mentioned earlier about what prison wise inmates would take into consideration, then she understood! She picked up the phone, called the Watch commander! This was the first time I actually witnessed that she was no light weight within Clinton's fraternity; I didn't know just what, but she was no joke! She gives the watch commander Darryl's number and housing location; then said, lock him down and come see me in the clinic now! She was just as calm; he must not have said anything to her, because there was nothing else said by her to indicate that she was responding to him! She told me to tell the CO to send the next prisoner/inmate in; he did, it was a prisoner/inmate whose stitches needed to be removed! Before they were removed, she looked at the wound to see that it had closed properly; then told me to remove the stitches! A few minutes after I'd removed the stitches and the inmate had gone to the waiting area, the lieutenant/Watch commander walks into the clinic! I'd cleaned the treatment area behind the drawn curtain; so I was sitting, behind the curtain, reading about the last inmate's medical history. It wasn't my intent to keep quiet to eaves drop; I simply happened to be reading. Mrs. Johnston asked the Watch commander: What have you heard about the rumor I called you about? Is that inmate locked down like I said? My aide doesn't think the inmate has heard anything of what's circulating; he explained why to me, and it makes sense! It's not going to be long though, before he hears something; even if it is a rumor! Look into this now and let me know something! I coughed; the Watch commander in a rough tone says; who is that? Before I could answer, Mrs. Johnston says; "My aide Lewis (saying the lieutenants name), it's only my aide"! He says: "What is that nigger still in here for? He then says, "Hey, get out of here until we're done talking"!! As I came from behind the curtain, I had the folder of the last inmate I'd treated, in my hand; what happened next blew my mind! Mrs. Johnston says in a very sharp, no nonsense voice; I told you he's my clerk, you didn't understand me, is that it Lewis? My clerk and I have a very, very, good understanding, don't we Anthony? Then to top that off, she goes a step further and actually introduces me to him! Anthony this is the Watch commander lieutenant. "Lieutenant Whitman this is (emphasizing the words) my clinic aide Anthony!" Anthony, have you completed your file entries? it's almost time for the count, so get your area in order, and you can go; I'll see you after lunch. I guess she could see tension in my face, because she smiles and says; relax, you're alright! Mrs. Johnston was a real mystery to me; but a mystery of which I was glad happened to be a part of my present life! It started to become clear what was meant the times I'd heard different COs say things like; not that one; or, not him; that one is hands off; or, not a good idea, belongs to Mrs. Johnston! I even began to wonder if my wife even had anything to worry about, if it was known who my wife was; which I'm sure they knew! I couldn't believe the way she'd shut the watch commander down after he lashed out at me; while referring to me as nigger! I was still where I was, and could therefore not let myself forget just how easily I could be made to literally disappear; just as easily as so-many others had "happened to up and poof" from the face of the earth! I remember a couple inmates who'd come up to the clinic one day; they were in the waiting area; playing chess and talking about how thousands of acres of land around the Annex being too much land to search for bodies! One of them had been in the Annex; the other inmate says to the one from the Annex: Are you sure such and such inmate isn't still there; his answer could have been like opening Pandora's Box! Tell me whether or not you think this could go on endlessly; the inmate says: I'm sure the guy is not in the Annex anymore! He wasn't there but about a week; he was assigned to the tree crew; we went out one morning; when we were rounded up to go back, we didn't see him and said one not here! One of the police said: We got a call about inmate so and so; he was taken down on an emergency hospital visit, to see his mother or daughter! You didn't see him when they brought him back? No, I thought he'd been brought back over here because he'd become emotional while on the visit! They could lose bodies all year long, and other inmates never know anything, if they arrange for inmates to be moved to the Annex, sent out on the tree crew; placed off in the woods, isolated from the other inmates, so when it's time for the go-back; an inmate, especially one working outside the wall, is assumed to have escaped; if he's not able to be counted! Everyone around the prison was like a knitted blanket; if you pulled one string of yarn, the whole blanket moved! One call from the "Grand Dragon" to any number outside the forty foot high grey wall (coon hunt/whatever); that, along with the designated blowing of the fire station horn; the Clinton fraternity of 'The Last Strong Hold' knew what it was time for; time to go hunting!! I'm not saying they needed to stage an escape if they wanted to kill a prisoner; because believe me, they would kill a prisoner, in a heartbeat! I hadn't heard anything about anything like that before, but I simply made what I hope was a joke; "and another one's gone and another one's gone, another one bites the dust!" Thinking back on it, I wonder whether there was any validity to what I'd said! Keep in mind where I was; just been called a nigger by the Watch commander, and ordered to get out of there; only to have the prison nurse step in and tell me I was alright and not to worry about leaving until my examination area, et cetera were in order; then she'd see me after lunch! I don't know if you see the significance in what had just taken place; she was bad, and people besides me knew more about what she represented than I did! As I left the clinic, shutting the door behind me, it felt like a chill ran down my back! It seemed to me like I'd never reach the door to the upstairs, fast enough! As I reached for the door, it felt like someone was looking at me, so I looked back; (ooohh crap) the Watch commander, Lieutenant Whitman was standing there with his arms crossed; an expression on his face, causing me to ask myself: Damn, what's he looking at me like that for?!

After lunch, I came back to the clinic from the staff kitchen. When the count cleared, the rest of the afternoon was slow, so I was able to review a few things having to do with abscess draining and what appearance may be reason(s) for concern! Though I was doing all I could not to think about what had transpired with the lieutenant, I was able to see him with arms folded, looking at me, after Mrs. Johnston had told me to go to lunch! What was, was real, and how much in the middle of it was I; even if I didn't want to be, hadn't asked to be?! The first nigger clinic and sick-call aide in the history of Clinton, I didn't ask to be; and believe me, whatever Mrs. Johnston was within the Strong

Hold of Clintons fraternity, it had nothing to do with her being a nurse!!! One day there'd been a fight in one of the blocks; three of the inmates involved in the fight were injured and had to be brought to the clinic; this meant several COs had to escort them! There was a lot of ruckus on the part of the COs, so they hadn't paid Mrs. Johnston any attention, though she'd been trying to find out from them what inmates' injury was more severe! She stood there a moment then simply cleared her throat; you would have thought she'd yelled "attention;" the way they spun around in silence! Usually I'd get into real conversations with her; talking about how I came up as a child, how I felt about having seen the struggles my mother faced, raising my sister and I alone; the type of woman she must have been as far as having pride was concerned; in that she'd never turned to public assistance, et cetera, et cetera! What I'm saying is there was never a day in the clinic that I didn't strike up a conversation: I can only assume she noticed something different this afternoon, because she asked me what was wrong! I explained to her that I was still thinking about what I'd caused to happen before lunch! What do you mean what you caused to happen? What do you think you did? If you're worried about the lieutenant being upset because you were still in here, while I was talking to him, whose aide are you? I answered; I'm your aide Mrs. Johnston. Isn't that what I told the lieutenant, Anthony? Everyone knows 72A2747 is my clinic aide! You're doing an excellent job in the clinic; I've never been more pleased!

When I got back to the block after the 3:00 pm count, the only thing being said to me by everyone was; he knows, Darryl found out, they got Darryl keep locked! Brother Anthony, go talk to him man; nobody know what to try and say to him brother! Different individuals dun walked by his cell, and a couple ovum said it sounded like he was cryin, man! I didn't know what to say to the brother; what does a person say as a prisoner to another prisoner, about something like his wife having been raped; and as though having been raped wasn't enough, she was allegedly raped by a prison guard working in the same prison wherein he's doing time?!! I started spending more time in the yard with the brothers (Muslim); cooking, then sitting on the court eating and discussing Islam. Sometimes we'd watch television (basketball playoffs); but you'd never believe it if I told you where we'd be watching them! In the, dead of winter; a hop, skip, and a jump from Canada, standing in the prison yard, watching television!!! Darryl, had been locked for about a week since the news about his wife being raped, and it seemed that he was going to stay keep locked even longer, because he was refusing to see the psychologist about his feelings! One thing about prison which anyone who's ever been there knows is, there are "no secrets"; well maybe I should rephrase that; there are no secrets amongst prisoners, we knew about administrative schemes, block shake-downs, administrative plans, etcetera, before the police/CO did! Word had made it around the prison, that Darryl had been heard crying nights after hearing about the raping of his wife! Like I'd just said about secrets, it was known, he'd received "no mail" from her, so, if he'd been telling himself it wasn't true (the rape), hearing nothing from her was not helping matters at all; especially considering that she'd stayed over after the bus had not arrived on time for the visit the day before! I'd not gone to try and talk to Darryl, not because I did not want to, but because I "didn't know what to say!" I went to the clinic one morning and confided in Mrs. Johnston about what was being said about the emotional state of Darryl, crying at night and not wanting to talk to anyone about how he feels, having him keep locked! Before he was caught in the homosexual act, he was a hospital worker, so she knew who I was speaking about; whatever it was, she was always straightforward with me, about how she felt! She says to me; he always seemed different than many of the other hospital workers Travis had kept up there. Anthony, you lock in his block, did he show that he might have had homosexual tendencies there? I had to say no, because of the rage I'd seen him fall into, that day! She and I talked a bit about him being married and having children (three daughters). She really couldn't perceive how a healthy, married man could become a homosexual! Anthony, I really can't understand it, is mans need for intimacy that strong?! How do they, those who become homosexuals in here; how do they adjust when they return home; or do they act like they're normal?! Anthony, I've been here longer than you can imagine; (she smiles and says) no, I'm not going to tell you how long that's been, you might guess my age (we laughed). She went on to say; I don't want to imagine "how often this happens, Anthony!" How often does this happen? Do wives ever find out about their husbands homosexuality?! Mrs. Johnston sat there shaking her head, staring pass me; almost like she'd stepped off somewhere; she kept shaking her head from side-to-side, back and forth! "Mrs. Johnston; Mrs. Johnston; I called her a third time before she'd step back as it were, into the clinic! I answered. "I don't think prison is set-up to answer such questions, even deal with such concerns".

At that time, I was as green as a new cornstalk; the questions directed at me then, to date still haven't been addressed by those in the multi-million dollar business of flesh housing! It's something, in 1979 and long before, our system(s) of government had gotten over on its citizens with the biggest farce ever put before its citizens to this day; what was that?! Crime is a defect of the mental state of what is at present a small segment of our citizens; to address the mental imbalance(s) responsible for driving individuals to commit crime; we need money, we need money, we must have the financial means to implement testing, as such that will enable us to better understand their psychological trauma, the possibility of such being hereditary, etcetera! The only possible way for us to do our studies is through imprisonment; thusly enabling us to "rehabilitate" the convict! Different dictionaries say different things, all alluding to the same thing; to restore, rehabilitate. In my English etymological dictionary, the word is given birth from Latin (habilitus), to invest with dignity! That was the farce which was eloquently presented to the money controllers; that in time, imprisoning the criminal will enable us to reinvest the criminal, with dignity! Decade after decade would come and go, reducing the rehabilitation farce to something which should have been absolutely undeniable, a hoax! Those behind it could very well argue that it was never anyone's intent to deceive anyone, trick anyone; yes, I might even agree, but what's to be said now, decades later in light of the hundreds of millions of dollars spent to imprison; if the results were laid before the civilized, honestly hard working, tax-paying human being, what would be said? Prior to Mrs. Johnston asking me the question about what the husbands who have been homosexually active while in prison do when they return home, I'd not spent a moment thinking about that, the bigger picture; what will those now branded do, if they've become men?! She'd asked some deeply thought provoking questions which didn't just stop with husbands who'd some day, one day have to face their wives after having succumb to his biological passions with a shit, faggot, gay person, Sodom & Gomorrahite, homosexual, whatever; one thing was real and I was now thinking about it; since NYSDOCS wasn't rehabilitating, whatever it was doing was "absurd!" I wasn't expecting that she'd ask me what I meant when I'd said: I didn't think prison was set up to answer her questions; but she did. Why do you think that to be so Anthony, after all, every inmate has counseling available to help him with issues; and upon a written referral, there's a psycho-therapist immediately available to you for weekly sessions as it relates to the mental health of an inmate! There was no mistaking it, she'd asked me a question, and an answer was expected! Remember what I'd said a number of times; I had to be very careful not to let myself forget "exactly" where I was! Whatever her position or status was within this fraternity which had and obviously would introduce a soul to death, and festively so; almost like a warning, everything in me was saying: Answer her Anthony! Answer her Anthony! Don't get too familiar with her! I knew she appreciated that I had a level of intelligence; but how prudent would it prove me to be were I to let on that I might possibly be astute in matters wherein it related to politics surrounding dollars and Clinton, 'The Last Strong Hold'! An answer! An answer; but what was it going to be; and why did I feel so strongly that the question was something of which I could not simply ignore? First of all when they ask you a question, there is an understanding which it's felt by them (I guess) that it need not be explained; our question to you is like a "direct order"; if they question, we answer! Secondly, I could not recall a single instance when I had not been forthright in a conversation with her; she was very sharp, keenly aware, and she was undoubtedly far removed from being insignificant amongst all who held rank here! OOOH, believe me, I was going to follow my gut feeling; I was going to answer her! "Mrs. Johnston, I'm with these prisoners, 24-7-365; and if anyone is able to distinguish who is and/or isn't incorrigible, it would be the one who has had to knowingly accept the reality of his present situation; and therefore agree to let those around him take the place of family, if only for the moment! What I mean by that is simple; in order for one person to really reach another person; the person has to be reached through his concerns! Now, there's one big obstacle in the way Mrs. Johnston; the greater percentage of the men here aren't even capable enough to recognize that they don't have a primary concern; because it's been so long since they've really cared about anything"! She sat there and, if you could have seen the way she looked at me; then she said something to me that would have never even crossed my mind! "Anthony, I've never felt this way about a prisoner, and I've met them from probably every walk of life; you have no business here; you don't belong here Anthony; you don't belong in prison!" Hearing her say that, really made me feel good; and I had no reason to think she didn't mean it!

After I went back to the block that evening, I decided to take a trip to the yard. I walked the yard alone, thinking about the day. While walking, I began thinking back on my poetry; I'd been writing long before prison; but it was only after getting to Sing Sing that I got into my writing again! I'd written quite a few poems since arriving in prison; but hadn't reduced anything to writing in awhile; though I'd had many experiences for writing material! I walked over to the back stop where a softball game was being played; there were different groups of individuals standing around doing what's done in prison; everybody tries to out-do everybody else with lies. There were four individuals from the five boroughs of New York City, and they were in it; I mean they were so caught-up in trying to outdo each other; I actually stayed and listened! No, not because I was impressed to any point of admiration; rather, impressed with the material I'd received for a poem or two! I walked the yard awhile longer; then saw an inmate on a cooking court, with a few of his homeboys; so I went and sat with them for awhile. They were talking about doing time and what they felt they were "getting out of it this time!" Since this was not a repeat trip for me, I chose to be a student in the sense that this was absolutely an opportunity for me to learn! It was interesting to hear them expressing sentiments common to those of so-many other prisoners. A few individuals had stopped by to talk for a few minutes; amongst them there were two who mentioned something which really disturbed me! Little did I know that Blue Eyes had been messing with Darryl's head, with a vicious onslaught of comments and remarks: (i.e.) "How are you going to handle that cunt when you get home "shit stuffer?" "Seen your wife lately, lover"? "Here he is, a real faggot's man!" "Wife coming back anytime soon; maybe she got something to come back for last time, whadaya think, huh; think maybe she was given something real good?" This particular inmate explained that he was on medical keep lock one day when he happened to hear Blue Eyes taunting Darryl! He said it went on for a long time, seemed like forever! He said, suddenly Darryl started screaming as loudly as he could: "Leave me alone!" Leave me alooonnne! Why don't you leave me alooonnne?! Aaahhh aaahhh aaahhhh!! The inmate said he could hear Blue Eyes laughin' and laughin'! He could hear Blue Eyes walking down the tier, laughing! The next morning when I reached the clinic I asked Mrs. Johnston if I might speak to her before it was time for lunch, explaining that I wanted to share an idea with her. The morning went like a finely tuned machine, no problems, no incidents, absolutely unlike prison anywhere! I was not going to remind the nurse that I'd asked her for some time to talk to her; what possible reason could I have for not offering up a reminder to the nurse about having asked to speak to her about a matter? If you recall, awhile back I stated that I could not afford to let myself forget where I was, what I was; nothing had changed; where was I still? What was I still? Though it might have appeared that I was in what some term (the loop); no, not at all; all I was, was an inmate; a prisoner, a convict who by the will of Allah (God), had a work detail under someone with undeniable secret power; it's source also unknown! For some reason I wasn't worried about asking her about it again; I just felt she'd bring it to my attention before I went to lunch. I was mindful of the time because I didn't know how long it was going to take or if she'd have any interruptions! It was 11:15 when she calls me and asked if what I'd spoken to her about this morning was still bothering me; if so, she had time for us to talk now! I explained to her that I was very concerned about Darryl's mental condition; I told her that he was still under keep lock because he refused to speak to anyone about how he's feeling! It has to be tearing him apart, what happened to his wife; but he has just closed himself in! I have an idea that might move him to open up and talk before it's too late. I went on to ask if it was alright if I spoke what I felt so strongly about; in no way will I be trying to tell you what to do; I'm certain you know something like that would never cross my mind Mrs. Johnston! She told me not to worry about that; because she knew I was smart enough to know how to express myself! They've been sending him to see a therapist who is a female; they should know he will never open up to her, simply because of the guilt he's feeling about his wife! As a man, if it were me sitting before a woman, I'd have to feel that she's looking at me and thinking I'm amongst the lowest things ever to sit in front of her! But if it was another man I was in front of, just that being a fact would make me feel different psychologically! I remember one day he and I were talking; and he commented about how he trusted you because you seemed to understand that there are some of us who did something stupid; but are sorry about the shame they've brought on their families; the hardship now on their families, etcetera! He respects you Mrs. Johnston; I think he'd listen to you if you tell him you would like for him to agree to talk to someone; because you're concerned about what he's trying to handle alone! Don't we have a male psycho-therapist who he could possibly see? I don't know whether or not you're allowed to write a note to an inmate; but if you are, writing something to let him know you're worried about how he might be doing, and have arranged for him to see a male therapist, etcetera; I'd take it to him, so he wouldn't have to possibly be ashamed of knowing you know about his homosexual activities! I'm really worried about him Mrs. Johnston; other inmates talking about hearing him screaming and making noise, like it's uncontrollable! Some of the inmates were talking after lock-in the other night, about CO teasing and taunting him! She didn't comment except to say she'd let me know about the possibility of a male therapist!

Things were normal in the clinic, files and everything up to date; so I asked if I could go the hospital for a few minutes. Things hadn't changed at all; beds full except one; hospital workers walking around half doing things for the inmate patients; only one of the other inmates who'd had that detail with me when we were in H-Block, was still working there; he too remained in Clinton after completing his classification; the other workers were new inmates from H-Block Classification/Reception! The hospital sergeant who'd taken me to see Mrs. Johnston months ago; was happy to see me; told me he spoke about me all the time to hospital workers since I left the hospital! I really appreciated that, and told him so. He had the nerve to ask me if I would like to come back to the hospital, and work; he went on to tell me he'd make me his senior worker and place me over the rest of the hospital workers! I told him he'd have to speak to Mrs. Johnston about that; not me. The farthest thing from my mind was going back to the hospital to work; but I wasn't going to say that to him. Before going back to the clinic, I said a few more words to one of the workers; then I went back. When I returned to the clinic, I was told to pull the medical folders of a few inmates; by the time I returned with the folders, the CO was there to escort us back to our blocks. Though Darryl was on my mind I didn't go by his cell to see how he was doing; I went and dropped my bag in my cell and went to the other side of my block to see an inmate who had just come in on a violation; I knew him from Yonkers. He wasn't there so I went back to my cell and was ready to call it a day, when an inmate a few cell past Darryl came by. He told me that he and a few other inmates had heard Darryl laughing like a madman; and talking about how easy it would be to stop wondering about what the fuck was going on; if he wanted to… There wasn't anything I could do about whatever he was going through; and it was definitely too involved for me to act like I could! I had to console myself with the knowledge of having spoken to the nurse about my concerns regarding him! While the brother was talking to me about Darryl and some of the changes he was going through; the CO did the mail call, and it included my name; two letters from my aunts; a card from my wife. Of course the first envelope I opened was from my wife, the card was really something I needed! Nothing fantastic in any meaning of the word, but it was two lines saying she'd be there for us, like we've been there for us! No, the words in the card were not those words at all; as a word person; I chose to sum it up as such. Had I let my wife's card close my day out, it would have been great; but I opened the envelopes from my aunts. The fact that both aunts had written me should have told me something wasn't good; but I missed the signal. It didn't take three lines of the letter from my first aunt to put my heart in my mouth; my mother was in the hospital, not in good condition at all! She managed to tell me that; using different words to describe what the doctor had said was wrong! As much as I didn't want to read the letter from my other aunt, it was as though I couldn't help myself. The first letter was the introduction; informing me of my mothers' health; the other was written to beat me up with fault and blame!

    In all my years of life and ease, I had never really "told" my mom how I felt about her sacrifices, heartache and pain, her stress and strain, etcetera! My mother probably didn't know she meant the world to me, and if the letters were correct, I'd not have another opportunity to tell her! I knew nothing about what the policy was in situations like this; I did know how off the hook my aunts were capable of being, so I tried to call on that knowledge to console me; but it didn't really help! I reached for a pen and pad to write something to my mother; with my eyes watering, I placed my pen on the paper, and when I'd finished writing, I had written the following:

---BLACK MOTHER OF MINE---

black mother of mine / you've fought for my every day standing firm / taking unbelievable pain /
black mother of mine / you've gone through hell to raise me...
i see the traces of hard times on your face /black mother of mine /
you've dreamt of peace in distant places/
all of this time gone by / mother i've grown /
black mother of mine / because of you / your struggles / i've become a man...
i have nothing to give / not a thing / nothing /
black mother of mine / such beauty in a tired / tarnished face...
lie down now mother / depend on me /
black mother of mine / your day has come / take love and wear a smile
your dream was magic mother / now your day has come /
i love you mother / and will always feel this way /
black mother of mine / with all of your struggles / hard times
you still managed to give me the love of an angel /

black mother of mine / from your lessons will emerge my power
to my children and to theirs / i'll teach them all /
black mother of mine / may you rest in peace / there it is mother
your day has come / take yours and rest in peace /
black mother of mine / good bye but go ahead
rest in peace / take your seat in the sky/
yes mother / i'm a man
but for you / I cry!!!

As I reduced my sadness to writing I cried, and shed silent tears which ran down my face! The grief I was feeling was so-intense that it was actually causing me to feel lumps in my throat as I swallowed! Through all the emotion, I didn't stop to try and gather thoughts of what I wanted to say to the best friend I'd ever had in my life; there was no need for thought, what I was writing to my mom was pouring forth from the soul of my heart! Though I'd managed to write through my grief; there was yet another reality which would have to present itself; was it going to be true! Was it going to be true, that the mother who'd been there for her son through everything I'd been subjected to in my life, never asking a question; was she going to surrender her life, and I not be there to at least hold her hand?!!! I believe that was the longest night of my life to date; other nights prior had been as such that I was too occupied and overwhelmed with fear, to even think about the lengthiness of those nights! The next morning, yes death was on my mind; and that was exactly what would start my morning; Death! Someone was not responding to the count; then I heard a voice which sounded like the Grim Reaper, Blue Eyes! I hear him say; Darryl, I'm coming pass your cell one more time for this god damn count; you better pray to fucking god that you're sitting up, looking at me! From what I was told, he went down the tier again; but Darryl failed to respond to the count! The CO must have thought Darryl was playing possum, because the CO called for additional CO before he had the cell open to enter it! Darryl was dead! He'd killed himself during the night, he'd cut his wrist and wrapped them, making sure the blood wouldn't be noticed! One of the advantages of working in the prison clinic, my job in particular; Mrs. Johnston had absolute knowledge of everything having to do with the prisoners; their injuries, etcetera! Now what do you think that meant? Right; she'd talk to me, if I managed to present myself in the proper manner...! I was able to learn that Darryl had cut both wrist, but he hadn't wrapped them; but after cutting his wrist, he put both hands under his pillow and laid on it! She said there were a number of other cut marks on his wrist, indicating that he'd possibly attempted suicide on other occasions; but may not have had something sharp enough to cut deeply enough to do more than cause bad scratches on his wrist! The few times I'd gone down to talk to Darryl he wouldn't; so I have no idea what it was that drove him to kill himself! Like I mentioned earlier, when two inmates are caught committing a homosexual act, the administration doesn't tell the families of those involved, what role each played; that's left up to the families to conclude! I may be wrong, but I don't believe Darryl would have been so thoroughly defeated because his wife had been left to wander what part he'd played in his homosexual activity; but any man knowing his wife had been taunted with words of her husband being a faggot and involved with one; then raped because she'd come to visit him; just how much could the average man bear! Perhaps had he not been taunted by Blue Eyes and other CO, thus being made to possibly feel like even less than nothing; then unable to do anything about it; all of this together became too much for him to bear.

The night I'd endured as a result of my aunts having written me about my mother being in the hospital, and how critical her condition had been made to sound was over shadowed by Darryl; his suicide! Before the morning was over, I was able to show Mrs. Johnston the letters I'd received from my aunts; and asked her if she could possibly help me get a phone call so I might find out about my mother. She asked me about the phone number in the letter; I acknowledged that it was to the hospital; possibly to my mothers' room. She was able to get a direct line; dialed out and gave the phone to me! As the phone rang my heart was beating so-hard I felt light headed; so I sat down, waiting for someone to answer the phone! Finally someone picked up the phone, but no one said anything for a couple seconds; then a faint voice, it was my mother! I remember whispering; ma; ma; ma is that you ma? It's me ma, Anton, ma… Then I could hear her voice sounding stronger; Anton! Anton, is that you Anton?! Where are you? It's mommy! I sat there, tears running down my face; I couldn't talk for a few seconds, and then I managed to say: You alright ole lady? Mrs. Johnston reached out and rubbed me on my back (trying to help me settle myself I guess) she asked me if I was alright; that calmed me! I said to my mother; surprised you, didn't I? Left you speechless; I don't believe it; you, speechless; not my mom! I told her that I was still in Clinton; but was given a special call to find out how you are doing! I didn't mention the letters from her sisters (my aunts) because I didn't want to chance upsetting her! I told her I couldn't stay on the phone. She sounded brand new compared to how she sounded when she first picked up the phone! Laughing, she says; "Mommy's alright now Anton, mommy's alright now; I've heard my baby's' voice." I told her I loved her and would be sending her a surprise soon; but she had to behave herself if she wanted to be home to receive it when it arrived; I hung up.

It was early afternoon when an inmate was brought to the clinic with his front teeth broken off, top and bottom! Mrs. Johnson asked the CO who'd escorted the inmate, to step outside of the clinic; twice he refused! I'd only seen Mrs. Johnston adamant one other time; this time she sat back in her desk chair, looked at him very unintimidating like and said; "Young man, you "do not want to be here" to hear me ask you a third time to step outside; do you? Please step ou..." is as far as she got. Snatching the door open, the CO gave the inmate with the broken teeth a hard look, and stepped out of the clinic! As the door was closing he made a comment which I am absolutely certain he didn't mean for her to hear; just as the door closed, I heard the word, "Bitch!" Smiling, Mrs. Johnston picks up the phone and dialed a number; it must have been a direct extension because she didn't ask to speak to anyone. Mrs. Johnston: "There is something I want done, and want it done immediately! I was just called a bitch by one of your less experienced boys who'd refused to leave my clinic after having been asked twice to do so by me! At this moment he's outside the clinic with Officer Travis; he is to apologize to me; (with emphasis she says) then send him home for a few days!" (She was quiet, must have been listening to someone) No, "not one dime" I mean it; not a single dime!" I can only assume that she was asked about what she wanted done with the CO then what she wanted done about his pay if he was not going to be allowed in to work for a few days! A few minutes later while I was helping the inmate clean his mouth, that same CO knocked on the door. Rather than just entering, he knocked on the door and waited to be acknowledged before entering! I was behind the curtain with the inmate, so I was able to hear the CO say: "Mrs. Johnston I'm sorry for giving you a hard time earlier and disrespecting you; please accept my apology!" He stood there waiting for her to respond to what he'd said, but she never said a word about his apology; instead she says; I'll be speaking to the captain; you can wait outside! From that day, I knew she was no joke! If she picked the phone up on you, boooyy!!! My boss had juice, she had it like that; she just chose not to flex!!!

8

How Long Will This Keep Going On?

MRS. JOHNSTON, THE RN asked the inmate several times, who'd broken his teeth; who'd hit or kicked him in the mouth! Again and again the inmate would say it was a sneak jump, just as he turned the corner to go to his block! She told him over and over again that he did not have to worry about the CO if that was what had him afraid! He stuck to his story, though I knew better without the least doubt; and I'm sure the nurse did also! When you're in prison for awhile, you are able to read body language; and not just that of another prisoner! I'd later find out that it was the same CO who had escorted the inmate to the clinic, responsible for that inmates' teeth being broken; the CO had hit the inmate in the mouth with his club! (They call the clubs night sticks; I would say they looked more like bats for midget league ball players); many of the COs carried these bats in place of their standard baton! The inmate told me the CO hit him once across the front of the mouth! I'm going to tell you this prisoner was very fortunate; that one swing found a point of impact which happened to be the mouth. It would have been the same had the point of impact been the forehead; the unspoken three monkey law would have fallen over the prison; and Allah

(God) bless the child who didn't know it! Those COs, when their bats, clubs, sticks, batons were put into swing mode could have been likened to bullets once released from the gun not aimed! Though Clinton was the Last Strong Hold, if by chance you managed to get a healthy transfer; it had better not be the result of "court papers against Clinton! Because just as I'm sure many people have heard of the "Blue Wall of Silence" when it comes to and relates to the Police Department; the New York State Department of correctional Services has a similar wall! Little did I know that in years to come; I'd see, and learn of its workings; "first-hand!" Though time went by quickly while working in the clinic during the week; I'd be a part of and involved in so-much wrong, the week end was usually a relief! This particular Saturday; I was walking the yard with three other Muslim brothers; one of the brother's comments; "It seems like something is up." Though I had seen, and "boy-oh-boy" had I seen; I was not joint (prison) smart by a long-shot! I didn't see anything unusual about the yard! If standing in the yard, you did so in groups no larger than three or four; if walking the yard, you did so walking counter-clockwise! There was always a softball game going on; and on rare occasions; a "real mans" football game; "frustration release" on every tackle; wearing no gear! Prison, the epitome of a society engulfed in frustration! If you have some frustration which you want to get rid of and not have to worry about being written-up and/or boxed; this football game is what you got involved in! AAAHH!!! AAAHHH MAN! I watched the game enthusiastically at first; after a few minutes, it became brutal with capital letters! Some of the tackles, some of the blocks, the pile-ups were as such that the only way you could possibly get up; a driving force would have to be driving you! I'm referring to frustration; the type of frustration of which you might have been impregnated with in so-called free society; but fed and nurtured to maturity day after day, night after night and day in Clinton; the Last Strong Hold! In the midst of such a gripping existence, I was able to look past it at something which caused me to laugh loudly to the point that one of the brothers asked me if I was laughing at the game. Naaahh, I'm laughing because tomorrow the clinic is going to be packed! We started walking the yard again, but this time I thought I'd noticed something going on. The yard is usually balanced; what I'm referring to is the inmates are somewhat evenly distributed about the outer perimeters of the yard. It seemed to me that some shifting was going on; what I mean is one side of the yard began to thin out to the point that the number of inmates on the one side of the yard was noticeably less all of a sudden! I remember asking Obson what was happening; I hadn't gotten the question out of my mouth when all those who were still on that side of the yard began running toward the middle of the yard! Whistles started blowing and COs began showing themselves, and shouting 'line-up, line-up! Find your spots, line-up now! Find your spots meant the inmates were to line-up on their block locations immediately and not move from there until ordered to do so! This was a first for me; and I still had no clue! Well as we're walking towards the middle of the yard, I see a swag-bag lying on the ground; I stopped and was about to lean over and pick it up when Obson grabbed me by the collar of my shirt and pulled me; "ANTHONY, WHAT"S WRONG WITH YOU MAN?!" I still didn't have a clue what had happened; in fact, I didn't even know something "had in fact happened!" If this tells you anything about how naive I was still; listen to my response to Obson: I say to Obson; somebody's bag, somebody dropped his bag! (sitting here reliving this, I'm laughing; laughing at just how prison ignorant I was; "boy-oh-boy" was I vulnerable, I'm laughing again!) I don't think we'd taken ten more steps when a few CO ran through the crowd pass us and right to that bag! Obson says to me; brother, if you had picked that bag up, it woulda belonged to you; it woulda been yours! See dat guy lying on the ground over there, brother? Brother, I don't care what you see lying on the ground anywhere; if it ain't yours, leave it! I looked back across the yard; the inmate lying on the ground was being put on a stretcher and carried out of the yard! As for the mysterious swag-bag, what was in it that could have possibly opened the side of the head of that inmate? No, wasn't a rock; try a can of crisp golden kernel corn; yep, a can of corn in a bag, fell just short of being a murder weapon! Fortunate right; I beg to differ, seeing that it left that inmate in a state of perpetual sleep, in a coma. From what I would read in his medical file; that would be his condition for the remainder of his life! Had I managed to pick that bag up; had Obson been a second or three late in grabbing me by the collar, in all likely-hood, I would have been facing an attempt murder charge as the sole owner of a swag-bag; which contents was a can of corn! In all probability Mrs. Johnston would have taken care of that, but I'm really thankful that I didn't have to find out! Before we move on let's linger another moment or three with this poor unfortunate prisoner now lying in a coma for the rest his unnatural life. This being prison, did the question why cross your mind? Let me entertain us with the answer to why one human being was driven to open the head of another human being, with a can of corn in a bag; a human being was now lying in a coma because he owed someone "two packs of Kool cigarettes;" and for two commissary buys, he didn't pay-up! Now, let's move on…

    The following Monday was scheduled for Mrs. Johnston and I to make sick-call rounds to one of the blocks; As usual, when we arrived at the block, the CO would pop the cells of those inmates on that block list for sick-call. They'd come to the front of the tier one at a time as they would be called, except the inmate or inmates on keep lock. Keep locked inmates would be seen by me in there cells; as I explained before, I'd do vitals of such inmates; and if necessary I'd change certain bandages. This morning would be anything but the regular cell visit for me; I only had one inmate to see, but when I reached his cell and looked through the bars; something about his complexion didn't look right. I called his name but he didn't answer. I called his name again, he didn't respond. I went back to the front of the tier and informed Mrs. Johnson that I believed the inmate was dead; she told me to tell the CO what I'd found! When I did that, the CO popped the cell and told me to enter the cell and do a physical check! I told the CO I'd do that, but the only way would be if he came to the cell and watched what I was doing when I entered. He looked at me and started shouting; you listen, you don't give me any terms ever; you just do what I tell you to do; I told you to do something, do it now; that's a direct order! Sir, I'm not trying to give you any terms, I'm just asking you to come to the cell when I go in; so you'll be able to clearly see whatever is wrong; was, before I entered the cell. Mrs. Johnson must have heard the CO shouting at me, because she calls out the name of the CO and says; "CO Druman are you giving my aide a hard-time?" With that he came to the cell with me while I did a physical examination to confirm that the inmate was dead!! See, a few months ago while in the mess hall during the evening chow, an inmate fell-out on the floor; another inmate stepped over to help him because he couldn't breathe! By the time CO reached the two inmates, one was dead! Before all was said and done, the inmate who had tried to help another inmate was charged with man slaughter! It was witnessed that he was seen making two attempts to resuscitate the other inmate! Had the inmate turned-out ok, perhaps instead of a man slaughter charge, maybe he would have been showered with praise and congratulations! It turned out that an examination of the deceased found a large piece of meat in his wind-pipe! It was argued, had the other inmate had not blown into the mouth of the deceased; what was found lodged in the wind-pipe, would not have been forced further down! Prison is where some of the most low-life examples of human beings can be found!!! Having charged this innocent inmate with killing another inmate, the state was now going to have to make it stick; how would that be done? This is where, those low-life mentioned earlier fit in; yes, proving to be an effective witness/snitch for the administration/state could turn out to be very rewarding should the snitch live long enough! Keep in mind, there is nothing that happens in a prison that the prisoners don't "know something about!" The prisoner facing man slaughter charges was about to be led to a conviction by a low- life snitch looking for an early release ticket! The warden had received a statement from an inmate alleging that he'd had several conversations with the inmate now accused of the death of the inmate who'd died in the mess hall! This snitch was stating that the inmate had told him he was waiting for a chance to get the other inmate because he'd been trying to write his girl friend. He further claimed he was in front of the inmate, who'd fallen to the floor, and the accused was behind him; when the accused saw the deceased fall-out. He alleges that the accused said; "He's done for, he's mine!" That is when he (the accused) went over to him and began blowing in his mouth! He said; he's done for, he's mine; before he ever went to him! So, he knew what he was going to do before he even went to him, to act like he was trying to help! A statement from a low-life snitch was going to be the cause of an inmate with three months to the parole board, being found guilty of a man slaughter charge; so that he (the snitch) might get an early release ticket! Again; little did I know that years later I would be in a position which would enable me to witness first-hand; the danger of a lie when accepted by those belonging to, a system with "ultimate power!"

Since my short stay in Clinton, I had witnessed atrocities of such degree that they call for the scholars of language to make a new entry in the book of words! But there was something else; what I'd witnessed to that point imposed a question on me; a question as such that it seemed everyone should have had! The fact that so-many prisoners were beaten to death and not being questioned could be understood; seeing that such was not known about! But how was it possible that all these inmates could be disappearing; and escape was so simply used to explain the disappearances away??? I could go on, but if these questions are just now being asked; then O Allah, you tell me something wasn't; that something isn't wrong!! I found out that the snitch, earned himself a move within the prison; a move to what was known as the honor block; (A-BLOCK)! But like I said, there are no secrets in prison! Hear me and hear me well; the life of the snitch is respected by no one; and occasionally they get what they want...! It was said that the CO found him in his cell for lock in; where word has it, he "fell on a few shanks" (47) forty seven times!!! Within a few days, word around the prison was that he died in/at the hands of "Prisoners of Honor" in the Honor Block! On the one hand, it was a victory and reason to celebrate; on the other hand, there was a fellow prisoner who'd now have to resign himself to the possibility that the only other person besides himself who knew he was innocent was now dead! There was only one thing left for him to count on if he was going to be spared an additional prison term for man slaughter; his faith in God!

There didn't seem to be a day that went by wherein I didn't learn or get a better understanding of something. For instance, Clinton kept record of every prisoner! Do you receive visitors, mail; do you make phone calls, do you get packages in the mail; do you write letters? If the answer to these questions is no, such is a recipe guaranteed to result in one or two things. If that prisoner happened to make himself the object of attention; he was either going to be beaten or beaten to death! If you remember, prior to telling you about the incident in the mess hall, and what ultimately happened to an inmate who had simply tried to come to the aide of an inmate who'd fallen out on the floor, unable to breathe! I was on sick-call with the RN in one of the blocks; I'd gone to see about an inmate who was on keep lock; but when I reached his cell I was able to tell something was wrong with him! I informed the nurse, who in turn told me to tell the CO what I'd found. He ordered me to enter the cell, but I refused unless he was there; this angered him, but he did come with me after popping the cell! When we reached the front of the cell, the CO pushed me and held me against the bars; don't you ever ignore me again nigger; (baton shoved into my stomach) do you understand me nigger; (shoving the baton into my stomach, harder) huh?! Mrs. Johnston had finished seeing the inmates who'd signed up for sick-call, so she must have been standing at the end of the tier, looking! She says, Officer William what are you doing to my aide?! What's going on with that keep lock? At that point, he tells me to go inside and see what's wrong with the inmate! As soon as I went to lean over the inmate I could smell an odor indicating he'd defecated on himself! He was under a sheet and blanket; both soaked with what seemed to be water, because it was all over the floor of the cell also! I pushed the button to the sink for water, but none came out; I pushed the button to the toilet, but it didn't flush! Who'd made the call to shut the water off to the cell of this inmate? The valves to cut water off to the cells, was between the two tiers on each floor; and to access this area, one would have to have the CO's key ring; so what was this saying?! Questions, questions, questions, and more questions!!! Why was this inmate wet; how did he get wet; had such caused his death…? Back to the last question;

had the fact that someone had wet that prisoner and let him lie soak and wet in his bed, "caused his death?!" What was wrong with him in the first place that made someone feel wetting him would solve something; stop something?! Whose hand was this death on; and what explanation would be given for it?! Had he only died last night; if not, how many days had he been dead?! The other inmates on the tier, what did they know; what had any of them seen, heard?! As for what other inmates on the tier knew, there was one thing they knew to be a certainty absolute; open your mouth, and you'd be one added to the absurd story of the list of inmates/prisoners who'd escaped and managed to vanish like the odor of a fart in the wind!! I told the CO I felt "no pulse" and that the prisoner was cold as ice! I slipped up and asked how the inmate could have possibly gotten soaked, and where the water came from that was all over the floor; if the water to the cell was turned off! The CO stepped into the cell, "hit me across the abdomen" with his baton, and said; I'll see how badly you want answers to your questions, later!!! NOW TAKE ANOTHER LOOK; 'WHAT'S WRONG WITH THE CELL? WHAT'S NOT WORKING? WHAT'S WET!! I didn't answer his questions, I just said: Look, I don't have anything to do with any of this; whatever is, is for you to report, not me; I'm a prisoner here; doing time! (The police/CO) You just remember that! I got ready to pull the blanket over the prisoner's face, but thought better of it; and left everything as it was when I entered the cell! When Mrs. Johnston and I were leaving, the CO locked the cell; the deceased was still there! I asked her if she knew the inmate was dead; she said yes, and told me not to enter anything in my notes; except that he was dead when I went to check on him! When we arrive back at the clinic; she got right on the phone and called someone! I want you to "listen to me;" I mean listen to me very carefully, because "I mean what I'm going to say!" My clinic aide has been no problem to me whatsoever; do you understand me? He is very co-operative and well mannered; does his work carefully, and "follows my instructions," with no problem! I am not going to repeat this, "not even once;" nothing, not a single thing better happen to my aide at the hands of "anyone!" I want you to call CO William and tell him however you want, but you tell him! Bye Bye hone. For me to say I was speechless is an understatement! I didn't have a clue that Mrs. Johnston felt any need or reason to cover my back! I'll tell you, she was really heavy! To see her, you would've never given a thought about how no nonsense she could become; and never show the first sign of being ruffled! I guess when you know where you stand, and are confident in and about that; you have no need for signs and indicators! Amongst the many things I'm thankful to Allah for, I'm thankful I wasn't of the convict frame of mind; because I can imagine an individual knowing he had someone with pull like that ready to reach out and touch someone... I didn't even think about trying to use my position to get favors or recognition in the prison!

I know one thing like I know my name; had it not been for my job in the clinic; let me be more specific; Mrs. Johnston's clinic aide, some things would have come down on me. There I was, standing in between the Captain Watch Commander, Deputy Supt; of Security, CO's and Mrs. Johnston! What I mean is; whoever it was she'd called about my well-being, had been told, not asked to do whatever without really saying; but it was understood and in no uncertain terms; that at no one's hands, was "any harm to come to me!" Mrs. Johnston and I were back in the clinic about an hour when the Watch commander and the Deputy Superintendant walked in! I had 2 ear irrigations, 3 bandages to check, 17 stitches to remove, after the noon count cleared; so I was getting some trays set-up! Prior to that day, I had never been asked to leave the clinic! The D.S. started to say something, but it was cut short; then the W.C., asked Mrs.

Johnston for the medical folder on the inmate found dead in his cell during our sick-call rounds! Mrs. Johnston asked me to get the folder from the table; when the Watch commander saw the folder he said; (a 68 number) was, and is this his medical folder? The number (68) represents the year in which the inmate was processed into the NYSDOCS system. What the W.C; had been given as a medical file on that particular inmate was not the entire medical file of a prisoner who's been in prison more than 12 years. It was only his most recent medical history; because others were too full to continue putting documents in them! Mrs. Johnston told him the file which he was holding was only for the past few months. The three of them were talking about something but I couldn't hear any of it! The nurse told me to go pull the entire medical folder of the inmate. His total medical history went back to his stay in Sing Sing; it was about eight inches thick! I took the entire medical history back to the clinic; then was told to sit outside with CO Travis! The count had cleared and some of the inmates who I was supposed to treat had come; we all sat outside of the clinic for over an hour before Officer Travis got a call on the phone; he hung up and went inside the clinic! When Officer Travis came back out he sent me in; the D.S.S; told me to put the inmate's medical history back from where I'd gotten it! When he (the W.C.) handed the medical folder to me, I stood there for a seconds thinking there'd be more; but I didn't say anything! Instead, he gives me a firm look and says in a cross tone; "What are you looking at, huh?" Why, are you still standing there with the fucking files?!" Mrs. Johnston jumped up and said to him: Is this the way you speak around your mother?! "Is that the way you speak to people when your wife is present?!" "Don't you ever, ever let this job make you forget that I'm as capable as you are; do you understand me?!" I have never had one of these men serving time disrespect me; and I've always been able to get what I wanted done! Then she says to me, Anthony take the files back to the record room and file them!

The report(s) which would eventually come to the clinic, explaining injuries, were always too convenient! By the time I'd return to the block from the clinic, whomever the individual (s) were who'd been admitted into the hospital, or come to the clinic to have injuries treated; now knew the truth about the CO's reports related to injuries for which they (prisoners) may have been seen for on a given day! There was no problem, the inmates knowing what the report(s) submitted by the COs contained; because they knew their reports would never be questioned! By the time a CO finished prepping other COs to back-up and support his story/version/lies; it was only a matter of showing the report to his sergeant to have it witnessed and signed! In addition to that, it was a matter of common knowledge; the prisoner found to be involved in trying to expose a Clinton CO would be made to regret the day he was born! Though Mrs. Johnston never said anything to shed light on what might have happened to the inmate I'd found dead in his cell, under his sheet, blanket; fully dressed, cell floor covered with water, all the cell water turned off; nothing in the CO's shift report coincided with anything I'd been told by twelve prisoners on his tier; "WOW!" As I've stated other times prior to this; little did I know that I would someday be in a position wherein I'd learn first-hand how dangerous a lie is; how dangerous a lie can become when someone has been entrusted with power; and uses that power to present and support a lie! Different inmates had told me the old man had been complaining for two days about having bad headaches; his arm feeling funny, as well as the tips of his fingers tingling! One inmate told me the old man kept flushing his toilet because he was trying to keep his water cold to put his towel in it, so that he could place the wet towel on his chest and head! A couple inmates said they'd heard him complaining about being real hot, unable to cool off! He had asked an inmate kitchen worker locking next to him, if he could try and bring him some ice for an ice pack! Someone explain how the following could have possibly not been mentioned in shift reports for two days! The fact, according to several inmates; the old man hadn't had water in his cell for almost two days! Do any questions come to mind? Questions like: Where did all the water come from all over the cell of his floor? Who had wet the old man? How long had he lay there, wet? Since shift counts are made, calling for live response, keeping in mind some of the statements made by different prisoners/inmates; what type of response(s) had he given coon their (2) days, six counts?! Perhaps there's an even more disturbing question; how long had that old man lay dead, soak and wet under a sheet and blanket, fully dressed?! How could I have been allowed to be the one to examine that old man, and nobody else be sent for to thoroughly examine the cell and the old man before taking him wherever! UMF! UMF! UMF! If you're asking how I know nobody else came to examine the old man or his cell; there were inmates all over the block and his tier! The cell was closed for about an hour; then two of the prisoners who were on the tier, were ordered to put the body onto a stretcher, and walk it to the front of the tier; two civilian from maintenance were there to take it wherever! What I just said was ordered to be done is unbelievable to the point that it boggles the mind; you have to ask how such was even possible?! What kind of power had the head running this fraternity been given? No, perhaps the more important question would be; who'd given him the power?! I know I was in prison! I know I was amongst what some would consider; some of society's most despicable low-lives! But, was what had been ordered correct in any way? Unless things have changed; unless the policies, rules, regulations and procedures have changed; I never imagined that the time would come wherein I would be involved firsthand with the policies, rules, regulations and procedures followed, when an inmate dies while in the custody of the NYSDOCS! I would also have the unfortunate opportunity to find out something else; the more things change, the more they remain the same!!

I honestly believe I would have been killed by other prisoners had it not been for one thing; I was a Muslim! See, prisoners may be ignorant about many things; but when it comes to the ins and outs of prison; and who's privy to what, there are few things they don't know! The prison population knew I had access to the medical records of every prisoner in Clinton. That meant I also knew or could find out at the pull of a file; exactly what any report submitted by a CO on an incident contained; be it inmate on inmate, or CO on inmate! I don't even want to try and count how many times I was approached by other prisoners about that very thing! In prison are, some of the best "legal litigants" in the world! Literally thousands of dollars are made by "jailhouse lawyers!" Appellate courts across the country review more appeals prepared by such legal minds than you'd ever imagine; and many have left their mark in law books for cases that have been successful to the point of "setting legal precedent" for future appeals to turn to in appellate courts across our country! One thing dreaded by any attorney is "the element of surprise!" Knowledge is power; and for the convicted felon, for the jailhouse lawyer; I represented their opportunity to have access to that element of surprise; "knowledge! Approach after approach, I refused request! Time after time I refused commissary offers, ($100 commissary buys sometimes)! When that didn't work, whispers of whether or not I should be trusted began to circulate! "Not being able to be trusted" doesn't mean but one thing in the joint/prison; it means the CO/administration own that particular prisoner; meaning that individual is a snitch! Boredom is one thing which has deep roots in prison;

rumor gives you something to look forward to! One thing you could count on being certain about is a rumor in prison; it was not going to produce anything positive! I'll say it again; there is one reason, and one reason only for me not having been shanked; the fact that I was a Muslim; especially after a rumor circulated that I should not be trusted! The inmate Muslim population in Clinton was large; and there were some individuals amongst our Muslim population who were very well known! It was no secret to the prison administration; if something caused the Muslims to have to respond, it was going to be final for whomever it was we were coming for; be it an individual or a group! Other than information about what coincident reports contained; I can't recall a single incident wherein I was asked to bring back a single item from the clinic; not so-little as a Q-Tip or a band aid! Oh, let me make a correction about what I was asked to give from the clinic; medical information pertaining to treatment or the lack of such for an inmate looking to put in a lawsuit against the prison, was something requested from me! As I stated before; I could have had a cell full of commissary or a substantial amount of money in my prison account had I complied with some of the many request from prisoners/inmates! Believe me; I could have helped my family financially had I submitted to even a few of the requests; but it was not of interest to me! I wasn't going to let someone buy Mrs. Johnston's opinion of me! There I was in a citadel of the Ku Klux Klan; and whomever she was, whatever it was she represented in that citadel; she sat, looked at me and said: Anthony you don't belong here, you have no business here! I'd seen and heard her take a stand several times against staff, for my well being; and made it clear exactly what her position was! I wasn't going to betray her for any reason! The three things Mrs. Johnston had told me to understand, I held on to them as though they were sacred!

There was a prisoner there who was part of a threesome,

guilty of killing a lady (white lady), for $1.68; he was always being made a joke of! The three were given 25 years-to-life; knowing what he was in Clinton for was "no secret" to anyone, and none of the police tried to make it one! That prisoner finally had himself put into PC (Protective Custody), hoping he'd have an easier bid! Little good that (PC) did, because his heist figures followed him; he was given the nickname (Cash Money), though the $1.68, divided three ways, didn't even amount to a penny per day, once the amount of time they had to do was factored in! As the weeks came and went, the tops from can goods would continue to be used to open the flesh of fellow prisoners! Prisoners would continue to fall on shanks; sometimes a dozen times or more; I became quite proficient at changing bandages, removing stitches, et cetera! I would learn of two other prisoners dying in their cells in Clinton; requiring me to make two more file laundering trips to the inmate medical records room, for the medical records of those two prisoners! One of the two prisoners died of a heart attack; I was told another prisoner saw the deceased, sitting on the toilet at about 9:35 that morning; and that he was seen still on the toilet, leaning over with his elbows on his knees, when that same inmate returned to the tier for the noon count! When he saw the deceased prisoner still in that position after the count cleared, he said he went and told the CO something might be wrong with this prisoner; because of what he had noticed!

Sometimes I would ask myself what the letters CO actually meant; it would have taken very little to convince me that CO meant "Comatose Officer!" (in the sense of lethargy); or Collusive Officer (someone acting to achieve a deceitful goal); Crafty Officer (an individual marked by deception, deviousness); Connivance Officer (individual giving his consent to illegalities by remaining silent)! I sat and thought and thought, trying to recall even a single occasion that I'd witnessed a CO actually "correct something." I am referring to the hundreds and hundreds of incidents that had been brought to a close by violence or profanity. Reading this, someone would assume I'm describing prisoners confronting prisoners, but sadly, it's not the case! I'm attempting to sketch a picture for you of the pathetically professional behavior on the part of NYSDOCS "comatose Officers, Collusive Officers, Crafty Officers, Connivance Officers! I can't imagine the "New York State Training Academy" even giving a multiple choice question that would have an answer as a choice like the following to choose from; (Question) If a prisoner comes to you and says; something seems to be wrong with a prisoner in his cell; how should you respond? (Well this is the answer which I received from that idiot of a CO?) "Okay, but if he's on the toilet, he might be taking a shit; maybe he's constipated; what's going on, the two of you got something going on?! Who's fuckin who?!" The sad shame is that was the response from the CO when he was told that something might be wrong with a prisoner, in his cell! As if that weren't enough; this same inmate after returning to his tier, would find the inmate for whom he'd expressed concern, lying on the floor; underwear at his ankles, still bent in the position of one who'd been sitting on the toilet! Though he had a (73#), his medical file would ultimately make "no mention" of him having heart trouble; or having ever been seen for such! I would learn from other prisoners that he had a few rather lengthy stays in the outside hospital! His medical files had not been stagnant; about 1 ½ to two inches thick when I was sent to medical records to get it; but it would be much lighter when I was told to return it!

    The third prisoner was found on the floor of his cell sitting as it were in a kneeling position on his heels, leaning back against his bunk. Word went around that he was known to frequently suffer from seizures, so when the prisoners on each side of him began hearing weird noises coming from his cell; they started yelling for the police; 17 is having a seizure! Yo, CO yo, CO, CO, 17 is having a seizure! Police! Police! The CO/police never came; but 17's cell was quiet, so nothing else was said. The next morning things were done as usual; the CO went pass the cells with the speed of light, and came back pass even faster! About a half hour later the cells popped, and they said they were out to start their day. Going pass, 18 cells saw 17 kneeling on the floor. Thinking about the noise he'd heard last night, he stopped at the cell gate to ask him if he was okay; inmate in cell 18 said, as soon as he saw 17's cell, he could tell the brother was dead! He said he ran down the tier to get the CO telling him to come because something seemed to be wrong with the prisoner in 17's cell! He went on, telling the CO about the sounds he and other prisoners heard coming from 17's cell; they'd called out for the CO but nobody ever came to see what the yelling was about! Nobody was able to say whether he'd been in that position from the time they'd called for the officer last night or not. But, the inmates in the two cells on both sides of him held to saying they heard nothing more after hearing what sounded like someone struggling with a seizure! 18 cell said he called to 17's cell twice but got no answer; so he convinced himself that the reason he didn't get a response was because after someone has a seizure, the person is usually drained of energy; so (17) cell is probably out of it now! I can't recall being pressured more about the medical records of any inmate more than for this one! This was a black prisoner who was said to have had a lot of home boys in Clinton! The pressure became so-heavy at one point that I actually thought about asking for a job change!

    This was the first time this tactic was used; "The white man is the devil, brother; and you know there's no heart of mercy in them! We created them from us ahki! Check dis out brother; if we don't stop deez crackas, day gon keep letun us die up in here! We were coming from the yard about a week later;

three black inmates were walking in front of me; it was obvious they knew I was behind them. They began making comments about knowing what they had to worry about more; getting sick in Clinton, being killed by the police in Clinton, being left to die in their cell, or the nigga they got in da clinic??? One of them says; does it matta, they all meanna same thing; they gon geddaway widit! A real punkass nigga, man! Then another one says; (turning around looking at me) otta set you da fuck-up; see what da fuck dat job mean nin; day lose you upinnis motherfucker to, cuz you ain't really nothing! I got a little angry and responded to what was being said; (using their diction) listen ta you brothas; I think I unnastan wa I was toll; ole black man toll me dat I was da firs nigga clinic aide in da history of dis prison! Lisinta you niggas man, no wanda day ain't neva had a brother up innis piece; a buncha crap inna basket niggas! Maybe it was something I said that afternoon, because things died down; or maybe I should say things returned to normal; request for files was occasional… I did take it upon myself to look into the medical file of that third inmate a few weeks later; it was no surprise that there was nothing unusual about his prison stay! Maybe this was because he hadn't been sick; perhaps he hadn't been there long enough, he had a (76) number. During the next week or so, I asked Mrs. Johnston a number of times about seizures, but she asked me to be more specific; because apart from muscle spasms, the subject is vast she said. Since she'd asked me to be more specific, I went on to ask if a person could die from an epileptic seizure; if so, would there have to be other medical conditions existing? She sat there for a few seconds, head down; then she asked me what I was up to! I told her someone had asked me how dangerous seizures were and were prisoners dying from them! Mrs. Johnston said, "What did you say Anthony?" I told him I had no idea, but I did know it was possible for a person having a seizure to have as many as five seizures back to back! What did you mean by that Anthony? I'm sure I remember one of the nurses, when I asked about a particular inmate suffering from spasms immediately after seeming to be alright; explaining that what we were seeing were actually both separate and individual seizure episodes! This same nurse went on to tell me that I should time each episode and note them in my shift report(s) if and when such happens. I thought it strange, not getting a comment from Mrs. Johnston then or after!

From the first night that I arrived at Clinton (The Last Strong Hold) to date, things had really changed. It's something that I'd have the feeling like there'd been change while still being in a haven for every type of filthy, foul, and unclean animal! What had happened? What was going on? What, if anything was different in the belly of the beast? Where was the change so obvious that I was able to feel it? "This change was inside of me, I'd changed!" The way I saw and understood things had changed! The way in which I rationalized and accepted things had changed! The way I now expected things to happen had changed! In spite of all I'd seen, there I was; able to lay my head on my pillow at night and sleep like a baby with his head in the arms of his mother! Prisoners were still being beaten to death by any one of, if not by all of the four CO I'd mentioned; the (comatose officer, crafty officer, connivance officer, collusive officer)! Prisoners were still disappearing! Blue Eyes was still himself; prisoners were still stabbing, slicing, raping, and extorting each other, etcetera! Yet like I'd said, things had changed; but, the more things changed, the more they remain the same!!! It was something to really think about; the reality of what must happen to the mind of the individual who spends a decade amidst such "mind altering decadence!!!" The way I was now able to come and go with no noticeable signs of apprehensiveness of reluctance after such a short time was hard for me to believe; especially considering where I was!

I couldn't remember the last time I was unnerved by anything that had happened; or by anything which I heard was going to happen; especially considering where I was! What might someone say about that? I don't want to imagine what the evaluation therapist would say was wrong; what had happened to me emotionally as a result of the psychological trauma; there was no doubt about the trauma! To me, what was being shown was the ability of the human being to adjust and adapt! What I was seeing was a human being showing how strong a mind in a state of denial can be; such as when I told Judge---: either he was a liar, or Allah/God was a liar; because I would not serve a single day; due to the fact that time was a thing created; that Allah had said He created creation to serve the human being! Therefore time was meant to serve me; so every day would only serve to benefit me! Such being true judge, you are a liar; I will not serve one day; Allah is not a liar! I can still see and hear Judge in his fit of rage; stating how much time he'd sentence me to serve; but I was truly of the state of mind which told me I would not serve a day; perhaps I was in denial; but to date, I'll say the time served me! Though I had said what I'd said to the judge, and meant it with every beat of my heart; I had no idea that in some future date I would show the days, weeks, months and years had served me better than any Harvard, Yale, Oxford University, etcetera could have ever even begun to! More than that; the fact that I would someday re-enter the same system of power (NYSDOCS) and observe it as it were, through different glasses; wasn't even part of any far gone conclusion! I would get a better understanding than I ever had about something I'd heard; that being: The names and the faces have changed, but the game is still the same!

Working in the clinic, I'd see the D.S.S. (Deputy Superintendent Security) and the W.C. (Watch commander) often! When they'd come into the clinic, it was like they were making rounds because they would never stay for more than a few minutes. There was something I noticed after the third or fourth time they came and left; I realized that I had actually seen one or the other of them carrying files. For a while I didn't put things together; didn't really think anymore about it until one evening in the yard; here comes one of my cohorts asking for a favor. Do me a favor; hold it; (as I'm turning to walk away) just hold it a minute, ok? I ain't axin fano files or nutun like dat; I jus wanna axya ta do one thing; all ya gonna havta do is say yes or no! The other day, one of my CO-defendants refused to take a free ass kickin from a CO. I already talked to some of the guys working in the hospital; they said he ain't up there! Dat mean day tookim tada outside hospital like I heard somebody sayin! I asked him how long he'd been here; he said he and his CO-defendant had been in Clinton almost three months; six weeks of that, spent in reception. I asked him why he felt it was necessary to tell me he wasn't asking for files or anything like that, as though I had access to them! I went on to say to him; you just got into population, what reason would you have to come to me? He said it had cost him a pack…Imagine that, for information as accessible as that was it cost him a pack of Kools; simply because he'd not been around long enough to know anyone! I must assume it cost him for the names of each hospital worker too…I stood there looking past him for a moment, reflecting on the unfortunate naivety of this convict standing before me! Someone had told someone that his CO-defendant had been taken outside; and he'd over-heard what had been said. Realizing they were talking about his buddy, he concluded outside meant outside hospital! I looked at him, smiled and asked him; if it's not a file you want or anything like that, what could you possibly want that could possibly only require a yes or no answer? I jus wanna know what hospital they took him to, thasall. From what I understand, they only have one hospital around here; right? Thasall I'm askin ya; did they take him there; yes or no? I said to him; you said you heard some of the men talking about him having been taken outside right? Do you have any idea how far the prison would have to travel to take him somewhere else? What do you need to know that for any way? So I can at least write my CO-defendants' mom, and let her know he's in the hospital! Hearing him say that, I told him that would not be the wisest thing to do; depending on what he planned to include in the letter(s)! A moment or so later he says something which made me wonder if he was really naive or just hard-headed! He says to me; I don't need the prison to give me any free letters; I can sendim right out, insteada dim bein put by hand throughda stamp machine; know what I mean? I shook my head and said to him; you don't have a clue do you?! You don't have the faintest idea where you are do you?! "Man, I am going to tell you something which you need to take to heart for the rest of your bid; you got sentenced for yourself, do you understand! When it's all said and done, if you live long enough; you're going to be called before the parole board alone! You are going before them by yourself, do you understand?! You better make up your mind that you have your own time to do, and do it! If you don't understand me now, if you live long enough; you will…! Do you know who can possibly help you with all that information, and address your concerns? Write to see your counselor! Don't go into any real detail; just tell whomever it is that you're having some problems and need to speak to him/her! If you're going to write home, don't be stupid man! I turn to walk away; he grabs me by the arm and says; so does that mean you're gonna git the name of the hospital for me! I just snickered, shook my head and walked away! I did speak to a couple guys in the yard (pointing him out); asking if they knew who in the heck he was! They just said he had a partner who'd gotten himself carried outta here, trying to be bad; (someone else said) trying to impress these convicts! I reacted like I didn't know anything about him having a partner, and asked what his partner's name was; and where did he lock? One of them told me to wait a minute; he went across the yard and came back. He aint back yet (ha ha ha); aint comin back; fool ass cracka, know like I know; he know the dude aint commin back! He was in B-Block; one of the guys in the block packed his shit up and gave it to the police! We stood there talking for a few more minutes; I told them about my conversation with him, and what I thought of him; based solely on that conversation. One of them commented that the guy hadn't been in population long, and that he was like what people refer to as a "mark!!" I didn't say anything, but I certainly knew what he meant! Before anything else could be said, the same prisoner/inmate says; the dudes in this spot sure gua get fat offa him (ha ha ha)!!! He stan out like he gotta a sign onniz back! Stan out jus like a "mark!" The brother was right; it was like this poor guy was a neon sign! The everyday person reading this book would not recognize him as being any different than any other prisoner walking the yard! But he was anything but the average convict in Clinton; and just as he had already; he was going to continue drawing attention to himself; that is if he lived! My next day at work, I did attempt to locate a file on the co-defendant of the mark. I was able to thumb through the files, though there was no file on him; and the nurse simply stated he was supposed to be missing! Though I didn't mean to; I laughed out loud and said; imagine that! As I stood there thinking, it clicked; that was one of a number of files I'd been sent to pull about a week ago! I hadn't given any thought to it; because it wasn't the first time I had pulled files and didn't return them the same day; but the next! Is it possible that this missing file was one of the file I'd seen the DSS or the WC leaving with during their rounds last week? Of course Allah knows best; but was I to wager; I'd say that particular file was amongst the files taken by the DSS or the Watch commander!! I didn't have that answer, nor did I want to know the answer to that question! But not wanting answers didn't change that human curiosity! I was seeing things being done with aim and purpose…! Yes, there was a lot of stuff going on; but in a manner of speaking, something kept my suspicions numb! What I mean is; it seemed that with all I was seeing, with the level of hands on involvement related to medical file reduction on my part; I should've been a nervous wreck!

I recall an inmate who managed to get a letter out while we were in reception; to date it isn't known how it was done; just that it was! One afternoon a sergeant came to H-Block and told us that we were to put our ear-phones on that night after the quiet bell; an announcement was going to be made! He went on to say it would be in the best interest of us all to take seriously what we would hear! That night after the quiet bell, an announcement was made; I do not remember the entirety, but it began with: When you arrived, you were all told to send your letters to the mailroom, with envelopes open! You were also told your letters were read; then closed prior to leaving the facility! A few things were said after that, then he says; one of you managed to smuggle a letter out of here! At this moment we don't know how it was done, but we have a good idea! Some of you probably know who this individual is by now, even how he managed to pull it off; but we want you to tell yourselves what would've happened to him, had he failed! Oh, one last thing; the warden told me to tell one of you, your letter made it out; but, what about you? The following morning an inmate was put on keep-lock; the infamous Blue Eyes could be heard telling him he'd be keep-locked until transferred out; he'd receive no mail, have no commissary buys; none of his letters would go out unless approved, word for word; he'd receive none of his in-coming mail, if there was anything questionable in it! Then to clear up any doubts there may have been; he says: "Any, of you assholes stupid enough" to try and include a message through your mail, to the family of this ass wipe; you can give your soul to God; cause, your ass belongs to me!

It was Friday and time for Ju'mah (Muslim Prayer Services); I was allowed to go. I don't have to say I was more than happy for the change of scenery; the change in the reception blues which came with being there! The Imam had a lot of time to say what he wanted to say; so, he gave us a lot to think about! There were some brothers there who remembered me from the county Jail; they gave me different food items to take back with me! At first I was reluctant; but, listening to them, I accepted that I would not be searched coming back from Ju'mah! We talked for a while; then the Imam announced it was time for reception to go back; I was okay with the food stuff as long as I was in Ju'mah; but it was a different story once I was back in route to reception! The images of the cells I'd cleaned, kept coming back to mind; the police doing whatever they wanted to prisoners! But, it was too late; I was going to have to go along for the ride; whether it was going to be bumpy, was up to me; how was I going to ride this horse? I could have pushed the "panic button" and got busted; or let things play out! As it was, you had to really look if you wanted to see that I had anything; this must have been something the brothers in population were use to; because, everything went like clockwork! As I think about all that there was for me to look forward to in the way of consequences, Allah was blessing me to be overcome with a sense of apathy and atrophy! I don't know of any other way to explain my state of mind, except with those words; because I was not tense! I can't say I was nervous any longer; or that I moved about with uncertainty!

I'd been getting visits from my wife, once a month; she'd bring our sons. Though I was thankful beyond words, it was hard for me because; beside the trip taking all night, it was costly!

Even something like $25.00 could have been money used for a bill, food in the house, even clothing for our sons! Prior to the bus full of wives, girlfriends, mothers and children arriving at the facility, they'd be taken to a public type of rest area where the women can shower and dress for their visits. Besides the cost of the bus round trip, the visit was all day; our sons could not be expected to be there all day and not eat anything! I'd see other visitors making trips to the machines and returning with food, drinks, snacks, et cetera; while our sons sat and watched them! AAAHHH!!! You have no idea how I felt, sitting there helpless; unable to do what a father and husband should have been able to do! But to my surprise, my wife would make strategic trips to the vending machines, never failing to ask me if I wanted something! Believe me it was easy to say no, you and the little guys eat, I'm just fine having the three of you here! Sometimes I would just sit and look at my wife going through all of this, burden because of me! It may not have been obvious to others, but it was clear to me; she had loss and was losing weight. She was already petite, so losing weight was not suitable for her at all! She shared with me that she was working a full-time and part-time job, as well as going to school in the Bronx a couple nights per week! It wouldn't take a rocket scientist to realize my sons were really missing out on that most beautiful unit, (family)! As if missing me in their lives wasn't enough; my sons were being deprived of their mom also! When they left home in the morning for school, they'd not see or hear the sound of their mother's voice until she was waking them at the home of the baby sitter sometime during that night; to take them home! Loving my wife as much as I did; appreciating her as much as I'd come to; it was so painful, knowing my sons weren't the only ones dealing with deprivation; their mom was dealing with it like a world class champion! Walking as it were, through the bowels of hell itself; with a courage and committed willingness to give her very last! For a second there, I was going to say my wife had a heavier burden than my sons; deprivation more intense; but who am I to make that assessment? What qualified me to say the depth of the hurt being felt and experienced by my sons was any less intense; or if they understood any less, what they had a longing for? It was said a while ago; "Kids are people too!" I wander how much thought we'd really given? In fact, I wander if beyond a slogan, has anyone really stopped to give it thought at all!? There was more sitting before me than a visit with my wife and sons; the past was sitting before me, the future was sitting before me; sacrifice, struggle, as well as the hopes and dreams of my sons was sitting before me! There were times when I'd try to fool myself by telling myself my sons were lucky to be little guys; because they couldn't really understand what was going on! I had no right to try and make light of what my two little buddies were being made to accept and if possible, make sense of! What I was telling myself even worse was; my reason for such thinking! That being; so I might feel better about the sad, sorrow situation! It didn't work; I knew better!

There was something I noticed years later that was just as it was when I was in prison; on visiting day in the male prisons; wives and girlfriends with children, would pack the visiting room for every visit, every family day event! On the other hand; you could count on a hand, the number of husbands and/or boyfriends coming to visit the wife or girlfriend in a prison for women on visiting day!! Even when women prisoners were mothers being visited by their children; it was an extremely rare occasion that the father was the one with the child/children on that visit! Were it not for the grandmother of the children, the imprisoned mother(s) would do the entire prison stay without ever seeing her child/children! Where is someone who can explain to me, the imbalance here?!

One weekend I got a visit from my wife and sons, along with

a surprise; they were staying overnight! I was not comfortable with it at all. The incidents involving Darryl and his wife were still fresh in my mind. According to word going around the prison; a few weeks prior, the girlfriends of two prisoners had been raped while staying across the street at Kay's Hotel! With all the talk going around the prison, it was my understanding that there was no report even made about it by either girlfriend! Before I said anything, my wife said to me: "I heard more rumors about prisoner's wives and girlfriends being raped while making the mistake of spending the night at THE HOTEL!" Then my wife said something to me which I hope wasn't meant to assure me that I had nothing to worry about! "See I've been told that I don't have anything to worry about; isn't that right guys"?! My little guys started jumping on me, telling me; they were going to protect their mom! It may have sounded cute, but "reality was real!" I told her I didn't understand how she could have made up her mind to stay up in this place; knowing women have been raped up here, and not a single thing has ever been done about it! The evening and night after the visit were the longest I'd spent in Clinton since hearing about my mother! Every sound that night, I was up and at the bars; straining, trying to hear! The next morning when they called my name, I was so anxious; it was difficult, trying to walk slowly! When I arrived in the visiting room, I didn't even look at my wife's face; I looked at my sons, because if anything was wrong; it would show in their faces! When I said hey buddies, and saw the excitement and smile on their faces, I knew everything was okay! When I hugged my wife, I hugged her so hard! I held her for a long moment, whispering in her ear; don't you ever do this again, please! I have to admit it though, having a back-to-back visit with my wife and sons, was nice!

It was all the better, seeing as how I'd figured out a way to see to it that my wife and sons were able to visit and enjoy snacks and drinks as other visitors did; I'd become a letter artist for a couple guys! People are of the opinion that African American are the illiterate group when it comes to writing, spelling and the correct use of words; believe me, nothing could be further from the truth! There was one white guy who was suppose to be so well known for the mail he received, and the females he had coming to visit him. I overheard him talking to another prisoner he was walking in the yard with; about being charged too much for the letters being written for him. The other prisoner said to him; unless you intend to let everyone know you can't write, you're going to have to continue paying for the service! Do you think you're going to just find someone to write for you, just like that; and it not get out into the prison? Well, that sounded like an opportunity for me; I took the first opportunity I got to make him an offer. Of course you know he responded as though he had no idea what I was talking about; so I repeated some of what he'd said, and what had been said to him; then turned to walk away! He says; hey, hey; you're the one working in the clinic, right? I turned around, saying yes; and that should make talking to me easy to explain too, when your friends want to know what you're doing talking to a black guy! You and I know what's really happening. How do I know you're any better than me, or can even write? I told him to write what he wanted to say as best he could; I'd then make all the corrections necessary, as well as put some mixing in and taking away from; while adding some romantic compliments to it. I'll give it back to you to read; if you accept it, rewrite it and mail it. What I want is simple; I will write five letters per week for you; three pages each letter for $15.00! You have visits every week; whenever my family comes up, you'll pay me; see to it that they get $15.00 in items from the vending machines! I thought about it; my family came once every two week; so I agreed to do ten letters every two weeks for the same amount. He did, I did; it worked, he was happy!

This particular Sunday we both had visits; two convicts pulled it off (the $15.00 vending heist)! This is how simple it was to make the buy happen: He and I had already talked about what I wanted his visitor to get from the machine. When his visit went to the vending machine, she'd buy what we'd agreed to. She'd then tell the CO my wife had given her money at the stop because she had no change; and they'd agreed to it being given back with items from the vending machines, rather than exchanging money in the visiting room! "Having made history, it was no secret what was being said about me." I was said to have been the first nigger clinic aide in the history of that prison! That along with it being very well known that I was Mrs. Johnston's boy, things went without incident! My wife did not know about the vending machine arrangement; but I didn't do it again. In spite of that, I still did letters for him; instead of a month of letters, I wrote seven a month for him; no charge.

Believe me, there'd be few things CO would be able to prevent in any prison, if and/or when prisoners would decide to put their differences aside for a common deceitful end! There is one thing prisoners have that those hired and thought to have been trained to control, don't have; that one thing is, 24/7/365! Twenty hours per day, seven days per week, three hundred and sixty five days per year! Regardless of the number of correction officers the state has; these CO don't have "24/7/365" time together! Time is unlike anything man can create! Few people if any have as much of it at their disposal as prisoners! Few places shelter abuse of people, with immunity; like prisons! If you live a hundred years, a century; you will never come to experience the multiplicity of personalities that exist amongst convicts! Years ago there was a program on television; before every show it would say: It's a different world than where you come from! Make no mistake about it; prison is a different world than where you come from! Many of you will think I'm referring to this world being different; solely because one is dealing with and judging the behavior of robbers, murderers, rapist, child molesters, kidnappers, drug dealers, and so on! I would ultimately be hired by the department of "New York State" wherein I had been imprisoned as a convicted felon! Yes, I would be hired some years later as a "Muslim Chaplain" for the New York State Department of Correctional Services. Later, I will walk you through that world, a system of government which will cause some of you to find yourselves in a state of aphasia! As it is, much of what I've shared with you is a "direct result of some New York State Employees who were of the "worst type of criminal/criminal mind!"

There have been days in which I've traveled back in my mind and cringed at the images that seemed to be haunting me! Images of some of the sick, sadistic violence which had been meted out against prisoners, black and white alike! Images of some of the blood and gore that I had been ordered to scrub and clean off of floors, wall, ceilings, bars, sinks, toilets, stairs, etcetera; of cells and so on; after prisoners had fallen victim to savagery beyond even the most abstract definition of the word! "MY GOD, I've shivered sometimes when I've thought about these individuals having licenses to carry guns, and the power or freedom to "kill with anonymity!" That part of this truth, will come soon enough; but for now, I will continue with a "2 1/3 to 7 and a 3 to 9 years education; unparalleled!!

Prison could be different for each individual. I guess it depended for the most part on where your day had you. What I mean is; for the prisoner whose day has him in the mess-hall all day, he saw mess hall stuff; the prisoner whose day put him in the package room, he saw package room stuff; the prisoner whose day put him in the lumber mill, forest detail, etcetera;

that's what they saw! I would venture to say with a certainty; that there were few details where CO didn't get "beat down workouts" at the expense of a prisoner! I say this because working in the clinic, I rarely recall two prisoners being brought up to the clinic for treatment needed because of a fight they'd had with each other! On those rare occasions, I could tell because of bruises, that I was cleaning/treating, as a result of two prisoners fighting! But whenever a CO would drag a prisoner up to the clinic, alone; not followed up by another CO and prisoner; I knew the deal! "Not only that, the, bruises are as different, as night and day!" The manner of treatment is totally different! What I mean is; when Mrs. Johnston would ask a prisoner what happened, after having a fight with another prisoner, the prisoner would answer! But when a prisoner who'd been brutalized/beaten by a CO or CO's, the CO would tell Mrs. Johnston what had allegedly happened! There was another thing which stood out as different about the behavior of the CO every time it was an incident involving, two prisoners fighting, the CO who escorted the prisoner or prisoners, would step outside the clinic and talk with CO Travis; but just the opposite when it was a CO beat down! The CO would remain with the prisoner for the entire clinic examination; and the only question answered by the prisoner would be where he locked, his din number, his name, and whether or not he might be allergic to aspirin; (the last question, may or may not be asked)!

It might sound strange to hear me say prison's no longer overwhelming to me! In spite of all the underhandedness, deceit, willing-readiness to help in the utter covering up of correctional Law codes and Ethics violations, resulting from the sadistic brutalization, and even the outright murder of prisoners, etcetera; which I've had first-hand knowledge of starting from the night I arrived in Clinton. Just why I went about my time in this dangerously sick citadel, like there was nothing to worry about, I can't explain! Perhaps there's really something to the saying: The human being is a very adaptable creature! There was one place where anyone with sense paid attention; the one place where you had no idea what you might see, what might happen; the yard! When I tell you, if it could happen, it was going to happen in the yard, and in "wide-open-cover!" Like the rape of that "young white boy" by four prisoners, right there on a "cooking court," on a bright sunny day! On the street, when a group of males do a female one after the other, they say they ran a train on her! You don't want to even try and imagine, how often, it happened in the yard and in cell blocks! What category would you put the prisoner in, who happens to adjust to having been victimized by such? Would you say this prisoner should consider himself, fortunate or unfortunate? Fortunate because he got use to it and therefore didn't commit suicide; or unfortunate, because he will live with the memories of being dehumanized; robbed so-to-speak, of his manhood, and forced to walk around known as what they refer to in prison: somebody's bitch, for years!! Oh, and don't forget the secret; will it remain his secret?!

9

The Home Plate Umpire

THE YARD IS one place where you don't know what you might see! In a few weeks the "championship softball game" is going to be played! For weeks, everywhere you go, the jail house bookies are taking bets, on the "down-low!" There is going to be a lot of money won! On the other hand, it goes without saying; if there are going to be people winning money, there are going to be people losing money! Prison is one place where you stand to lose more than your money, if it turns out that you're on the wrong end of things; what might that be? Money is one thing which will cause one to lose his life in the blink of an eye or quicker! Though there are some prisoners with large sums of money; the thing which takes the place of money in prison is cigarettes! Every day that passes leading up to the big game, the wages get bigger and bigger; more and more prisoners get pulled into the betting! One "gang" has wagered to the max against another "gang!" Just like on the streets, bets are made that one team will win by this, that, or the other number of points; a certain player will hit a homer or bring in so-many runs, steal bases, etc!

Reading the above statement may sound like typical betting games. Is that what you're saying to yourself? Let me share just one incident with you, related to a prisoner who had wages placed on him that he'd steal two bases! A carton of cigarettes for each base stolen; six prisoners were involved in this simple bet; twelve cartons of smokes! His first time at bat, he was thrown out. The next time he got on base with a double, and stole third! The next two times, he popped out! His last time up, he hits a single; steals second but was thrown out or so the umpire said! I have a question for you now: Who is in trouble?! The, empire who made the call, was shanked twice; the one who stole the base had nothing to do with anyone betting on him, because he didn't tell anyone he could steal the bases! It doesn't work that way though! See, he knew he was going to be held accountable for causing the three prisoners who had bet on him, to lose their money; so he was pressured! Was that the extent of his blame? He should be so lucky; his team loss the game! Now, why did they lose the game?!!! Exactly! Had he not been caught stealing second base his team wouldn't have lost!!! No, not just yet; there's much more to the end of this game having been won or lost! See, it's like this; yes, the one prisoner was caught stealing second base; but that wasn't the last out! Remember, it's not over until the fat lady sings; and in this performance, she has just now stepped to the microphone!

There were still two innings to play, and his team is down by two runs; he would not get up again, and his team would have to score three more runs; there were two outs, men on first and second! The ball was hit high and far, over the head of the second baseman; one run scored, second run scores, the batter rounds second for third; the ball's been thrown towards home! In a few seconds, a tie game was going to be either won by a foot on home plate, or loss by when a glove touched the runner!!! Keep in mind where this game was being played; don't doubt for a second that depending on one word, blood was going to flow; life was going to come to an end; because in order for there to be a winner, there'd have to be a loser! Every year a game just like this has been played; one team wins, the other loses! There'd been only one game which didn't end peacefully; there was a fly ball to center field; bases loaded, two outs; the field team was up a run! What looked like a game over catch, turned out to be a miss judged fly; over the head of the center fielder! One, two, three runs score; the one who hit the ball stopped; the game was over with the second run having been scored!

Here it was again; many of the prisoners watching this game; saw the last nail biter! Some probably sitting on the same cooking courts, having placed similar bets; looking at an almost carbon copy of the game played a few years ago! The runner a few strides from home plate; the ball coming down; the catcher standing on the plate, with hands up to catch the ball; suddenly you hear: pumff (ball in glove); sllluump (sliding home); then an unbelievable silence! It was as though time stood still! Everyone looking at the umpire, waiting for a call! You can imagine what he was asking himself: Oh Hell, how did I get myself in this mess! Suddenly: He's out!!! He's out! It was total mayhem!!! Players from the losing team were all around the umpire; yelling and screaming, pushing and shoving! I felt for this poor guy; to the best of my knowledge all he did was; volunteer to help a game be played fairly! Some of you probably have the same question I've had; why in the world would someone take a Russian roulette responsibility?!

Not only is the umpire at home plate; but the umpire at each base is in the exact same position if he makes a call that could have gone either way! Now, I'm going to ask you again; who lost the game? Was the game lost because of a missed stolen base or because an umpire made the call one way rather than the other? Whatever the reason, one thing was certain; blood was going to be shed, and death would not be far behind!

The intensity of this yearly game was not new for neither the facility or for security; so what followed almost immediately, can't be explained away! In spite of all the commotion, we (the prisoners) were able to clearly read the moves and gestures being made; telling us to clear out! It was amazing; how the appearance of disorder was the total opposite! You would have had to witness how it unfolded, in order to appreciate what I'm presenting to you! The yelling, screaming, cursing, pushing, collecting, payoff arranging, etcetera; gave no indication that signals were being given, and cooperation was taking place to make way for the home plate umpire to have his head burst open with one swing of a bat!! A low voice says: Just want ta show ya, you ain't got nothing ta worry about after this... Just as the ump, turned, swoof (bat being swung); pooth (sound of the bat hitting the head of the umpire)!!! If you can imagine someone swinging a bat and hitting a melon as hard as he can; AAAHH MAN! The inside of his head splattered all over; the prisoner passed the bat, and before the CO even knew what had taken place, the bat was on the other side of the yard somewhere!!! Prisoners didn't run from the area; most simply walked a few feet away and just stood there; looking at the prisoner sprawled out on the ground, with most of his head gone! The prisoner who'd committed the gruesome murder, walked back and forth past what he'd just done! I'd been standing behind the backstop with a prisoner known as Oscar; watching the game. Understand what I'd just witnessed; I wasn't moved, disturbed or shaken in the least; having seen the head of another human being busted open; and less concern given it than might be given to a dropped water melon! The CO came in a swarm; grabbing everyone or ordering those to the area to get on the ground! Whistles blowing crazy; and the population in the yard are being ordered to fall in lines! Fortunately for me and Oscar; we'd gotten away almost as soon as things happened! Security questioned that one prisoner for a week; but wasn't able to get him to own up to doing anything! I was told the explanation he gave for why he was seen walking back and forth past the body was because he saw the head busted open, and was in shock! Security knew he was lying; he was in there for murder; had been locked down a few times for assaults on other prisoners, since being in prison! He was suspected of being responsible for a number of assault incidents connected to gambling, etcetera! In spite of all these things, nothing could be proven; and security could not get any other prisoner to snitch/rat on him! By the time the yard was cleared and security finally located the suspected bat; the bat had been cleaned; where does security turn, who can really be charged?! You would think all is settled; considering what transpired, causing one prisoner to lose his life in such a brutal and savage manner! Perhaps were this not prison; but, there were other individuals who were going to be held responsible for the money and cigarettes having been lost!

By the way, it was well known that CO placed money (sometimes, large sums) on different events! It was also known that there'd been contracts put on prisoners by COs. A prisoner might have been the reason a game or event may have been won or loss!!! As for this championship ball game; different COs might be overheard talking about one, two and three hundred dollar bets on it! The prisoner, who didn't succeed in stealing the bases, had himself placed in (PC) protective custody; because three (2 cigarette pack) contracts were put on him! The prisoner playing home plate on the losing team paid 6 cartons of cigarettes to the two guys who'd loss them; he was being blamed for the loss, because he didn't block home plate right! Because he paid the cartons of cigarettes bet, he saved his own life! In the joint, you will lose your life over 2 loose cigarettes; you owe it and don't pay; these fools don't have anything left except their reputations; they have to protect them! Yes, even for 2 cigarettes!

A softball game, the winner takes all game! Collectively, those who won would win thousands and thousands in prison currency! There'd be some prisoner in debt to other prisoners for years before paying their debts off; some prisoners unable to pay their debts, escape death by signing themselves into PC/Protective Custody; those in debt but unwilling to run, fall victim to any number of physical injuries; most of them are caused by being shanked or stabbed! If you convince yourself to bet on a game in the joint, know you're going to pay one way or another, you are going to pay! You are going to get up off of that money! I'm sure people dismiss any thought of just how much money flows through the hands of convicts every day in prison! It would be thought to be untrue, just how much it "cost to put a hit on another prisoner"! How much would you start at: $500.00, $1000.00, $1500.00? Depending on who you ask, one hundred Kools (a half carton, five packs) of cigarettes might be enough to get a hit carried out! Believe it or not, there was a patient whom I'd attended in the hospital, he fell on a knife six times, 6, because of a "debt", something that even in its second hand, is dangerous; "a pack of cigarettes!" The one thing anyone with a sound mind would not do would be to volunteer in the Clinton Champion Softball game (in the "Belly of the Beast) as the umpire at "Home Plate!

After Clinton's long anticipated championship softball game, you can be certain that some six months are going to pass before the debts incurred by this game are settled, one way or another! There's no such thing as a defaulter; you're going to pay one way or another! Keep in mind one thing; this is prison, a place where a rep (reputation) is something you can't afford to lose if you're respected for it! It may only take one sign of being soft or weak, to give the impression to others that your rep doesn't have to be feared; imagine that! Something was made very clear to me after that game; life did not stop because of the vicious outcome of the game! Individual after individual thought to have played a part in the winning or losing of it, was made to deal with the consequences! Looking at that; as time came and went for me, I realized that many of the things I was witnessing; however barbaric and unnatural to me, had become as natural as life itself for some of the men who might never again see or know any other world; ever again in life! I remember one old man whom everyone, even the COs referred to as Pop; he shared with me that he had been brought to Clinton, by horse and buggy; and that he'd seen three generations of turn-keys (CO) come through there, right out of high school! He said he'd even had a couple (17) year old punks call him, or refer to him as boy!

The administration at Clinton was going to put someone's head on the chopping block for bashing the head of this prisoner; even if it wasn't the right person! Ultimately, the prisoner who'd be prosecuted for literally knocking the brains out of another prisoner was already serving two consecutive life sentences! What does that mean? How much time is that? That individual was going to "have to serve" the complete minimum of one sentence, then serve the same minimum of the second sentence, before he'd even be eligible for parole consideration! This means he'd have to be in prison for fifty years before going to the parole board! What would taking, the weight (blame) for one more body matter? Don't let yourself just sit there and read "fifty to life," like you're reading a TV Guide about what's on television! Hearing about that amount of time is one thing; knowing it to mean, such will be the absolute corralling boundary in which the rest of one's natural life will be played out is another!!! When I talked to this particular individual before he stepped forward to take the weight for busting open the head of that prisoner; he said almost word for word what I just said;

but he said it like this: What the fuck brother, I'm gonna do fifty fuckin years any how; why not go on and do twenty five more, and have money to spend for a while?!?! It shocked me when he later said to me: Tone (he called me Tone), don't think I don't know what a lot of the men feel about you shouldn't be trusted because of who you work for; but I been in this joint longer than most of these niggas talking; If I can't tell by now, then I need to be set the fuck up! It's easy for you to call me stupid and crazy for taking another body and getting some more time; when you have not been written off by your family! Man, I ain't had a letter from nobody; a card from nobody; ain't had nobody even accept a collect call in eighteen years! How many visits you think I dun had all the way the fuck up here, when they wouldn't even come see me in Sing Sing! I don't try and fool myself Tone; I ain't gon never walk the streets again man! I'm gonna die right here man! If I ever make it to the board, I will say what I want to say to them then; but until then, I'll see how I can use ($2500.00) to try and make the only life I know, comfortable! I've heard black guys talking about how their families have written um off; I think white families write us off more than your people do, because we don't have any business here! I asked him whether or not he really thought somebody just up and killing another human being was so meaningless as to be willing to make a way for the person who killed, to get away with it! He said something which was so sadly true: think about it Tone; you and I both know security won't find out who did it, regardless! One thing I know about this spot is what is well known; the life of a jailhouse snitch is real short here in Clinton! It's believed that administration/security puts the snitch back into population, after the information needed is received! I must have had a strange look on my face; because he asked me what was wrong? I said; that doesn't make any sense at all; who is going to come forward and tell security anything, knowing security is going to let the prison population know who the snitch is? He told me something that never crossed my mind; "some people have to be a part of reality man!" I know of (4) four incidents (prisoners) who were promised transfers closer to home if they came forth with what was needed, only to be thrown out to the wolves; to be shanked to death! Then he laughed and said: But if you look at it, they did get transferred closer to home; even if it was in a box!

This is a question for my readers: Can you imagine yourself ever becoming so comfortable, so resigned to being locked away; that fear is no longer a factor! What is it that could have possibly been done to the mind of a human being that would make accepting the blame for a murder, as easy as just stepping up and saying, I DID IT?! Everybody should take note, including the criminologist, psychoanalyst, psychotherapist, psychologist, etcetera, of what was and is done to that mind of the human being all day; everyday. In one way or the other, everyday of the year; people make up their minds to accept and do things which they would never even entertain the thought of; were it not because of the one thing which burns desire into the heart, unlike anything else man can name; money! Money was dangled before the minds' eye of an individual who said; he might as well be paid for doing time, since he was going to have to do time any way! Think about his logic; this was $2500.00, two and a half grand for something he didn't do, free money: he was getting this money for doing what he was going to do any way! Think about it, this was not being calculated in cartons of cigarettes; this was "money in his account!"

Prison is a haven for illiteracy; men of all nationalities and ethnicities are found to be unable to read past the 4th or 5th grade level! Many prisoners' math skills don't go beyond counting petty sums of cash; petty criminals counting the petty cash made from ($5.00 & $10.00) petty sidewalk drug sells! Male prisons are full of fathers and husbands convicted of nickel ($5.00) and dime ($10.00) heroin and cocaine or crack sells for suppliers who never serve a day! What is it about the whispering call of money? Is it so seductive to the mind that sons would shame their mothers; husbands would destroy their homes for it; fathers would abandon their children for it; what power!

Let me share a sad truth with you; you can be in prison and never say a word to anyone, about anyone; and have someone walk up behind you and stick you with a tooth brush three or four times; only to have the truth come out days later; that someone lied on you! The truth is; you'd not spoken to any CO about anyone, about anything! Why would I mention this? There was an incident which got a prisoner killed in the yard! It was all the more unfortunate because, the man who lost his life turned out to be a victim of mistaken identity! He was not the prisoner who a (two pack of cigarettes) contract had been taken out on! Yes, I said two lousy packs of cigarettes had been paid to have the life of another human being taken! But, guess what; that sick, demented individual still had a decision to make; what decision do you think that was?! Why would he still have a decision to make?! "This murderer still had to decide what he was going to do about the person he'd already been paid to kill, but didn't! What I mean is: The one who'd been paid still had a contract to honor; what was he going to do?! No, he wasn't going to be paid any more money! Yes, it meant just that; two lives were going to be taken; two people were going to be killed for (TWO PACKS) OF CIGARETTES!!! There was only one way to cancel this contract out; the individual who paid the cigarettes was going to have to accept being repaid! I guess, you'd say that's great; at least a second person won't be killed behind this sick mess! This is prison; a society which few of you reading this know anything about! The one who'd done the hiring agreed to the return of the money, but...; but not the same amount! Prison is cold hearted! The contractor was told; in order to cancel out the contract; instead of two packs; it was going to cost two cartons! You have one week to come up with the money; if you don't, you know the deal!! This hit, believe it or not; turned into a betting incident! How much do you wanna bet he's gonna do him; I have 5 packs he won't, etc.! Unfortunately, the guy couldn't get anyone to loan him two cartons; especially after one of the prisoners with (50 packs), spread around that it wouldn't get done; was found almost poisoned to death after trying to put up the (two cartons) needed to cancel the contract! Damn; when it was all said and done; two prisoners would be killed for (two packs) of cigarettes! I know how savage this sounds, but what's to be said about the cold, hard hearted, stupefied re-action(s) on the part of hundreds of other men who'd just witnessed a fellow prisoner 's brains splatter; from being hit in the head with a bat!!! Prisoners went back to playing cards, tossing footballs, lifting weights, cooking court chefs, and a prison society of other things done every day to keep our world going around with some semblance of order! It was nothing new, violence after the annual championship softball game; security knew two things had to happen with the game having been played; a team had to win, a team had to lose! That meant the prison was going to have victims of violence resulting from bets having been made and not paid! Though this was a prison, belonging to a system of prisons within a NYSDOCS; it (Clinton) was its own governing body; worried about and/or accountable to no one! Prisoners being shanked! Prisoners being killed, as a result of gambling which was commonplace for us! And administration put such incidents to rest with less concern than one might have; were a gnat in his face!

    The administration may have been able to hush-hush past incidents; but at least one time, the victim was not an insignificant number; this time it was a prisoner with a family who'd not written him off! This time Clinton was going to have to call someone front and center for this vicious murder!! This time there might be questions which someone outside the forty foot high wall may want answers to! One thing Clinton had were plenty of suspects; and even in prison, it's still the law of the land; to kill another prisoner was a crime of murder! Especially if it were the wrong prisoner; someone was going to pay the price for murdering this particular individual! As prisoners, if nothing else; we'd know who was who! Even if we didn't do anything, we'd know who we had to be careful around; who'd kill first, ask questions later! We also knew there'd be a reciprocal response; if the mistaken identity had gotten a prisoner with prison buddies, killed!!!

There's another brief insight I want to share with you; take a few moments to read it a second time, so that it might really soak in! Over a period of some three decades, I've shared many aspects of these societies from within; it hasn't failed; expressions of distain, disgust, ridicule, listening to people of and in ignorance, scorn rules, regulations, policies, the unwritten laws of prisons; established by prisoners, and withstanding the test of time! I'm going to share something with those reading this book. You will probably never hear prison administrators ever utter; at any given time, there's not a prison in the state wherein the prison guards could not be taken, were the prisoners to decide to do so!!! The blood of prison guards would flow like water, the sounds of their agony would be made to sound like thunder as it were, in a valley! Think about it: when I was a prisoner in Clinton, most times there were 144 of us in 6 tiers, locked in, locked out by "a single prison guard!" How much of an imagination do you have to have to picture what they could have done had they "chose to do so!" Right now they'd be able to make widows and orphans of almost an entire tour of prison guards in any/every prison across the state; by the time the governor were able to call out the responders, it would be too late! There are almost double the number of prisoners and prisons today than thirty years ago! One of the best decisions that the state administrators has made is to hire Chaplains, especially Muslim Chaplains. In part two of this book I take you into the system as "NYSDOCS" employee for ten years as a Muslim Chaplain. Had I not seen the employee filth and administrative corruption with my own eyes?

What happens when the mind of a person has been so thoroughly conditioned, that the only surroundings wherein he can function, exist behind a forty foot high wall?! In Clinton, I met and sat with individuals who'd been sentenced to prison for the "REST OF THEIR NATURAL LIVES!!!"

I would become acquainted with two prisoners from different walks of life, but with a common deficiency; they were both functionally illiterate! These two individuals had been given names that would cause you to stop and ask yourself: What did he say his name is? You have got to be kidding me, I can't believe he said his name is Trash; Ha ha ha ha; Bullet Proof; gee wiz! What could possibly be wrong with the mind of a person, to have him take pride in being called "Trash"? Let's look at the name; being called garbage, rubbish, litter, debris, clutter, filth, waste and the like; which one would you accept as a pet name?! How about Bullet Proof; he told me the name was given to him after he'd been shot (11) times, and walked away! There was something about him though; to see him, you would have never imagined him even knowing anything about guns; much less being bullet proof! He was quiet, easy going; even came across as shy! Those two were as different as night and day in their personalities; and if taken on their surface, the true lion might be viewed the lamb, and vice versa! Trash had been down (11) years; as alone as anyone could possibly be! Having burnt bridge after bridge, after bridge where his family, friends and associates were concerned! Eleven years without as much as a visit or response to even a letter he'd written! I mean (a) letter, in the literal sense; being illiterate, he didn't feel good about even trying to write anything! I'd hear people calling him "Trash", and he never had a problem with it! For some reason, I couldn't call him that; so I asked him his name; Trash, call me Trash! I asked him quite a few times why or how he got that name, but he never told me! Prison isn't a place where you want to be alone!! It's hard enough doing time; but having nobody on the outside or inside, while possibly doing time for the rest of your life; has to be a terrible future to look forward to! When I looked at the brother from that perspective, I began to better understand him accepting being called Trash! I might possibly look at myself as something thrown away, something worthless, defective, useless, rejected, dismal, despicable, inferior, of no value, of poor quality, et cetera, if I had concluded that nobody wanted to be bothered with, or cared about me! Being called trash would definitely distinguish me from everyone else! I don't know whether he knew it or not, but the name trash was very impactful! There were perhaps hundreds of people I'd met, been introduced to, whose names were forgotten; many times, as soon as told to me! But trash, you'll see what I mean: His name came to me immediately! I have no doubt whatsoever that you won't forget the name! Just think about it; I've just introduced the name to you a few sentences ago, but it will come to mind for years to come; trash!

I don't really know how it happened, but I found myself walking the yard with him a few times per week! After a while, he and I began sitting at the bottom of the cooking courts, talking or just sitting, looking and/or commenting on things going on in the yard. I finally got him to feel at ease enough to agree to sit with me on the cooking court assigned to the Muslims! He made it clear to me that he wasn't interested in Islam; and I assured him that I wasn't trying to convert him! Laughter didn't come for a while, but he did smile at progress; not that he saw progress as such! It was interesting; prior to spending time with me, in a decade, no one had so much as asked him how he was doing! Within a month and a half, the brother said seven individuals, of them police (CO) had asked him was he becoming a Muslim. He and I laughed because as far as he knew, Islam wasn't even being talked about! But, there wasn't a sitting wherein he and I did not deal with Islam; because, the manner in which I'd respond whenever he'd become impatient, etcetera; caused me to respond to him with verses from Qur'an and hadith (sayings) of Prophet Muhammad, (pbuh)! And guess what; there were times when he, unbeknown to himself, would correct himself with different things I'd stated from Qur'an and hadith (saying) of Prophet Muhammad (pbuh)! Those occasions were really rewarding for me, because I was seeing something prove itself to me; """Anything that sends a message to the mind is a word; and, words make people!!!" The brother and I melted a lot of ice, and I guess you could say he and I became to each other what I said everybody has in prison, sahabah (companions)! It was odd because he still had no one, who'd do anything more than acknowledge him (Trash); if he happened to be standing alone in the yard. He still seemed to have that distanced manner about him; and put forth that, "I'LL KILL A BRICK" persona! But I'd been given a chance to see different; I knew about a side of him which was being hidden! I saw a side of what was still a human being; I had been given a chance to see inside the mind of someone who'd not yet been totally broken down inside of the "digestive system of the belly of the beast!" Like I said, the brother and I melted a lot of ice; even found reason to laugh together. I asked him if I could ask him a question which might lead to another question. I told I wanted to try and help somebody, but I wanted some advice or a point of view from someone else. I explained to him that I thought he was the best one to ask, because the individual whom I wanted to help had a situation similar to his! You want some advice from me; you want my opinion?! (ha ha ha ha) He laughs. I responded; Yeah, why not? First of all; you need to start trying to see yourself the way I'm seeing you! Look, I'm serious brother; I need your help! This guy has a lot of time in, just like you! He's had no visitors, mail, or packages; just like you! He's a loner just like you; almost to the letter! I want to try and get him to tell me what's on his mind; how he feels having been disowned by his family; if he had an opportunity to write them a letter, what would he say... Check this out brother, you can't tell me you don't have thoughts about these same things! Let me say this though; I don't want you to think I'm asking you to help me with this because of what we've been doing. If you say you don't want to get involved in talking about this kind of thing, I won't mention it again! I just felt you could better understand what this guy must be feeling, than anyone else, that's all. Do me a favor brother; think about it tonight, before you say no! I'd given him cell work the night before, so I asked him if we could check what he'd done. This was going to be a big day for more reasons than one; maybe even the door opening to change for the rest of his life! I'd given him a whole paragraph of words which I'd scrambled for him to put back in their correct order (3 sentences), along with (20) simple words; a letter either missing or miss-placed, to be corrected! What expectations did I have, if any at all? I can't really say an agenda existed; I believe for a person to expect something, you will have had to consciously entered into whatever, with some preconceived conclusion! What I had done and was still doing, I had been doing as far back as I can remember doing as a little boy in kindergarten! Wow; as I sit here recalling and reflecting on that incident as a grandfather (54 years of age), the heart of that little boy awakens in me! I, (48) years later; wipe tears from the cheeks of the "skinny little girl" whom everyone teasingly called "Olive;" picture the cartoon Popeye, the sailor man, just maybe you'll understand! Allah willing, in my next book I'll share this incident which causes a smile to run through my mind, and a question or two to run through my heart, as I sit here wondering...

As for the paragraph, the sentences and words, he aced them; except for (2) words and (1) sentence, he aced the whole thing! I don't know who was more excited, me or him! I jokingly said to him; Naaa, I ain't gonna believe this; when I gave ya the work, we agreed to what? We agreed you wouldn't open any books to find any words! The sentences, I have to accept they were done by you; because, I know you wouldn't ask for help; because people would know you had problems! He sat there laughing at me; you don't understand the gravity of what I'm saying to you; I hadn't seen anything in my adult life, more fulfilling to me, than seeing laughter! Yes, seeing him laugh was probably the most gratifying thing I'd ever paid attention to! I may be wrong, but I don't think 2 months had passed since this individual sitting before me had told me his name was Trash, call me Trash! This was the same human being who'd resigned himself to being nothing more than something you might step in, walking in the grass; nothing more than rubbish, something discarded! This two month ago solemn being, was echoing with a sense of reason, a purpose! He laughed at me and challenged me to give him another list right here; if I thought he had to cheat! Picture what's being said here; he's accepting the accusation of being told he's expected of cheating; but he's beaming with confidence, and almost daring me to give him another list of words right there! He kept saying: Haaa, I musta done it! Haaa, I musta done it! Haaa, I did, right?! I did it, right?! I knew by the way he'd reacted, he'd done it; my brother had done it alone! The person, who'd written himself off, was now cheering for himself about something that meant more to him than anything since time had stopped in his life!!! He cared! He felt good about it; "you could see it in his eyes!" I hugged him like a brother hugs a brother; like a human being hugs another human being; he hugged back!! Apart from visits from my family, that day in the yard was probably the best I'd felt since I'd been in prison! Little did I know that I'd made a friend "in prison"; my reason for emphasizing that I'd "made a friend in prison" is because, I don't believe one makes but a few in life on the outside! Just remember what I emphasized; it will become clear later as you do my time with me!!!

At work the next day, the clinic was business as usual, except for one thing; I'd not been given the slightest hint that I was going to be presented with what Ms. Johnston said to me! Anthony, people want to train you to work here in the O.R.! I had no idea of what she was talking about, so, I had to ask her what she meant? She says: Well, the boss wants you to go into the "operating room" here in the prison! You'll be trained to be an "Operating Room Nurse;" This means, you'll actually be certified and licensed as an "Operating Room Nurse" upon your release; receiving all of the necessary certifications and licensing required to work in any hospital in the state! Anthony, I know where your heart is, I know what you're looking forward to; getting closer to home, closer to your wife and sons! Anthony, it's a chance of, an opportunity of a life-time! You have to decide, I will not let anyone pressure you in any way, and I mean that! He's asked me, and I agreed with him completely! You've been exceptional with me here as my clinic aide! There is only one thing Anthony; you have to agree to stay here in Clinton until the completion of your training which might require that you're here until your conditional release (CR)! Your training is a very intensive education, and is going to require that a lot of time be put into you! Keep in mind what's being said here; you're going to be trained to do everything an operating room nurse does in operating rooms on the outside, in hospitals!! Ms. Johnston, can I think about it? Ms. Johnston, staying in Clinton my entire bid was never something which crossed my mind! I know I can't get a transfer out of here if the warden decides to keep me here; but, you know how much I talk to you about my wife and sons! You know I send the money that I make here, home; trying to help! Ms. Johnston, please let the warden know I would like to think about it. On the other hand, like I was going to say a few minutes ago; I know it doesn't really matter what I might decide, because if the warden has made up his mind that he wants me to stay here, the matter is settled; I remain here! know you said you'd not allow anyone to pressure me into staying, if it's not what I really want to do; but I don't want to cause you any problems! I just pray that it will be taken into consideration, how dire the need is for me to get closer to home, for the sake of my sons! I'm sure I sound like a wimp or something, always whining about my wife and sons; the struggling my wife is going through, etc! Who am I kidding, I don't think I'd even be able to concentrate on such a level of intensive study as would be required; because I'm sure I'd be so preoccupied mentally! Staying to be trained for the position as an operating room nurse in the prison hospital wasn't mentioned anymore; I didn't mention it to my wife at that time. I'm not sure why! I've given thought about a few reasons why, but after weighing everything, the pros and cons; the cons were strong that they made anything else irrelevant!

    The reality of what had been offered to me was heavy on my mind, though I tried to dismiss it! I hadn't mentioned the matter to anyone, though a month had gone by. Trash noticed that I seemed to be off to myself; he asked me several times if my family was ok; asked if someone (another prisoner) was pushing up on me, etc! I assured him that everything was alright; but there was something other than the everyday prison routine on my mind! Keep in mind, he wasn't a Muslim; but he noticed what none of my Muslim brothers had noticed, or at least said anything about; maybe it had something to do with what he and I were doing together! We were actually enjoying being around each other; though just a few months ago we weren't even names in the vocabulary of each other! He assured me that he had no problem whatsoever making it clear that I was to be left the fuck alone! Brother, I know you know I ain't neva leavin here, except to be taken to another joint; so it ain't like not telling me is gonna keep me from makin things worse! Brother, you probably don't know what it feels like, finally finding a friend, having a friend! In almost 12 years, you are the only person to treat me like I was worth something; even when I was on the streets, if I had something to give, I had friends, brother! (He laughed) I'd been trying to figure out what game you were playing, what you were up to, what it was you wanted; you had to want something! I knew I didn't have anything worth anything, so I could only think of one thing which you could have on your mind, if you were looking to get something from me; take someone off the count; take somebody the fuck out We sat there for a moment, not saying anything; finally, he said, "I'm sorry brother Anthony, but I'm telling you the truth! You're looking at Trash; think about it, some- body like you wastin your time on me!" I asked him if he still thought it to be true; No, he responded; because when I offered to take care of things if someone was pushing up on you; nothing stopped you from naming somebody! I looked at him and reminded him that I was no less a convict; doing time in Clinton, just like him! I went on to tell him that whether or not I'd killed one person or six people; the fact that I wasn't doing time for such, might possibly be because I did what I did well! The look he gave was as such that it said he had a million questions! As the weeks and months passed, he and I grew closer; he improved in his reading and writing, to end up doing something which brought me to tears! I'll share that with you just before I leave Clinton; for now I'll simply say; the brother I was now spending time with was not the person I'd met a few months ago! I was really having a hard time with the fact that I wasn't telling the brother about what had been offered to me by the Warden! For the most part, I was concerned with how he might react; finding out the Warden had offered me something! Remember; I was a prisoner, in prison; but not just any prison, this was Clinton; the Last Strong Hold! The Warden had offered to train me to become an (Operating Room Nurse) in the prison hospital... What all did this mean; where did this mean I'd possibly be able to go, and with whom? The brother had already expressed having concerns about what it was I might want from him, though he'd said he really didn't still have those feelings; because of what it was I could have said when given the opportunity came up to do so; I was, none the less, concerned with how he might react! Time passed as such that I really didn't have any opportunity to think about the fact of him not being able to either read or write, just a few months ago. It was really hard to believe!

It seemed like time was flying, and he and I behaved like two people who'd known each other for years. One afternoon I asked him about his family; his disposition changed! What?! What about my fuckin family is going to do you any fuckin good?!!! I've done just fine on my own, wifout countin on none of what you call, my family! Don't expect anything from nobody, so ain't no disappointments, let downs, or nothing; I ain't expectin nothin; know what I mean! Responding to him, I said; I'm going to call you what you want to be called; Trash, listen to me for a minute; brother, we can spend the rest of our life's running from what we've made of the years; but we will never be successful, regardless of how many weeks, months and/or years we run! Do you know why Trash? You can't get away from you, yourself! We will find ourselves seeing the many different parts we've played in chasing away and pushing away those people who'd loved us! He didn't comment; just stood there. A few days passed before I brought up the subject of his family again; but, this time I used a different approach! Trash, check this out and tell me what you think! Since I've been down, one of my aunts has made some comments to my wife; other members of the family have teamed up against my wife, also! There was my wife, with two little boys; 3 yrs and 4 yrs of age. Asking myself, almost every day, while thinking about things that happened; how many of them would have happened had my family been there for her; been there as support?! I asked my next question, "Trash, what am I doing?" What was I trying to do?" "I was doing what's done every minute of the day; every week, every month; all year long; had it not been for anyone but me, things would not be as they are right now Trash! It was easier for me to find fault in any and everyone but myself; so that's what I did; faulted anyone but myself!" During the next week, I'd learn what it was he really felt, and how much he longed for a connection of some kind from someone; anyone in his family! Little did he know, he'd given me a fountain of information to help me help him do what he wanted so badly to do, but didn't know how to go about trying to do it! Though Trash hadn't actually admitted how much he missed hearing from his family, he could not have shouted it out more loudly! Trash, the other day I told you about my wife and how my family chose to hang my wife and sons out to dry; but I didn't walk you through any of the step by step details possibly given birth by and/or as direct result of their unwillingness to offer up support! I'm sure you remember me blasting and condemning my family; but what did I offer against myself for having the ability to choose between right and wrong, and choosing the wrong as my course of action? Blaming someone else makes the outcome so much easier to accept when we end up in trouble for our actions! Brother, when is the last time you've tried to contact your family? I know you couldn't write, could barely read; but a card, sending different family members cards would have done something to try and stay in touch! You mentioned one aunt, more than anyone else in the family; even smiled sometimes when talking about her! I'm going to make a suggestion; if just thinking about this particular aunt can make you smile, even after 14 years; what do you think of at least trying to write her, making the first letter you've ever written, to the aunt whom I'm going to say was/is your favorite aunt?! If you're like most of us, I'm sure you took advantage of opportunities to use your aunts' love and generosity, for your own corrupt desire! If this is true, I think she'd really be surprised to receive a letter, even a card from you; first thanking her for having been willing to trust and believe in you; then letting her know you're sorry for the many times you were other than truthful about why you needed money! Trash, you're not kidding yourself, you know doing this time alone isn't what you want to do! How would you really feel, even getting a piece of mail (letter, card) a couple times per month? Even if your aunt doesn't write back, just knowing you finally thanked her, and acknowledged you were wrong would probably mean a lot to her; in any case, what will you lose?! Keeping in mind some of what you'd done to hurt her, name even one thing which she did to get back at you! The brother just sat there looking down, saying nothing. A number of times you could see in his face, strain, uneasiness! There's one thing which puts you in the company of most of the convicts in here, and it's not having been convicted of a crime; the unwillingness to admit you were wrong! I don't know what it is about people, not just us, not just criminals; but people in general; we'd rather live a life alone, than bare witness against ourselves! That's what you're doing right now, but why? Then I said: Oooh, I get it; at least you can say: She might know I'm a liar, a thief, a conman; but I didn't admit it; so she'll never be able to tell anyone I admitted anything, at best she'll only be able to say, I think my nephew...! Brother, if I was still talking to that brother who'd so-convinced himself that he was nothing more than garbage, worth nothing, rubbish, etcetera; then I might be better able to accept such reasoning; but, it's no longer so; that person can and will only exist if you want him to, if you let him! He looked at me and said something which really shocked me! He began with: "Check this out man; you don't really know two of nuttin bout me; don't you think I know you made me your fuckin pet project up in nis motha-fucka! Huh? You think cause my fuckin name is what it is, dat I ain't got no sense man? All dat fuckin talk bout us being the same up in here; dats bullshit brother! What, the administration pointed me out to you and told you ta work with me; see what you could do to get me to act like I give a fuck? I started to tell you to leave me alone the first day you came to me outta the blue! I knew it! I knew something was up with you brother! Been doing my time by myself, on my own, alone, no fuckin friends; ain't never tried to make no friends! Why you mess it up for me brother? I trusted you; thought something was different bout you! Brother, I'm gonna tell you straight out; you might of used me, but you helped me too; I can really read now, and I know how to spell and write! If it wasn't for that, I would do you (take you out/kill you)! I know you think you gotta do what you gotta do; but, what if I was to do what I think I gotta do? Did you know a transfer can't happen when the prisoner is recovering from an injury or is real sick? I know a lotta prisoners that didn't get transferred because accidents happened, know what I mean!

While Trash was venting, I stood there trying to figure out

what could have possibly bought this on! I'd just finished talking to him about issues which could quite possibly bring him into a reconciliatory position with an aunt who seemed to be one of his favorite, if not his favorite aunt! I stood there looking at him, listening to what was being said; trying to figure out what was going on in his head at that moment! I was lost until he mentioned transfer; though he had not mentioned it to me since I'd told him about what the warden had told the nurse he wanted me to stay there and do! It was like he'd not heard a word said to him related to he and his aunt; about people in general not being willing to bear witness against oneself if or when in the wrong! Just what it was that triggered thoughts of me leaving him, thoughts of me possibly being transferred after being a real friend! To possibly understand the trauma which such a happening might cause; keep in mind, Trash had been in the locked down a total of 15 years; 4 years in jail, going back and forth to court before sentenced; 11 years in the NYSDOCS, (Clinton)! According to him, he stopped trusting other criminals after a CO-defendant turned on him; his family cut ties with him even before he was convicted and sentenced to life. Listening to him didn't take a psycho-therapist to understand that it might be wise not to take issue with him, not immediately! I turned and walked away, leaving him alone, sitting on the cooking court! A few days later, Trash surprised me! I'd been walking in the yard about half an hour when he caught up to me; "Brother Anthony, need to talk to you a minute." I didn't stop, we kept walking together until we reached the cooking courts; we walked up and sat down. He began talking about some of the things I had suggested he might think about doing to start a possible reconnect with his aunt! He asked where I suggest he might start, and if I could help him with it. I sat there with him, a lump in my throat, eyes filled with tears; I wasn't ready for what had just happened! Remember, I'm telling you about Trash, a convict who according to everything acted out before others; seemed as though he was cold enough to give ice, frostbite! How much of what he'd paraded before his world for the past decade or more, had been nothing more than that, a parade?! Not so fast; just hold on before you concur; on the other hand, let yourself give thought to the other possibility; perhaps something within the past few months, passed through to his heart; the one he had as a child! We all remember that childish heart; the one which nothing can get you down!? Maybe he met someone who made him believe he'd found a friend! How many people have you met in your life who've been made angry, been let down, been told about something hard to deal with, etc; and they cursed you out; talked to you like you were nothing; accused you for what was happening or was going to happen! Days, weeks, even months pass since clearing you; but the person was too proud and arrogant to come back to you with humility! None, of the people you know, fall into the category of Trash; yet they did not have the integrity within to return to you, with the humility which Trash returned to me! We sat and talked for a few minutes, allowing me to think about things. Having done so, I said; "Trash, the way I'd contact my aunt after such a long time, would be with a card! A simple but nice card; on which I'd own up to having been deceitful, lying to her a lot of times about money; why I needed it! Let her know how it made you feel, what it made you feel like; but only after you got away from things that took over your life and what mattered to you! Aunt Jane, I'm sorry for taking advantage of the love you had for me! I know you don't care about an apology from me; but, it's the least I can do; knowing I owe you so-much more! Since I'm probably being truthful to you for only one of a few times since I grew up; I may as well let you know I feel like a coward, apologizing this way; but I might never get a chance to apologize face-to-face; take care of yourself Aunt Jane!" He didn't say what he was going to do, and we went on; like nothing was ever talked about!

A few weeks after our talk, a brother whom I'd seen regularly in the yard, came to the clinic to be seen by the dentist. I came out from the medical clinic to get a file from the medical file room; a prisoner was sitting on the bench around the corner and down the hall, outside the dental office. He called for me to come there for a minute; he wanted to ask me something. I pulled the medical file, took it back to the clinic to Ms. Johnston, and went back to see what the guy wanted! The last thing in the world I would have expected to hear from this guy was: "Word is going around the prison that you're supposed to be helping one of the guys in here, read and write! I have somebody who wants me to ask you what you will charge to help him with writing; but keep it between him and you! He said he was able to read, fairly well; but couldn't write worth shit!" I asked him; "Why can't you help do what this guy needs help with? If I help this guy, it won't be as though nobody else knows or won't find out! Just like there's a rumor circulating in population that I'm supposed to be helping somebody read and write; if that's true, the same leak will open up again! If I'm helping someone now and, it's not supposed to be known; why would I acknowledge that, to you here?" He says, "I don't know what to tell you man; take it easy man!" I couldn't believe it; first of all, this was a white prisoner asking me about teaching somebody how to write! Secondly, out of the blue, somebody who's never said a word to me; calls me and asked if I (an African American convict) would consider teaching or helping someone with his writing!

A couple weeks went by, I was walking the yard, guess what happens; exactly! Exactly, but not only that; the prisoner who was supposedly being represented that day at the clinic, was actually the same prisoner who'd asked me if I'd consider helping;

he was asking for himself! He stops me in the yard, wants to know if I'd thought about what we'd talked about! He says to me, "Tarver, look; I was asking for myself, but I can't let none of the guys I hang with know anything about my situation; nothing Tarver! The way I know about Trash is because I've heard you and him talking, the cooking court I use is right above yours. Everybody has been wandering what the fuck was up; you hanging out with that sick bastard! I decided to find out for myself. I found out for sure just the other day, when Trash musta been mad at cha! I heard him say something about being helped by you to read and write, or he'd do you!" He went on to tell me he'd pay me, but I'd have to promise not to tell anyone about it, because he has a lot of followers in population who have a lot of respect for him and look up to him!

I didn't know what to think; what was this guy up to? As if that wasn't enough; guess what his nick-name was; Bullet Proof! There were actually individuals in population who called him "Bullet-Proof!" There was no way I wasn't going to ask him what that was about, but I couldn't help myself! Richie, you've got to be kidding me man; Bullet-Proof, where did that come from man? He didn't laugh about it, didn't even smile when he explained where the name came from! "Tarver, I spent time with and did things for some very interesting people, and made a lot of money! I've been shot 11 times. I don't mean one day I was shot 11 times; but eleven different times, after I was shot from two to seven times! Somebody heard me called Bullet-Proof one day, it caught on!" After coming to grips with that over a period of weeks, I agreed to try and help; though I was still skeptical about the story told to me about why he needed me! In short, this is what he explained to me: "Look Tarver, I can read but can't write worth a shit! My wife writes me letters a few times every week, but I've never wrote her a letter back!" Of course I asked him how he was able to get away with not answering any of the letters his wife had been sending all those years. His explanation (I must admit) was an easily acceptable one! You tell me what you think. He began, "Well, you know how you have to find things to talk about on your visits; when my wife asked me why I never answer any of her mail; I just told her I look forward to talking about her letters, when she comes to visit!" I had to ask him how his explanation went over; he continued, "Oh, she loved it, she loves it man; said she looks forward to it!" Though we'd talked about helping him with his writing, he never said he had something specific in mind to be used for the purpose! Not that it would have mattered, but I was surprised to see what it was! Past letters his wife had written him; he wanted me to read them, several at a time: then help him answer them! I realized something after reading the first letters he'd given me; he was able to read, but not well, not well at all! His spelling was poor also! Being led to believe he'd read the letters before I did, I began asking him what he wanted to say about different things his wife had written about! I asked him to read the first (2) pages of a letter and tell me what she was talking about, what had happened, had she ever gone there before, etcetera. Some of what he responded with didn't fit; I noticed the same thing with another letter, so I said something to him about what I thought! At first he tried to explain it away; but, finally admitted his reading was bad too!

What began as something simple, turned into anything but; why he would ask me is still something I don't understand! He was able to explain it away when asked by his group, what he was doing spending so much time with me! Instead of me helping him with something, he was helping me with some problems I was having in the street; that was his explanation to his boys! After all was said and done, I hadn't done as much to help him improve his reading and/or writing, as I did to just print letters which he could copy and send to his wife! It was something, how he'd been able to get away for as long as he had; telling her he didn't answer her letters, because he wanted to really have something to talk about during their visits! Over time I found that he had a bigger problem than he'd owned up to; though he could read, that ability may not have been beyond a third or fourth grade level. The idea was that I would sit with him, read a few of his letters aloud, he'd comment on them a few lines at a time; I would print his comments on another paper for him to put a letter together in his own style. It took a minute or two for him to see the importance of closing his letters in script not printing; nothing fancy or artistic, just simple script saying, loving you much, With love, Much love, Always loving you, and his first name at least! He had a very pretty wife in his corner, and though he could be heard talking that player talk sometimes; if he was, you couldn't see it in the visiting room! Between him (Bullet Proof) and Trash, with whom I would sit on the Muslim cooking court; along with my clinic job; time really flew by! Before I'd know it, the day was over and it was time to lock in for the night.

Throughout my imprisonment I wrote prose, I wrote poetry. When the cell gate would slam shut, I'd sit and think about feelings; the cacophony was deafening. Another day has ended and a sense of calm falls over Clinton Prison; for me it will afford me a few hours to write again about all of the feelings, I had through the course of my busy day. It helped me act as though things didn't exist! Were I to intertwine the thoughts, experiences, events throughout this period, prison would seem like a walk in the park, an occasional school yard fight, a brawl in a bar on the corner, even a normal disagreement between two human beings; something that got out of control and became violent! "For someone, anyone to be allowed to come to such a conclusion would be sinful". To approach this reality like its part of someone's normal day would be criminal!!! What was done during and throughout this period in which I struggled to hold on to my sanity was in every sense, every definition of the word, "criminal!" The mind boggling, sadistic brutality, the utter disregard for human life, the fact that correction officers killed prisoners at will, because in Clinton they could, this should not be called "pleasure reading"!

There's no such thing as a secret in population when it comes to who's been turned out! Each year there are additions to the list of sweet cheeks, prostitutes (prisoners) given a chance to pay the debt off by giving up his manhood to whomever, until he's paid his debt, or catches a shank at some point and time, by someone! Those were the choices given you by the prisoner you owe; but there are choices you can make for yourself; you can request protective custody or request a transfer to another facility! Protective custody is his best choice, because this can be done immediately by privately requesting to see a sergeant and explaining what's going on! You can request a transfer in writing, but this will take months; in the meantime you're still in that prison and amidst the danger! One thing about prison, information travels throughout the system from prison to prison; you can get transferred while in p.c; there you might feel that you're no longer in need of p.c., because you're in a different prison; when in the twinkling of an eye, the death from which you fled finds you!! Like I said, months passed and fallout from the game was still obvious; men being brought to the clinic after getting a beat down to remind them that their payments were too slow, far and between; a prisoner would limp in with some stab wounds in his thigh. Two men came into the clinic, but insisted on standing; both had just been shanked in the ass cheeks, to possibly let them know that it was going to be very, very unhealthy for them, for not having made any payments in three weeks. This was their way of saying they weren't paying any more! Let me share what was explained to me by different individuals: Think about it; wouldn't it make more sense to give a wakeup call to the person who's been paying, but has slowed down or stopped; before "let-un-num know you ain't fuckin round wif-fum!?"

There's one more incident of fallout which I'm sorry to say, yet glad to say, was just that; a single incident! Rather than trying to continue enduring the unmanliness of the sodomy which comes with being owned by whomever, until he paid his gambling debt; let's just accept that he was killed; the prisoner in debt, was killed! If I had to, I'd make a bet; whomever he owed, if he was bothered at all, it was because the dead man hadn't finished paying what was owed! In case you've forgotten, the main currency in prison is cigarettes; yes, there's a lot of regular money in prison also, but the main currency is cigarettes! The one who swung that bat and made contact with the head of a fellow prisoner, had 750 "cartons of cigarettes" to pay out! It doesn't take doing time in prison to understand that there was a lot of money, if he was on the street, free to move around! 750 cartons of cigarettes, owned by any one prisoner, could put him into a position of financial power; wherein he could have anyone killed! I remember a prisoner in Clinton sending 300 cartons of cigarettes home, after a visit; all it took was $100.00 to one of NYSDCS finest! Depending on who you are in the joint, you can be the owner of some of everything imaginable, and not have a single item in your possession; but in a heartbeat, put word out that you need whatever when the count clears after dinner! An entire payment will take place right under the eyes of the police/COs and they do not have a clue!!! A hit/contract is carried out the same way; the police know it after it's over; either that or they've been paid, to look for a rock in a rock pile! Like I said, prison is no different than so-called free society; life goes on in prison, regardless of what happens!

Trash and I had become quite close since I'd begun working with him. I'd told him about someone I knew who reminded me of him. Some time had passed since I'd said that to him; in fact, I had forgotten about it. One evening on a Saturday, he and I were walking the yard; he says to me: You remember the brother you said I reminded you of; you said he wanted to write his mother but wouldn't, because he didn't know how to tell her how he felt about the things he'd done! He should just tell her about the things he did; he should just own up to it, own up to being wrong, brother. You know; don't be tryin ta find some jive ass excuses, or putin na blame on somebody else! I ain't sayin itta be easy, because, when I think about all da things I dun dun ta my mother and my family, man Anthony; what can you really make up dats gonna help you feel better about yourself; know what I'm sayin?! I know if I could get a chance ta do what this guy got a chance ta do, I know I'd be scared as hell!! I didn't interrupt him or bring to his attention what he was saying; but think about what's being said; more unbelievable is, who's expressing these feelings! A few months ago, this same physically existent person had probably been deemed incapable of even possessing such sentiments; much less expressing such to anyone! Remember, this is the same prisoner who had taken pride in introducing himself as "Trash!" He went on to say: "All da lies I dun told, all da phony apologies I dun made, axin for another chance and shit; then another chance, cuz I dun learnt my lesson; all da fuckin beggin, jus so I could git out; but soon as they'd git me out, all dat beggin ain't mean shit; not a fuckin thing!!! I was really fucked up then brother; ain't even feel nothing was wrong…!" "I use to think about da stuff I did ta my mother, and da stuff I use ta do ta other people in my family, when I would get busted and was locked up for awhile; kickin cold turkey, throwin up, woke all night, chills and shit; then I would think to myself, and admit to myself, how wrong da things were I was doin; but when you're chasin nat whitelady, dat heron; you give less than a fuck about nothing, I didn't care brother; I didn't care at all; ain't giva shit!" Little did he know I was able to relate to some of what he was saying about that "white lady". I also had been introduced to her...It reminded me of a poem I wrote about her over thirty years ago while in "Clinton/The Last Strong Hold!"

(Me and My White Lady)
I met her one day, after a long heated conversation;
With some friends who left me in a state of total meditation.
In the back of my mind, I could see her coming from a distance;
In time there was no way for me to deny her existence.
It was as though she was camouflaged, because she was such a mysterious thing;
Sometimes she could make bells ring, she was bad; she'd make birds sing.
In her absence she'd make you shake, shiver for many an hour;
But, to see her from a glance, you'd not believe she possessed such power.
I fell so deeply in love with her, and she looked so innocent;
Yet as time went by, I could not explain,
and no one could understand where my high spirits went.
It was so plain to see the change, Dr. Jekyl, the change, Mr. Hyde, the change;
You see, since I met my white lady, I lost weight, stayed sick,

my friends thought it strange.
Quite often you've heard people say love is blind;
Therefore I was unable to see that she was not the loving kind.
I had fallen in love with a lady whom I found I could not trust;
For like herself, in time she would have also turned me to dust.
But with help I found she had but one intention;
To kill; leaving a total impossible to mention.
So to the world outside my tears, I refuse to explain;
Behind a face which hides my fears, I just wish it would rain.
Yes, I am what I never could, being what I never should.
Sometimes happy, most times sad;
Maybe good, maybe bad.
I feared the future for it had to come;
Total destruction for all or some;
Because mass confusion had come to town;
Turning both the young and old around;
Yes there is a lady who's very well known;
And we know she didn't come here alone.
It is terrible how she paves her way;
As she leads both the weak and strong astray;
She'll make days which use to feel so gay;
Slowly but surely fade away.
Those days will be dreary instead of blue;
Will make you a person, so different, so new;
She is hunted constantly by D.A. Dix;
But even more constantly by those who need a fix.
Do you know this lady the way many do/
Because, I know this lady, she had me too

The brother kept talking and talking about knowing how this other guy felt, and what he'd say himself, if he could; I sat and took mental notes, careful not to interrupt!

As I sat listening to him, I understood clearly what he was saying! Think about it; we all know we've done something which at the time we didn't really give thought to; perfect example, impulse buying; a decision which often causes years of regret! No, it doesn't mean whatever your situation might have been is of the same nature; simply that it's possible to act on something that you've not really given thought!

Don't let yourself forget; just a short while ago, this same individual had been written off, even by himself! Everything synonymous with the word trash, would not make you better appreciate the lowliness which had become second nature to him! But now something was happening that could not have, would not have happened just a few short months ago! The brother was expressing interest in problems or concerns of someone! I was actually looking at something that had been said by W.D. Muhammad many years ago, unfolding; manifesting itself! That being: Anything that sends a message to the mind is a word; and, words make people! The message which had been sent to the mind of this brother was a devastatingly demeaning message of worthlessness; but, sent by whom? What is the more important question; who sent the question or, just how long had the brother succumb to the message of devastation that had been shaping him?!

In a few short months, look at what had transpired; a mind which had been wasted and lulled to sleep; had been disturbed! The apathetic outlook was being overcome with a desire and a will to do; a desire to be! Trash had been in Clinton for a long time and was not a part of anyone's cooking court; not really befriended by but one or two other convicts, and even they didn't seem at all disappointed if he wasn't around! This being so, I doubt that there was anyone in population who wasn't wondering what the hell was going on between Trash and me! Our relationship had become one that I would appreciate! I don't think there was a day that would pass without it being asked in one way or another; what's up brother; Tarver, is everything okay between you and Trash; Brother Tarver, need help with anything, etc? At first I didn't understand what was causing all of the concern; it wasn't until Ms. Johnston asked me straight out: Anthony is there something you want to tell me about concerning you and Gary (Trash)? If you're having problems with him, he'll be gone tomorrow! I assured Ms. Johnston there nothing was wrong; I went on to explain in brief what had taken place.

Ms. Johnston was really a beautiful person in heart; I don't doubt for a moment that had Allah not placed me in this prison detail job, I would not have lived to leave Clinton! On more than one occasion I'd overheard Ms. Johnston emphasizing: Honey, believe me; you don't have to worry about him; I think I've put him through enough and have not noticed any change in his behavior yet; he doesn't get into conversation about his detail; even when other prisoners are doing such, he chooses to talk about matters unrelated! I'd, asked myself a number of time, what was the reason for such concern! Had it not been for Ms. Johnston, I still would have not really known the brother's real name; Trash would still be Trash to me! I'll say it again; I really don't understand the reason(s) for all of the concern! Then again, maybe I do; after-all, this was prison! No, there was nothing going on, nothing at all; he and I were friends, plain and simple! I had managed to do something which no one else was either able or simply cared not to do; get him to open up! All-in-all, he and I were loners! I'd do my work with and for Ms. Johnston, go upstairs to the dining room for "lunch," back to work, the block, the yard, the block...

Trash was set until I got myself involved with different matters involving him and his life!

This is true, I went back to work; had really given no thought to any transfer! When Trash was talking, I became really excited, after-all, this was new; a new stage in his growth and development!!! Months passed, I basically did my usual, and Trash was always leaving me to wander! I don't know where it came from but, Trash came to the yard, he wanted to talk! I wasn't sure what to think; again, Trash seemed excited and anxious; this was a first for him! He began with possibly writing one of his aunts, but simply using a card; I thought it was a great idea and told him so! He said he'd use the one inside flap to say a few things, he went on… When all was said that he wanted to say, he simply walked back inside! I let him go without another word being said; in my opinion, he'd already said volumes! Truth be told, he needed for me to listen, but his mind was already made up!

Over the course of the next month or so, some of the brothers sat on our cooking court, cooking, eating and talking; we got into a number of topics, such as what we did at one time or another before life in the joint! Like a number of times before, it came to me; I spoke about things having to do with my volunteer work as an Imam for Westchester county; volunteering as Imam for the (3) facilities (Woman's Jail, Man's Jail and Man's Prison); you could do up to (2) in the prison. As always, different questions would be asked about how I ended up in Clinton. As usual, I'd simply say; One way or another we pay for our past, life unfolds as it should, or something of that nature!

In a different conversation one of the brothers asked about my boy, how he was doing; I could only tell them what I assumed; that being, he was okay. As for "Bullet Proof", it isn't that I didn't have concern for him, but it was more like I thought in the first place; it didn't take him long at all…In about a month, twice per week, either walking the yard or sitting somewhere, he was okay; in fact he was better than that! I really feel it was more a matter of him simply doubting himself, his capabilities. In any case, "Bullet Proof" was doing just fine the last I heard! At the clinic it was business as usual, from sick call, the day to day treatments, to the "medical records," the game was still the same! Perhaps here or there you might have seen a minor difference!

Out of the blue, Ms. Johnston asked about Barry/Trash; stating, if there were even the slightest sign that something was wrong, he'd be gone in a heartbeat! With that having been said, I explained my reason for having taken interest in him! Hearing that, she understood what I was saying!! Knowing that she'd asked about the brother, I felt it best to pay him a quick visit, though I knew she would be told! The brother was doing okay, except he was in fact waiting on the mail; he'd sent the one aunt who'd not quite given up on him, a card! What was I going to say? What was I suppose to say? Thinking about the situation Trash was in, I started walking the yard alone; before long Oscar, Rashad and Karim had caught-up with me. For a moment or so, nobody seemed to have anything to say, which was fine for me because, because I was thinking about (Trash!). Finally (O) broke the ice, asking about my sister. Perhaps I could have led him on to believe he might get something going with her, but that's not where my head was! I was really thinking about (Trash)! For awhile Oscar would not leave the matter of my sister alone, he went on and on with it, to the point of even talking about how well off he was and what-all, he'd be ready and able to do for her! He must have noticed I wasn't commenting, because he finally got quiet and left matters alone! We just walked the yard a few more times, then went up onto our court and sat. One of the brothers started a fire, we all gathered closer as it was rather chilly! Rashad asked, if anyone was in the eating mood; everyone said yes! We left Karim there until we all went and came back with some items; we joined in and bought some steak; let the cooking begin! The weeks came and went; (Trash) would come out from time to time; until one day, who burst onto the scene, running across the yard to the Muslims court! (Trash) he had something in his hand; a letter! She wrote me, my aunt wrote me; she wrote back! All I could say at that moment was; (PBTA) Praise Be To Allah! I finally said; brother, everything pointed to her writing you back; everything! The police came running to the court; I assured them that everything was ok, that he was no problem on the court! More than anything, I really think the CO did or reacted as they did because they knew I work for Ms. Johnston, and someone would be able to make a negative out of something positive...Of course I could've been wrong, but it was just as I said; in fact, Ms. Johnston had something to say about the matter! I assured her again that nothing was wrong and the only thing going on was that (Trash) received a letter from the one aunt who'd not quite given up on him! I'd worked with him; he'd finally taken a chance, bought a card; wrote a little something inside, mailed it to her; after some time, she wrote back; he was very excited; it was just that simple Ms. Johnston, it was just that simple! Because it was (Trash), everyone had been trying to find something wrong; he had to be up to or doing something wrong! Now he could stay in touch with his aunt. They could now write each other on a regular basis; allowing him to really open-up and tell her whatever he wants to; whatever she might feel she wants or feels she needs to know!

Of course I could go on and on with any of the above, but I will be in The Last Strong Hold for what might seem to be forever; so I'll move on! Time came and went, all in the face of an offer to me, still standing; remain in Clinton to be "Trained to be an Operating Room Nurse"! I finally told Ms. Johnston I had to get closer to home, that I can't stay in Clinton! Ms. Johnston simply said: "Okay Anthony, I understand, I understand!" I went back to work, nothing else being said about the matter! Time came and went; (Trash) and I continued our relationship, in spite of people! He became angry; in fact, I might even say he was furious when he found out about my transfer...He accused me of using him, etcetera! He even stopped coming to the yard for awhile, if or when I was there! When he did finally come out, I caught-up with and told him we had to talk, it was very important! At first he was adamant about not being bothered with me; then, he agreed to talk to me!!! I asked him if he really believed what he was saying; he was quiet for a moment, then he said no, he was just hurt by it (the news of and about my transfer)! We smiled; I gave him a hug, and we walked the yard for awhile! (Trash) had come a long way, I was both happy and proud of him; I knew he'd make it now, I knew he'd be okay, even if I never spoke to him again...

Eventually a transfer came through for me, and I was on my way to Woodbourne correctional Facility! Before leaving, I gave Ms. Johnston a big hug and kissed her on the cheek; after-all, I knew she was the real reason for my transfer! I shook CO Travis hand, told him thanks for everything! That night, I could not sleep, did not sleep; I lay there wandering about what Ms. Johnston was going to do, what I was getting myself into, et cetera! The next morning the warden sent for me, this was not done! The first thing I thought about was he had decided to block my transfer!! I stood outside his office, hands folded behind me, CO knocked and entered after being acknowledged. I was told to go in; doing so, I was told to have a seat! This is the gist of what happened: The warden shook my hand, told me I was an 'alright nigger', had no business being there, if I came back I'd prove to be breathing air which someone who deserves to live should be breathing, and that they'd have a coon hunt... He shook my hand again, told me that was all.

10

Transferred and a Return to a Calling

WHEN I ARRIVED, there were cells with doors; I was on the 3rd floor at the top of the stairs! As expected, things were different here! I was moved in and introduced to the Muslim community before I was even given a program! After I was introduced to most of the brothers, I went to chow (to eat); there wasn't any real difference, so I assumed all chow lines were the same! Having been on the road, in transit for a long time, I was hungry, I ate! One thing I missed immediately; the meals which I made for myself in the dining hall in Clinton! But I could forget Clinton. I had to because I was now an inmate in Woodbourne correctional Facility! I ate and went back to my cell; the CO took the count. I began unpacking; boy you can accumulate a lot of stuff! From time to time I'd stop and look out of my cell window, though it was only a view of an enclosed court yard! That was more than I had in Clinton. There was also a wooden door with a small window in my cell! I laid in the cell thinking, about life in general! No one else had come here or been sent here from Clinton since I'd been here; this said only one thing; a transfer had been ordered for me, from Clinton to Woodbourne; the only bed available! This is never done; there has to be a number of beds available in a facility before a transfer order even goes through, much less having it approved. Though I was grateful, I still couldn't help thinking about Ms. Johnston; what was/had been happening! Though I knew in my heart that if anyone was going to be ok, it would be her; she'd become more than just another person to me, she'd become someone who mattered in my life; she was probably the primary reason for me still being alive! Ms. Johnston was someone who'd hold a place near and dear in my heart; she'd probably never know that, but, her not knowing, would not change how I felt! The next day I was in front of the Program committee; they placed me in the welding shop. I tried my best but couldn't make my eyes adjust to the different welding lights! After a few weeks, I was back in front of the Program committee; I was asked a few questions, then, put into the Pre-Release Center. After a few days, I was assigned as an inmate counselor/resource specialist. This position is exactly what it says; I provided counseling to inmates, by compiling what I thought to be some of the best resources available for them! This not only proved to work out well for the center, but it proved to be great for us as inmates! I eventually replaced my concerns for Ms. Johnston, with the Pre-Release Center! There was more and more to do in the center, and the inmates really demanded my time and attention! They'd get the works; everything from where to go when they got out, to the actual interview… The population for the most part, consisted of the same type of people; they've just been moved closer to home, like me! Thought I'd make mention of that, as to make it understood that there was always the possibility of problem(s)! Hopefully, being closer to home would keep minds sober, though there was absolutely "no guarantee" of that!

  We never heard anything about a Coordinating Chaplain when I was in Clinton. Imam Rashad (an inmate) was the only person most, if not all of us knew about; he housed in the honor block. When I got to Woodbourne, the inmate Muslim community elected me as Imam almost immediately, even though I was absolutely against it; it was felt that since I was the Imam while on the street, I'd be best suited for the position on the inside! With that done, we went from there to making other positional changes and appointments for the community. This was all done within a matter of a few days; we didn't rush, as this was very important to us! We'd have different classes during the course of the evening; the primary classes being Arabic, Qur'an and Hadith; each taught by the person thought to be the most proficient in that area. Of course they wanted me to teach Qur'an, for which I had no problem doing. We (the community of Muslims) held our Ju'mah Service every Friday, with no problems. I'd find myself thinking about, and/or referring to Clinton and/or Sing Sing! I don't think any of the brothers knew where I would be coming from, though; they just knew I was coming… After the salat (prayer), we'd sit and talk about different issues. Sometimes an issue or two would get personal, causing us to run out of time allowed for our regular day and we would resume in the evening where we'd left off earlier in the day.

    As the weeks and months came and went, there were a number of "Family Events;" this is where I did my now well known "Push Broom Shuffle"! There was music, all kinds of food which we at the center provided; some of everybody who had been counseled and/or interviewed was there. We simply had a nice time during those occasions! One of the brothers was talking about having a sore throat and how it made him snore at night. That made me think about Sing Sing; I told him about the whole ordeal, from beginning to end! This brother literally cut another brothers' throat for snoring; I mean from ear-to-ear! Then went back to his cell like it was nothing; he said he was going do it, if the brother kept him awake again that night! The brother to whom I was speaking laughed, just like they did in Sing Sing;

until they saw exactly how serious the brother was about his sleep and someone keeping him awake at night...! I could tell it made him think; but he was just trying to play bad; like it was nothing! As for myself; even after seeing and being involved in all that I'd been involved in, in the Last Strong Hold; that was hard for me to accept; the guy getting his throat cut, for snoring! As the days went on, it was business as usual. Everything went well in the center, as it did in the masjid! The brother with the throat problem, toned down for some reason! [smile] The days came and went. I have to say this was one time out of my entire prison stay, that I was absolutely happy to see my bunk; it was really a welcomed sight! Though I was awake early, I was doing something I hadn't done throughout my entire bid; I was going right to bed and to sleep!

    I remained in Woodbourne awhile longer; doing my usual in the center, Mosque, chow, gym, cell, et cetera; then it was time for me to make another move! This was further away from home, yet still much closer than Clinton! I was transferred to Arthur Kill correctional Facility, but not before we had a going away party for me at the center! All the different comments and so-on from the brothers at the Mosque, as to why I shouldn't leave; along with congratulations from the administration! After we had stayed as long as we could in the Mosque, many of the brothers, including myself; cried and hugged each other; then we went to our cells. Much of the night was spent reflecting on the different aspects of my journey; and what this next phase was going to be like! I knew quite well that the population already knew I was coming; after-all, we knew about most of, if not everything, before the guards knew; that's simply how things were in prison! When I was leaving Woodbourne, having worked as an inmate counselor and resource specialist, and having been the Imam; many of the prisoners, and most of the Muslim community wanted to see me off! Again, I was being told to be careful brother, take care man, we're gonna miss you brother Imam, et cetera! Some of the Muslims were teary eyed; and others straight out crying; the truth be told, I became a little teary eyed myself! Woodbourne being set up the way it was, any good-byes had to be said within the actual housing area. The behavior of men whom so-called free society would have had no problem referring to as heathens, garbage, dirt, criminals, et cetera was remarkable! I have been present in the company of so-called civilized people; and have not witnessed such concern expressed; neither verbally nor physically!

When I arrived at Arthur Kill, from the van I could see people in the yard; inmates were exercising, etcetera; this let me know quite a bit about the place; or so I thought! After-all, I had already been an intricate part of the worst of them; so what could this joint possibly have to offer!? I'd made history in Clinton; I'd survived Sing Sing, and did the walk in the park at Woodbourne; how in the world could I not make it in Arthur Kill! The population already knew I was coming, along with a number of other prisoners; seven of us, all from Woodbourne! As we walked in, though we were shackled, it really didn't feel like it to me; it seemed more like a matter of mere appearance than actually being shackled! My first stop after checking in was the chow line; it was more like a dining hall; there were actual tables with chairs, pitchers and salt/pepper shakers on each table! The food was more like a regular meal than chow; in a sense that there was a choice of exactly what you wanted! When it came to the bread, you could take what you wanted rather than being force fed with just how many slices you could have! There was a real difference about the entire place; like an actual swimming pool and a life guard! There I was doing time, with amenities like that; it was all-but hard to believe! However hard it was to believe, it was real, it was true; I'd come to a prison facility where things were more like street than prison; more like I'd heard about in fed joints (Federal Prison)...The living area was a four man dorm; I was immediately known as [Clark Kent] because of my typewriter. Like then, I did and still do all of my typing with one finger on each hand! At any given time of the day or night, you'd hear a tick tick tack, tick tack tack tick tack... You'd hear me pushing out a poem, letter or something; yes, you'd hear this mild mannered reporter speaking a truth in one form or the other!

Then there was the matter of Imam; I did everything I could to avoid the position. I wanted nothing to do with it; tried very hard not to even get involved in with the discussion; but that was not going to fly with some of the brothers! The argument was different ahadith [Sayings of Prophet Muhammad]; it was further pointed out that I was Imam in Woodbourne, the Imam on the street in Westchester county Jail, Pen, as well as the Women's Unit, under a particular Warden and Captain; that was like the icing on the cake for everyone! I didn't argue, though I was still reluctant, and they could tell. I just wanted to get my time in and get out of there as easily as I could!

Before long, I was given my actual work detail which was more in line with what I'd actually done in the street; building and maintaining as it were! One of the first things we did was a floor outside; 2x12, 16 inches on center, with 3/4 inch plywood. This was a first for me since I'd been down, though it was right down my alley. I was having a good time doing something totally different than anything I'd done during my bid. Though it was nothing new to me, I'd not had the opportunity to make use of such knowledge for quite some time. After- all, there's no need for such when doing what I was doing in the other facilities! The man in charge saw that I knew what I was doing and was right at home as it were. He commented as such, and told me he had a surprise for me later! I had no idea that he meant my own work cart! Yes, he had made up a cart with some of everything in it, just for me! I went all over the facility; I actually went out front, though I'd go with him! He was a jolly old man, quite a fancy-free type of guy when it came to money. He got into a bit of trouble on one occasion when he attempted to help an inmate out. The inmate flashed at the wrong time, got caught and told on the old man! The old man was suspended for a short period, pending an investigation; then allowed to return to work; the inmate was sent back up north immediately! The old man owned a tug boat which he spoke about all the time; he'd speak about some of his many ventures, while I worked I listened! He'd have this glow about him, during such times; you could tell he missed those days! I remember one detail when I was in one of the living areas, on the first floor; had to fabricate a corner; I was really enjoying myself! Here comes the old man; he calls me to come and have some food! I didn't want to eat anything he had, not because he wasn't nice, but because he was simply one filthy person, literally! I told him; thanks, but I'm fasting; this meant I had to fast at least until I got off work that evening! I would've told him almost anything, to keep from eating something he'd brought in! From there he and I went to (Unit 1) where they were having problems with their dryer; we pulled the dryer away from the wall, tinkered with it for a few minutes; only to find out that it was not getting hot because the band was busted. He sent me back to the shop to get a band; he never bothered to lock the shop door! His thinking was: If someone was going to get in, he was going to get in; so, why not make it a situation that made less work for us; no broken doors, locks, etcetera! It made a lot of sense; he had a great insight for things, along with his own way of telling the truth …On the way back, the call was made for us inmates to return to our housing areas; I took the band to the old man, and started back to my housing area which was in Unit 2, on the second floor.

On the way back, I had to pass the mess hall; for some

reason I started thinking about being in Clinton, in the mess hall one day, during lunch! I remember that time in Clinton; at first, it was like any other day in The Last Strong Hold (uncertain); suddenly, there was an obvious presence of COs all around the mess hall! There had been a rumor out that two prisoners were going to have problems resolved, and that both had friends to side with them! You could cut the tension, with a knife! At the time, I was still in reception, and had just seen a Ku Klux Klan doll on top of the Christmas tree set-up on the 3rd floor in H Block! It was not a settling moment for me in any sense of the word; in fact it was quite unnerving! These guys did nothing to indicate that they were there for anything but to take lives and/or split heads; any heads which they felt were in the way of their main objective! I'm sure you know what their main objective would ultimately be; to return things to what they considered to be normal, return things to the rule of The Last Strong Hold…!! Well, nothing happened in the mess hall, and I was more than a little happy about that; because I was still in reception. I'd not yet gotten over the deadly beating of the brother on the third floor, or the two prisoners housed on the flats!! Bottom line, I was still well aware of the fact that these police had the green light to do whatever they wanted to do, and not have to feel that they'd have to actually answer to anyone! The warden was one of the primary killers there, in The Last Strong Hold; so they knew there was no reason to concern themselves. Though I was far from Clinton, I still thought about that place; I would probably do a lot of this throughout the years; after-all, I'd done much to make sure that those COs were able to do what they seemed to do so-well kill prisoners, split skulls, etcetera!

There was a lot going on in Arthur Kill, even though it was a Minimum Security Facility. Even with all that was going on I had a lot of my own time to do whatever I wanted to do! I had no idea that there was nonsense brewing on the first floor of

Unit 1! There was a Muslim housed there who'd gotten caught-up in some mess with a Puerto Rican guy. The Muslim was not carrying himself the way a Muslim should; so, the Puerto Rican inmate had no idea that he was even messing with a Muslim! By the time I got out of work, many of the Muslim brothers were waiting for me; "Imam, we gotta do something bout dis! If we let dis slide, we gonna hafta be takin all kina stuff from everybody here!" After finding out what was supposed to have happened, I agreed! I agreed with what was being said, though I didn't agree with the brother, his behavior, et cetera! The brother in charge of shurta had gotten many of the Muslim together without talking to me, so they were already in a let's take some heads mode! Though it was my responsibility to keep the Muslim community secure, it was not my responsibility to lead them to slaughter! What I did next was more in accord with Qur'an and Sunnah; I went and got ready to do what was possibly going to be necessary; then I met with all of the community, in the mosque! It was not an easy thing to; put a crew together to go to the unit where the inmate was, and attempt to talk with him! I wasn't sure he'd be willing to even have a conversation; but, I had to give him an opportunity to do so! I took the Muslim community to the top of the unit, told them to wait while myself, and four other Muslim went to the housing area where the inmate lived! There'd be a simple talk, if the inmate wanted to do so; should he decide otherwise, I'd have one of the Muslim go to the bottom of the unit, call the rest of the Muslim community, and we'd get busy!! When all was said and done, the Puerto Rican inmate admitted to planning to rape the Muslim, but he had no idea that the Muslim was in fact a Muslim! He (the Spanish speaking inmate) offered an apology, said he never would have messed with a Muslim, had he known; I had him and the Muslim inmate shake hands, and the matter was resolved! It was another thing where the brother in charge of shurta; and the brother [both Muslim] living in that particular housing unit, were concerned! As for the brother in charge of shurta; I let him know he should have never called any of the Muslim community together without talking to me first! The other Muslim brother was not behaving like he should have been; so, he was not even recognized as a Muslim; that bothered me greatly! That was not just bad, that was terrible; such almost caused the Muslim community to fight! Fortunately, the Puerto Rican inmate chose to talk to us rather than fight; had he decided differently, all hell would have broken loose! It was emphasized again and again, the importance of behavior and attitude; that we did not have the luxury of behaving like the rest of the inmates; we had to always be on our best behavior! It being said that we had to always be on our best behavior, caused many of the brothers to become resentful of their Muslim brother in Unit 1? Why was it so meaningful, how the brother behaved in the absence of other brothers? Maybe, just maybe it had something to do with the rest of the community being ready to go down for him! It's not that I was ever told anything like that; but I can't think of any other reason for such a reaction! Like in a number of other occasions, perhaps I'm simply in denial; just didn't want to look at things in a negative light! How I look at things should not matter; the truth should be the only determining factor! What truth am I referring to? Are there or are there not people who might be saying: If that guy was not recognized as Muslim because he didn't carry himself like one when other Muslims weren't around him in prison; what's going to stop him from doing the same thing when he gets out, on his own?! There is a sad reality; each person, ex-convict or otherwise has to be a Muslim for himself; every human being will ultimately return to Allah alone. One brother was so upset about things, until he said he'd rather be on his own, than with an idiot of a brother like that! There was really nothing the brother from Unit 1 could say;

after all, he was wrong! The other brother going out on his own was another matter! First of all, it was going to spread like wild fire; secondly, he was going to become a target for those who wanted to play the fool; and lastly, he'd not be accountable to anyone but the administration, should he possibly go off! It was not my opinion that there was any need to worry about him going off, but, such was not only for me to say; nor was it only me who felt that way! Such being the case, it had to be taken into consideration! A few weeks, the same brother from (1) Unit was boxed after our Family Day event (Eid ul Adha); he was said to have been seen smuggling drugs! It seems that his wife brought him some reefer in a balloon which he put up his rectum!!! He told me the truth about it, after he got out of the box; he said he took the drugs, and spread them all around the mats in the box; he broke the balloon up into small pieces and put them all around the box area also! He said he'd told me about it because he'd realized things weren't working for him outside of the deen, so he was going to really get serious about Islam; and this was a sign that he meant what he was saying! Allah knows what he did when he was finally released from prison! I didn't tell anyone that he'd spoken to me in detail about what had happened, since he'd spoken to me in confidence! The rest of the community seemed to place blame on the police, seeing that the brother was released without any charges; I never told them any different!

    I started putting time in the Law Library, I wanted either a furlough or work release, and this was the way to go about it. There were cases for some of everything, and I was determined to find a way to get what so-many others had gotten, using the law! Evening after evening, I went to the Law Library and sat with different books, trying to put things together which would work for me! There seemed to be all kinds of cases less fitting than mine, and they were not only getting furlough and/or work release, many of these prisoners were actually getting out of prison! I'd put in an application for a furlough or work release, when I was in Woodbourne, but it was denied because of the "nature of my immediate offense"! At first I was going to leave things alone; but, after receiving this transfer and finding things here so free and easy, I thought better of it! Like I said, there were all kinds of cases, and they were working for prisoners; I had to at least give it a try! Case after case after case; prisoner after prisoner after prisoner; I went through the books, putting my paperwork together! After I'd put together what I thought to be an excellent appeal, I submitted it to the Appellate court! This was only after I'd also been denied furlough and/or work release here at Arthur Kill; for the same reason for which I'd been denied in Woodbourne; (the nature of my immediate offense)!

I got involved with weights on my own time (no mosque or maintenance shop work). Since I began with cable weights, I didn't need anyone to spot me; for some reason, I did everything but legs. Perhaps it had something to do with the examination I had in Woodbourne; there were several doctors looking at my left leg; at the time, I had an unusual bubble protruding from one of the places on my left leg where I had surgery on the muscles, after I was stabbed in January of 1972! My left leg was paralyzed from the hip, down; I had surgery on the upper and lower leg muscles, leaving me with a drop foot and some foot paralysis! It wasn't long before I started using the 30 lb; dumbbells, to do butter flies. I also went to the 45 lb; single plate, for my sit-ups. In no time, I was using the loose weights for reclines (chest) which I began with two 45 lb; plates and the bar. It was fun, I'd go to the gym alone, workout alone, leave alone; I don't know, maybe the rest of the community was not into weights, or perhaps they came early in the day; whatever it was, I was alone and it was great, just great! Whenever I completed my workout, I was going to be bombarded by the community.

Muslims were going to have nothing but time, and they'd be looking for me to help them make use of it in the mosque. I had a very difficult time, getting us to "put the best construction" on a matter! It seemed to be so-much easier for us to find fault in each other, at the drop of a hat. But then, we weren't in prison because we were individuals known for having "good values and principles"! No, we were not in prison for doing the "right thing," we simply weren't known for that. So it wasn't and shouldn't have been expected, regardless of who we said we were! Truthfully speaking, putting the best construction on a matter was not something being done by anyone. Don't kid yourself, a human being, is a human being; right or wrong is not a religious issue, it's simply easier. I came into the understanding that no one gets away with anything in life. There was quite a bit of fault finding done amongst the Muslim community, and it kept me very busy! It might not have been as bad, had the frustration remained within the community; but, the frustration seeped out into the general population! There were non-Muslim coming to me with complaints about some of everything! I did what I could to get the community to understand how important it was to let what happened in Vegas to stay in Vegas, but it just wouldn't be. Some of the community members simply had a lot of mouth, and, shit happened!! There was a point wherein three brothers were going to be jumped by at least 15 white inmates. From what was said, it seems the brothers had taken something said in the mosque literally when it was meant to be literal. For about an hour I sat with the white inmates, trying to get them to understand that the three brothers had gotten the wrong understanding about what had been said in the mosque! At first it seemed like there was going to be a war. The Muslim community was not willing to let things just go; it was going to be an all-out war with the 15 white inmates and the Muslims. It took a few days, but, things worked out; we didn't have to war against anyone!

As time went by, I got involved with the Jaycees. Ultimately I became their V.P., then President; there was a pin given for each position. They came in from outside, making us a chapter within Arthur Kill (the county). We also had a Family Day event, allowing us to invite family members. The Jaycees events did not happen without incidents; there were a number of them, all dealing with drug smuggling! One inmate was caught smuggling reefer in; his wife was being watched from the very beginning! She'd been suspect as a result of activity in the visiting room! The police were watching the couple from the time the wife entered; so, when she did her switch, the police waited for the inmate to do his thing [balloon packing] up the rectum, then the police did their swoop. The couple was caught smuggling drugs, a felony for them both! Why would you allow your wife, girlfriend, or anyone to put himself in that position? In any case, he was put in the box, pending charges; she [the wife] was cuffed and taken into custody by State Police! I was somewhat disappointed that more of the Muslim community hadn't responded to the Jaycees; after-all, the Jaycees Creed was perfect for what we as Muslim believe!

The Jaycees Creed
We believe that faith in God gives meaning and purpose to human life;
That the brotherhood of man transcends the sovereignty of nations:
That economic justice can best be won by free men through free enterprise;
That government should be of laws, rather than of men;
That earths' great treasure lies in human personality;
And that service to humanity is The Best Work of Life…

One particular Friday, I dealt with the creed, almost word-for-word! From the beginning, I spoke about having faith in Allah, and that this was not a temporary or part-time faith. I went on to speak about the brotherhood of man when it came to nations being recognized! I talked about the human family being serviced; and how that family is humanity, every human being on the planet; free or otherwise (in prison or on the street)! Was it understood that I'd actually talked about the creed of the Jaycees; I wasn't sure. I didn't say so for whatever the reason. There were a number of guest, a few were there for the first time. Three took shahada [one black, two white]! This made five white inmates in the Muslim community; can't say any of them were there for protection, because Arthur Kill was just too laid back for that. It was too easy going, even though prisoners were being beaten, prisoners were being raped, and prisoners were being extorted! Arthur Kill had its problems, but being protected by the Muslim community wasn't a need.

I thought about Clinton, there was "no day room, TV room", for us to watch inside! I was able to watch TV in the kitchen/officer's mess hall on the fourth floor where I ate lunch as the clinic and sick call aid, if I wanted to. Other than that, if a prisoner wanted to watch TV; it was done in the yard. There was one in the area where the wood for the cooking courts, was chopped. It was under lock and key, in a box mounted to the wall; whenever the TV wasn't being watched. In Sing Sing, there was a TV on the flats (bottom tier), in the back, in a box also mounted to the wall, under lock and key. There the TV was watched at night during recreation time, while prisoners played cards, checkers, chest, et cetera, or just sat and talked; the prisoners were all from the same block (flats, tier [2] & tier [3]). As for Woodbourne, I don't recall ever seeing a TV. If you didn't find something to do with your time, you were just out of luck! At Arthur Kill my day was spent in the Pre-release Center or in the mosque; otherwise, I was in my cell. As Imam, I did go from block-to-block occasionally; but for the most-part, if I wasn't in the Center or the mosque, that doesn't include time spent in the yard. I was not the Imam in Clinton. As Imam, you had no freedom in Clinton as far as going from block-to-block was concerned. Your freedom as Imam came from your recognition by the other prisoners. Everyone knew who you were, and they came to you if they had an issue with the Muslim prison population. Though the police and prison administration gave the Imam "no freedom of movement" around and/or throughout the prison, there was one thing he had without question, he had his "honor block" cell; he was in the "honor block"!

Throughout the course of my stays, I'd done quite a bit of writing. You'll be able to tell writing from when I was in the N.O.I. [Nation of Islam] with Elijah, Malcolm and Farrakhan, from when I began to be a follower/supporter of W.D. Muhammad. In order to really read my writings, you'll have to read my book of Poetry in motion which should be out soon! In fact it had long been my understanding that not all Muslims in the outside communities were truly on the haqq [truth]; worshipping Allah/God, according to Qur'an [Book of God] and Sunnah [Sayings/Practices] of Prophet Muhammad. It was my knowledge of this that made it much easier to deal with and accept what was going on with "many" of the Muslims in Arthur Kill. There were in fact many differences between us as time went on; but it always came back to the Book of Allah [Qur'an]; and the Sayings/Practices [Ahadith] of Prophet Muhammad. There was never any further discussion when it came down to those two things; at least not with me! There were brothers coming in from up north occasionally; they had a much different attitude [more serious] about their Islam. I'd give individuals a few weeks before they'd get into the swing of Arthur Kill. Most of the brothers had never even heard of Islam until they came to prison or jail.

They'd been any and everything but Muslim in the past. It was clear to me that Muslims were for whatever the reason(s), held to a much higher standard! Anyone else could say and do anything; and nothing be said; let a Muslim sneeze without saying Al-hamdullah [The Praise is to/belongs to God]; it was talked about for days by almost everyone [Muslim and non-Muslim alike]! As Muslims, we are supposed to praise Allah/God when we sneeze; but that's not the point I'm making. What I'm saying is we are under the eye of scrutiny about everything; regardless of what it might be! I did not think most of the brothers would be actively involved in a Muslim way of living when they got out! In some circles Islam was known as being a religion for the black man or individual of color. People from other countries were not in any great hurry to let it be known that they were Muslim; and they certainly did not want to be attached to anything the black man was known for! This was one of the things which I found myself having to deal with when some of the brothers would come to Arthur Kill, from up north. Some of those brothers were really that far behind in time! I am not going to say I was then, where I am now; but, I was not simply lost. In fact, there were brothers who'd come in from up north who questioned having the devil (white man) in the mosque! Perhaps if we'd had a connection with the outside world (Imams from Central Office in Albany), we would have been better equipped to deal with those things. I saw no one from the outside, the entire time that I was in Arthur Kill. The State of New York is huge; for two men to cover the entire state was all but impossible. But, in my opinion; for two men to touch base with each prison, at least once every few years was not too much to expect. This was not done, and it showed. But, I was doing exactly what I'd told the judge I was going to do; this time was serving me, I was not serving it!

I don't know what it was, but I thought about Trash, his

situation with the aunt that hadn't given up on him; though he seemed to have done everything he could to burn any bridges which might have existed between the two of them! It was not a matter of there not having been a stable home, or Trash not being introduced to people who cared, early in his life! Trash was just Trash because he'd messed up early in his life, and didn't think things would catch up with him! He'd been down a long time and had given up on life; he was Trash, plain and simple; nothing more, nothing less! What was he doing now, what was he up to since I'd left for Woodbourne? Had he reverted, or was it enough of a start for him to be in actual contact with his aunt?! Then there was Bullet Proof, how was he doing? His situation with his wife, with the crowd who propped him, looked up to him and followed him around! What had he decided to do with and about that nick name?! He definitely had props as a result of that nick name. Was Clinton going to allow him the room/space necessary to be his own man, or would prison smother him?! I thought about many of the brothers in the Muslim community in Clinton, comparing them with the community in Arthur Kill. I understood the shock on the part of the brothers, once they arrived at Arthur Kill; it was like night and day! Those who had truly changed would be alright over time; those who'd taken hold of the deen of Allah, to merely help them pass time, would fall apart, over time! There was something people didn't seem to grasp; the fact that the shahada was not a mere prison utterance; when you took your shahada, it was for life, the rest of your life! It was strange to me when different Muslims would come to me, wanting to take Shahada again because of what they'd done/not done in their past; it wasn't until many years later that I really understood what they'd felt, however incorrect it might have been! Both in and out of prison Muslims have said: "Imam, I got caught-up in this, that, or the other thing! Imam, please let me take my Shahada again; because I stopped making salat/prayer!

Ya Imam, when I came to this country I went to work in a bodega, and I sold so-many things which were haram (unlawful). Imam, I won't go into what I've done, that's between me and Allah/God; but, I need to take my Shahada again; please give it to me again...!" The list could go on and on. It's sad, but true. The very thing which we as indigenous Muslim fight or struggle to rid ourselves of; brothers/Muslim from other countries fight/struggle to get a hold of! Over time, things changed for me; but, like I said; this took time! It was years later that it became clear to me what one was actually saying in his uttering the shahada! Had I the understanding then, that I do now; many of the individuals would have been dealt with much differently; they would have been given more clarity of understanding; of this I'm certain.

Though it wasn't as open, all of it was there; rape, robbery, extortion, et cetera was all there in the spot which Killed Arthur! As Imam and President of the Jaycees, there was nothing that happened which I was not privy to! As Imam, I would talk about different rapes, robberies, extortions, etcetera, but the talks would fall on deaf ears; as President of the Jaycees, dealing with the general population; I'd take issue with what happened here or there, but like with my khutba, what I took issue with, also fell on deaf ears! Prison being in itself, a society with laws, rules, regulations, values, principles and ethics; whatever, was going to be, was going to be; that's just how it was! Again I thought about Clinton; what happened there amongst the prisoners, I grew to expect; but not here in Arthur Kill. The madness in Sing Sing was even easy to accept, it was Sing Sing; a mad house, a filth pool; with murderers, rapist, child molesters, the works. Thinking about Woodbourne, I can't recall any of this madness happening there; what was the difference?! There was extortion and robbery I'm sure; but those things were for the most-part, isolated happenings! It took some time, but, old laid back Arthur Kill was a beast, waiting to be awaken; it had no problem claiming victims! There was nothing about a minimum security facility that gave me any indication that you'd have to worry about somebody victimizing you in such a way as might have you wanting to kill yourself. That is, until I got to Arthur Kill! That old, quiet looking spot had a lot going on! Yes, there was a swimming pool, a nice weight room, a gym, a beautiful yard, et cetera; but there were demons, beast; they were alive and real; who would make war with the beast!

The middle of the week meant my family, was not coming, my wife would not be inclining an ear! For some reason, I wanted, more than ever, to sit with my wife, laugh at and with my sons! My wife brought my oldest, son her step son, to visit me; it was my first time seeing him since being away! They would not allow him in to visit me because he was not on my visiting list; that was ridiculous to me! My wife and our two sons were already inside without him; I was told that he was outside, and that they'd not allow him in because of his name not being on my visiting list; I went off in the visiting room! They knew who I was; I remember everyone trying to calm me down; but nothing seemed to be working! I hadn't had a write-up since I'd been down, they were told that; but they didn't seem to care. They were not going to allow my oldest son in! It got to a point where they called for the Watch commander, because they knew they couldn't afford to have me (the Imam and Jaycees President) in the box; and on the draft [shipped out] behind some nonsense in their visiting room! I was taken to another room where the Watch commander and I talked about the matter of my oldest son and why he wasn't on my visiting list. The bottom line was that there were no visiting list requirements at any of the other prisons; so I didn't expect that there'd be any such need here! He went on to ask me about why he'd never visited me elsewhere; it was not even a matter of trying to answer that. I asked him what did any of that had to do with the present situation? He saw that I was getting frustrated; so he told them to let my wife put his name on my list, and let him in! After all was said and done, we had a nice visit; though it was much shorter than it could or should have been! During our visit, we laughed and talked about some of everything! The yard was open, so we went outside where we were able to enjoy the fresh air, bright sunlight, and other amenities available in the visiting room yard! I thought my two little guys had gotten bigger; but my oldest son had really gotten bigger. I hadn't seen him since I was down! That night, I thought about him; what did he feel? How did he feel? What was he thinking? Me not asking or talking about him; did I love him any less; what was it? I could tell myself what I wanted to hear; but was I telling myself the truth? In my heart I knew I didn't love him any less; but what was my mind telling me about his wants, his needs? While in Clinton I hadn't mentioned him even once; just how badly I wanted to get back to him was not even an issue! Was that something to be considered? That visit with my oldest son made me think about many things that I'd given no thought to at all! Why was that? He was not from my wife, but he was none the less my son! Not talking about his mom was understood; but not talking about him was not something that should have been tolerated; much-less understood! Was my being a part-time father going to affect him adversely? Would the time ever come that I'd wish I'd done more for him or been a better father to him? I mentally beat myself up.

There was not a day that I didn't go to the weight room to work on some part of my body; by that time I was all-cut-up! I'd gone from the 30 lb. to the 80 lb. dumbbells when doing inclines and reclines for cutting chest, and working on my wings; on the loose weights, I went from two 35 lb. plates and the bar, to double and triple 45 lb. plates and the bar; both wide and close grips when working my chest! I'd gone up from 100 lbs. to between 240 and 280 lbs. when working my back; I was also doing curls on the universal machine! The only place I recall any of the brothers being was upstairs in the gym, playing basket ball; as quiet as it's kept, that was fine with me because I did not need the interruptions while I was working out! The minutes, hours, days, weeks and months came and went, little, if anything really changed, until a boat [draft] came in one day!

There was one inmate/ prisoner in particular who came in; he was the prisoner from Sing Sing who'd broken his ankle [bones coming through the flesh, type of break]! I knew him immediately, but, he didn't remember me! I confronted him, asking him how he felt, how his ankle was! He wanted to know who I was and how I knew about his ankle! I told him that I'd been in Sing Sing, on the other side of the fence when it happened; that I saw some of the basket ball game! I went on to explain that I saw him and others go up for a rebound, and how he came down on the cross-bar at the base of the basket! He became very excited, wanting to know where I locked, et cetera! The fact that he'd been hospitalized and everyone else shipped to the four corners of the globe, keeping them separated, may have had something to do with how he responded when I told him who I was and what I'd seen! That was the only time I'd seen the brother; he must have made some noise, and was transferred out immediately! I'd been thinking about his situation; the brother was not letting it be known that he was finally in the joint with someone who actually witnessed what happened to him in Sing Sing! Yes, I told him my name, rank and serial number, so to speak; he should have had no problem locating me, or having me located! As for the noise; he was right to make noise; I just won't say he went about things, the right way! With what I knew, I can't imagine not running into or seeing him anymore; he must have been shipped out! In any case, I hope Sing Sing did what was necessary to correct that backboard situation!

One evening, I received some mail from the courts regarding my appeal for furlough/work release; I was instructed to go to the first floor conference room where I'd be afforded a chance to represent my case! I'd been denied both furlough and work release on two separate occasions; once in Woodbourne, once here in Arthur Kill! What would I say which was different than before!? I had about three weeks to get my presentation together, so I thought! Trying for a furlough and/or work release in this day and time, to be denied would be expected; seeing as how the media is doing and has done everything imaginable to discredit/condemn us [Muslims]! Being a black man was not, according to many, a gift from God; to be a black man and a Muslim, would have to be considered a curse! The day of my hearing came; being excited and anxious, I was early. There were several prisoners called before me, only one came out smiling; he was in for possession, and it was his first known offense. In my opinion, he should not have been here in the first place! They finally called for me; truthfully speaking, it was a waste of time; they had decided to deny me, before I even went in. I'd have done better, between a rock and a hard place! There was even a point wherein I broke down, crying; reflecting on, and talking about my family. To them, the only issue was my immediate offense being so serious in nature! Rather than sit and listen to all of their rhetoric, I got up and walked out. After-all, they'd made it clear that I was being denied again! The lawyer I had, had not even bothered to review my argument. He was a creep; he could have given less than a damn about my situation (my family)! After running things pass the guys with whom I played spades, I decided to bring the lawyer up before the Board of Attorneys; for inadequate and ineffective counsel. I know he could have made a much more persuasive argument than I had given him, had he put forth any effort at all! What I'd given the lawyer was simply for the purpose of ideas, not to present as my appeal. He did exactly what he should not have; he used what I'd given him, nothing more! It was a few weeks before I went to the law library to begin my paper work against the lawyer. Finding a lawyer to be inadequate and ineffective was new to me. But, I guess it was similar to how most black people felt about white America. This country didn't really give a good shit about what happened to a black man, an African-American, and it showed!

I thought about what Mr. Peterson had said about, "always know where you're at". I began to give circumstances and situations another look; only to realize that what was, wasn't as it seemed! I don't know what it was, but a week or so later; a psycho-therapist called for me. At first I wanted to have nothing to do with him. Even he saw it for what it was at the time; a waste of time! He called for me again about a week later, but he presented himself differently or so it seemed! Unlike before, he did most of the talking; he talked about my doings; wanting to know about my emotions during the last hearing! Again, like the first time; I was quiet, still didn't trust him; didn't think he was anything other than a means to an end for the administration! It took a couple more weeks for me to begin to open up to him; while I was feeling him out, he continued to talk to me about life and some of its liberties; almost as though he knew what I was doing! He did something which surprised me to the point that I was speechless for a moment; he told me he knew I was Muslim! It was not that I thought such was unknown to him; it's just that I didn't expect him to openly acknowledge it. He went on to let me know that he knew I was the resident Imam, as well as the President of the Jaycees there! I became more open with him! Twice weekly I would sit with him for an hour. We talked about me, what it was that made me tick. It was something, the way he was able to attribute many things I said and/or did, to my position as Imam or Jaycees President. He was very much on track. I was a person interested in the well being of others; wanting the best for whomever it was, regardless of race, ethnicity, et cetera! It made me think about Mr. Peterson again; him not having ever gone to college, and why he said he'd never done so! He said: "When you sign-up for a particular thing, you let the powers that be know one of two things: what you know or what you don't know! I made things even more simple; If they know one, they'd have to come to a basic conclusion about the other; meaning, if the powers that be know what you don't know, they basically know what you do know"!

Over the years, I've come to realize something which many people take for granted; there is one thing prisoners have plenty of, time to think; in fact most prisoners do nothing but think about how they can get over on the system; or another prisoner! Some prisoners look for the opportunity to sue the system (anyone who's a part of the administration); to them there are times when it's nothing personal, it's just a payday! I don't know what Mr. Phillips did or didn't know about what was going on in Arthur Kill; what did he know about was how the drugs were getting in; who was being extorted, raped, et cetera! As the weeks went by, the way in which he spoke to me changed; was he fishing or what? Whatever it was, I let him know my feelings; I was very direct with him! When he said to me: Anthony, those who work in the field of law enforcement (i.e.) policemen, detectives, correction officers, and so on, become overwhelmed by the stress of the profession at a much higher percentage than the public is aware of! I looked at Mr. Bob Phillips, and shook my head; I was literally awe struck for a moment; to the point that all I could do was chuckle and shake my head! Before I ever realized, it came out of my mouth; and it was probably all the more shocking, because I don't resort to such language. I said, Mr. Bob Phillips, please, please Mr. Phillips, the one thing I asked you not to do with me was what? I asked that you not to talk to me like I was stupid! Spare me the bullshit man! I know damn well that what you said to me isn't in any of those idiot books you're turning to trying to explain the mental state of those of us in this society! Don't tell me you believe that shit you just told me! If the commissioners of parole who sit before prisoners, do so with those types of sentiments; as asinine, and twisted as what you just told me; they deserve to have their asses kicked with steel toe boots! I started shaking my head again and chuckling, couldn't help it; I looked at Mr. Phillips as I chuckled. I said; I've heard some idiotic things before. If police on the street, law enforcement officers, peace officers, correction officers, those who work hands on with criminals, are covered and pardoned due to stress when they commit crimes; if individuals who go home every day, are unable to control their situation[s], then tell me how prisoners/convicts who live 24/7/365 for years and years are expected to correct a state of mind which is already vulnerable! Mr. Bob Phillips that's bullshit and you know it! He was happy that I was opening up and saying what was on my mind. He told me he was really pleased to have someone not afraid to be straight forward with him. He wanted to know why I was so adamantly against what he'd said about policemen, correction officers being overwhelmed to the point of committing crime themselves! I told him you have to be honest, these people have excellent paying jobs; with no reason in the realm of logic, to steal, push drugs, get into aiding and abetting, et cetera; but when they do they're forgiven. He is someone suffering from the affects of his job, he's therefore, not responsible! On the other hand; we have men, women and children who've had their personalities, characters, dispositions, morals, principles, values, and ethics; molded and shaped by the decadence of everyday crime; filth, evil and every indecency known to man almost from birth; viewed by the same system as pariah! You know as well as I, that this is simply a mouth full of crap! Here in prison are men who have become part of another society, 24/7/365. In order for many of them/us to survive, they/we take on a different self image; an image which many hold on to for years; others for the rest of their lives! You have many men who've never learnt how to read and/or write, being convicted of crimes. These same felons, many of them only go from bad to worse; because they learn what they didn't know; what they'd never thought about even wanting to learn! There is a system of government that is truly about one thing and one thing only; confinement, incarceration, imprisonment; say rehabilitation if you want to, but I know better. I live in, with and around it!! A rose by any other name, is still a rose; so, confinement, incarceration and imprisonment is one and the same; it has never, nor will it ever have anything to do with rehabilitating. Mr. Phillips, prior to my first day of high school, I was probably one of the most naïve black kids on the planet! If I, were to share what my mother and I experienced since that day, you'd label me a liar! There is nothing about this criminal justice system I trust, absolutely nothing Mr. Phillips! You think you "know" why I'm in prison don't you? I bet you're one of those individuals of the mindset, who believes; if it's on paper, and in the possession of the city, state or federal government, it must be the truth! Mr. Phillips look closely at my face; if I told you I had a 3" to 4" full beard at one time, what would you say? He smiled, and without hesitation he asked me what point I was trying to make. I asked him to just go along with me for a moment and answer the question! He said; "Anthony, anyone looking at your face would know you've never had any facial hair. I asked another question; would you believe I was between 5'7" and 5'8" tall when I was sentenced!? Of course you wouldn't; in light of the fact that I'm about 6'2" tall now! Well, in spite of the police being given that description, here I am! Besides, the burglar was brown skinned; do you know what I was threatened with Mr. Phillips? Furthermore, though the doctor told the police that I "was not" the individual who'd come back and forth to his home one day or night, and robbed him and his wife, with a sawed-off shot gun; it didn't matter; because when the DA found out about that, rather than call the doctor/surgeon; he called the wife to the stand to supposedly identify me! This is our criminal justice (just-us) system: If you don't admit to the charges, and accept our offer; we will indict you and take you to trial separately for each charge; and believe me, you'll be found guilty and sentenced to the max on each charge!! Mr. Phillips said our time was up; so we wrapped things up, with the understanding that we'd pick-up where I left off!

That meeting caused me to look at black inmates/prisoners differently; how many of them were here for no other reason than not having any money? For a long moment, I stopped thinking about any actual guilt factor. The fact that Arthur Kill was predominately black and Latino; there was no one who could tell me that we were majority of the committers of crime! I found myself thinking for a moment like I didn't have a care in the world; like people of color had become victims of the system; that they, just like me; had been victimized! It would not have mattered; except for a handful of people; me being/becoming an average black man would have gone off without a hitch! Looking at reality for what it was, that meeting with Mr. Bob Phillips had me on a roll that wasn't good. Being able to share my emotions with my card buddies really helped me come back to myself! For a moment, it was like I'd gone on a journey in time. There was a certain unreality that I was allowing to step into a real world! No, I am not saying the system is just; but everything isn't just cut and dry against black inmates! What I am saying is; though there's greater percentage of us in prisons/jails; we'd not be if we were not so readily available. Even with all of the stereotyping that goes on! Throughout the evening, I talked to different people on the unit about how I was feeling. After getting the much needed feedback, there was something that I had to admit; I was allowing my personal realities to impact how I felt about things overall! After looking at things from a cross section of guys, I had to agree; because I'd been forced into my situation, I was looking at the imprisonment/ incarceration of all black and Latino inmates, in the same light! Prior to this, nobody knew why I was down. I know how everyone says that they are innocent and don't belong in prison; but in my case it was true in part. I was innocent, whether or not I belonged here was another thing! I'd allowed myself to forget about the many things I'd gotten away with. In any case, things got back to normal for me; and I was able to do whatever I had to with only the usual problems!

The next week, Mr. Phillips called for me again; he seemed to expect me back into that condemning the white man, condemning the system mood/mode! I began with where we'd left off; but I was more pleasant. "Mr. Phillips, what do you think of when a DA resorts to clearing cases, he does so on the back of some poor individual with no means to buy justice! To me, a crime is a crime; and what's being done, what's been done is criminal. Or is this type of thing only criminal when we do it?" Suddenly things go from Mr. Phillips being pleased with me being open and willing to express myself, to: "Anthony, you're very bitter aren't you!? Let's talk about that…!"

There I was, sitting in front of someone who'd been thoroughly indoctrinated! I remember saying to one of the Deputy Superintendents of Programs where I was working as the Imam/

Muslim Chaplain for New York State in 1998; that prison is a world of its own! Prison is an apprenticeship program; prison is a graduate school; prison is a nightmare; prison is able to turn a caring heart, into a piece of cold flesh; prison is unlike anything ever misunderstood! Until I made the complete journey, I didn't and probably never would have understood all that prison is! I understood prison to be all of that from having been in prison myself. I found prison to be what it is, and possibly flourish as it does because of the deeply rooted corruption existing from the front door of the prison, to behind the doors where the shots are called, and the corruption condoned! I made it clear to Mr. Phillips that he would have been correct in saying I was bitter had he talked to me earlier in my incarceration. I didn't tell him that I'd taken a journey back in time just last week! I did tell him that it was conclusions like his cause men [prisoners] to not have sessions with therapists! I went on to ask him how many of the books which he'd read to get his different degrees, had been authored by men who'd been in prison!? I answered my own question for him; not a single one! It amazed me how people could sit behind desk, before professors; and listen to years of bullshit based theoretical, speculative conclusions which are anything but conclusive! They graduate with different degree levels wherein it's viewed that they're qualified to go out and spread theoretical evaluations about the hows, whys, whens, ifs and causes of behavior; criminal or otherwise! I observed something about the sessions which was very noticeable.

Mr. Phillips took obvious notes on our sessions in the beginning; but as we continued meeting, he'd seldom open his note pad; why do you think that was?! He asked me why I thought I was so angry, so bitter before; and why such was no longer so? I explained that when I was first sent to prison, I knew I was there for two crimes I'd not committed; that such had made me angry and bitter! I knew it was known by the detectives in both cities, that I was not the burglar with the 3 to 4 inch afro and full beard. Nor was I the fool who'd robbed the surgeon and his wife, [3] times in one night, with a sawed-off shotgun. That fact had been confirmed by someone while I was in the Westchester county Jail. It was hard enough having to deal with hearing a detective tell me while in the precinct viewing room: The doctor said you're not the one. To have Dollar [an inmate in the county jail] tell me [while laughing a bit]; it was his buddy who did it. He even bragged about it; damn right I was angry; bitter! Many things had happened since then; many things which I would have never been a part of otherwise. I've grown in Islam; as well as in my values, morals, principles and ethics! Grown in ways which I'm quite sure I would not have; on top of all of that, I've gained a lifetime of wisdom not available in any societal institution of learning. I told Mr. Phillips that this was if fact one of the last meetings he and I would have; but that it was very important that I share something with him! "Mr. Phillips, I don't want you to think I haven't appreciated our talks; they meant a great deal to me. It's important to know that only Allah/God knows whether or not I belong here; but I will say again what I said the day I was sentenced by the judge; I will not serve a single day; every day will only serve me! In my opinion, each day has done just that; they've served and will continue to serve me!" "Mr. Phillips, I don't want you to think I'm saying I've never done anything wrong; though I've never burglarized any home which people occupy. I've done my share of shop lifting; buildings that I'd entered were always burnt out, enabling me and a few others to rip out the copper, brass and lead; we'd take this scrap to a junk yard! The Lord of the worlds is always just in His punishing; I now understand and accept that I'm here as a result of punishment for some of my many indiscretions of the past!"

Though Arthur Kill was a minimum security facility, it was

casing an illusion. We know that some security staff and police are criminal and corrupt! They are looking for someone to place your faults and human frailties on; rather than owning up to them. I'll never come back for such! Allah has told us to "travel through the earth, and see, what was the end of those who came before us". The time I've spent in prison has put before and around me, criminals of every mindset; from just about every walk of life and up-bringing; what does it tell me the end was for their criminal behavior?! I refuse to give another human being that type of control over and of my life, ever again! Some make excuses by blaming the one he was with at the time. Like, I was with this brother; I was standing with some friends; this brother was giving me a ride...! Out of all the people in so-called free society, you happened to befriend a loser! The same holds true where the police are concerned. They know the difference between those who violate and those who do not violate the societal trust! When all is said and done, they claim to have nothing to do with the ones who violate. We know those police who feel that they have to play the part of second judge and jury of convicts. As for me, I was a guest in the house of the NYSDOC; and like any house that belongs to someone else, if it's not mine. Whoever the owner might be sets the rules and decides what the guest can and can't do. It's up to the guest to weigh things and decide what manner and method of approach will best benefit them immediately and over the course of time!

    I know I've come a long way to get to where I am today; but how far? Is something, either not clear, or simply taken for granted by most?! There didn't seem to be any doubt about the attitude of the majority of the prisoners; they really didn't seem to care about anything but trying to impress other prisoners negatively! I just couldn't accept the idea that people caught in crime, were involved in crime as a result of their jobs! I was equally against prisoners wasting their lives away, trying to impress; it was something which very few prisoners could attribute to anything but prison! Mr. Phillips could have set me up had he wanted to; because I was anything but polite, and easy to deal with. Instead of trapping me up, or trying to; he did what in my opinion, made it sense; he got what he could from someone capable of giving direction, focus, from a position of confinement [from a prisoner who was not simply going to say what he wanted to hear]! On a number of occasions I was told I seemed different since I started meeting with the therapist; that it was like I thought I was better or something! It's said that you don't see yourself the way other people see you. But, personally, the only difference I felt was that I finally had an opportunity to voice; to vent to someone who could make a difference, if he chose to! So I did really talk freely for what was probably the first time since being down. I'd felt like expressing myself many times; but something always said no. Only Allah knows; I could at best only guess what it might be! In any case, people were seeing a difference in me. I was a convict who'd run the gauntlet just like many of them. Perhaps the actual gauntlet course was not the same; but never the less, I'd run and survived! Yes, I'd picked up a few perks along the way; but that was, in my opinion, par for the course. Having been told by different individuals that I seemed different; like I thought I was better, I made it a point to give more of myself. I'd make sure I was available if and when needed! There were occasions when I'd show-up even if I wasn't called upon.

I'd not used a few of the nick-names of my card playing buddies on my housing unit. There was one brother name Bone Crusher, a big brother; another brother who made the throat cutting sandwiches, one can of tuna for eight sandwiches; he didn't have a nick-name, but he ate slowly all the time; I'll call him Eat Slow; the third and last brother, my roommate Fareed was already mentioned, so there's no need to introduce him to you. All three brothers; my card playing buddies had the same thing to say about me. Since I'd been meeting with Bob Phillips; I was more direct with what I had to say, I didn't seem to beat-around-the-bush, I didn't seem to be as vague; to me, they were saying the same things. How it's so easily forgotten or over-looked; the reality of the time being done now, serving time! This made me think about one of the Meccan Sura [Chapter revealed in Mecca]; Sura Asr [Chapter, The Time]: By the token of time through the ages, verily, man is loss; except those who have faith, perform righteous [good deeds], and come together, for the mutual teaching of truth; and exercise patience and constancy. There was no doubt in "my mind," the element of time had caused these guys to be in loss; even where the basics and fundamentals were concerned. As for faith, they had none; they had no intention of doing righteous, good deeds; they were not going to show forth any degree of patience, and constancy was absolutely out of the question; these guys were in serious, serious trouble! There was something even more distressing knowing there were a number of Muslims in even more trouble; because they (most, if not all of them) recite that chapter often, only to be amongst those lost! I can say the nick-names were serious components of time done; for each of them; they could have chosen to refuse being called such. Even if there are others coming against you, would being on the outside make a difference; or were you just a low-life; a dead-beat; et cetera!? I know you've all heard: To thy own self be true, for he who cannot be true to thy own self; cannot be true to any man. The only three things that changed since I was in that prison was, names, faces, and an occasional position change for me; but the game was no different; the game was still the same as it's been for only Allah/God knows how long! As Imam, I tried to direct us to a direction which would show us the realities of life that had eluded us! I was not going to force any of the guys to accept any of what I was presenting. There wasn't one of us who were there for being best in conduct; each of us was in prison for not being able to stand with or for dignity; in the literal sense of the word! There is another reality. For just about everyone breathing, it was so easy to find the fault[s] in a human being. It is so-terribly hard to see that human being as one with virtues. Why? I've talked to and had dealings with thousands of prisoners. I don't really believe or think I've tried to see good in any of them; not the type of good which is unselfish! Thinking about it for a quick second, I find it easier than I expected.

Just because I was the Imam and President of the Jaycees, that didn't mean I was liked by everyone. For some, I was just another nigger! Then there were those who thought I was just another jail house wanna be who'd go back to the street and do what convicts do best; get over! The fact that I held two important positions was insignificant; because I was a convicted felon first and foremost; the positions were only a way for me to do my time; as far as most were concerned, I was simply going back to the hood! It never crossed their minds that there was in fact a Muslim amongst them; from day one, I am a Muslim. This was known about me when I was in Sing Sing, when I was in Clinton, and when I was in Woodbourne; there should have been no reason to doubt this now that I was in Arthur Kill. I'd grown to know prison, even if I didn't want to! Yes, Clinton had done it all for me; Sing Sing was boot camp for me; boot camp, nothing more! Never in my wildest dreams would I've said to anyone, in truth: Sing Sing was not where I got my prison education; but, having been sent to Clinton for reception; then put into population there; I'd have to tell anyone; that Clinton was indeed "The Last Strong Hold!!!" My work detail[s], gave me an education unlike any other; I saw what few, if any see, first hand; in Clinton reception and population. I'd been and become a part of my own education! However, in truth, it is no different than any prison in New York State. Except for their classification, they were all up north in their manner.

What I'd proven to do best was, work with other prisoners. I'd shown that I was able to talk with them, and get them to talk when nobody else could! The Muslim attitude in the outside world was not going to be as it was in prison! Being around people whom you thought cared; doing what might have kept you in good standings; having Muslims brothers constantly around; worrying about getting caught doing wrong; getting help or being asked about needing help, et cetera; are not going to be a part of life on the outside. The race card was going to be played; leaving Muslims, especially Muslims of color to wander what in the hell is going on!

Having worked for the NYSDOCS for ten years, after having been a prisoner myself, I see that what I thought would happen actually is true. Prison has become a haven for gangs and gang members! In Downstate, the prison in which the majority of the prisoners in NYSDOCS come through; the prisoners actually come from every corner of the globe! It's a "maximum-maximum security" prison. Every gang, in the state is there! It's gotten to the point that they (the gang members) don't care; they care nothing about you or your life! While I was employed as an Imam/Muslim Chaplain there; I saw some very interesting things happen in the reception yard. Two incidents which I'll mention have to do with a gang member wanting out of the gang, and a quiet CO. I'd gotten information that a prisoner was going to be taken-off or killed for wanting out! Instead of letting him out, he'd been given orders to off (kill) one of the COs in the yard! He was not in agreement, that was known; he was supposed to get beat-down. The "BLOOD" who was supposed to push him into a cell had already been arranged. I arrived in time to save the individuals' life! The CO who was on duty was in too much of a hurry to get off work. He did not listen to anything that I said about the prisoners involved; or about the police being in serious danger. The next day in the reception yard; as sure as the day follows night, the quiet CO was almost killed while in the yard. The prisoner whose life I'd saved ultimately tried to do what he'd been ordered to do! The prisoner told me: "Imam, I had no choice; who was gonna protect me; you couldn't help me do my bid (time)!" What happened to that particular CO is well known by most of the CO in Down State! The fact that it could have very well been prevented had the CO listened to me the day before is not something ever talked about by anyone. Down State suspended me for allegedly "trying to incite a riot!" Even though I was allowed back to work, the intent was to humiliate me by having the front desk (entry) post a "Do Not Allow to Enter" on my Muslim Chaplain picture. Putting the picture up was a reminder to everyone. Everything they claim took place will be talked about in another book (Allah willing)! Wallkill was/is a "medium security prison." Everyone wearing glasses and receiving Public Assistance or Social Security in New York State is eligible to receive their glasses from Wallkill. All of the glasses for these people are made in Wallkill. The prescriptions are sent to the prison, from wherever the patients go for check-ups. Prisoners are tested to see whether or not they are capable of doing the necessary math to fill the prescriptions. Those who qualify are then trained and given jobs in the prison "eye glass" shop. There's much to be said about both prisons and about my NYSDOCS employment (Allah/God willing).

Brothers came to tell me that I was wanted back on my unit. They said I'd made "work release!!" I told them to stop playing games, and kept working; but they insisted that I'd made "work release." For them to say that I was wanted back on my housing unit to pack up because I would be leaving tomorrow! It wasn't funny any longer, and I told them so! They all knew

I'd been denied both "furlough and work release." I'd put in a complaint against the guy who was suppose to be my lawyer; for inadequate and ineffective council! They also knew I'd been told a number of times that I was just wasting my time trying to complain about my lawyer. I was waiting to hear from the Bar Association! All of these things ran through my head. It got to the point that I told them I'd go back, just to get them to leave things alone! So I put everything back into my cart; took it back to the shop, and went to my unit. When I arrived, the police had bags waiting for me. He told me to get my things packed, and that I'd be leaving for Fulton in the morning! I asked him to stop playing. The police told me I was about to get myself in trouble because he didn't have time to keep talking to me about packing up. At that point I didn't know what to think. So I went ahead and packed my stuff, though there was still that element of doubt saying: They're full of jive, why are they messing with me like this!? After I packed my things and took the bags up front, the police told me I had to remain on the unit until I was called down to leave. At that point I was just about convinced that something had happened. I wasn't sure; but something seemed to be going on. I could not believe it!!!

I am a Muslim, and I've grown and changed quite a bit; prison life had enabled me to see things in a way that I'd never seen them! As for knowing, that's an understatement; my knowledge of life had all but made a complete revolution! The person I was years ago, I no longer was. All these years later, with all the time that has come and gone; having given years of my life to the system of NYSDOCS (both as a prisoner and an employee); I saw life for what it was, for what it is! Whether or not I would approach life that way, only time would tell! The next morning, I was up and ready to go. I realized that the only change was going to be in the names and faces; the game was and would always be the same! That was something which would be the cause of many men going to and/or returning the joint (prison)! I had to think about something which Prophet Muhammad [pbuh] was reported to have said: "Live every day as though you will live forever, but as though, you're going to die tomorrow!" It would have been so easy to get upset with things not going my way [having to wait]; but life was going to be just like that! There'd be times when I'd have to wait; and times when I wouldn't. What was I going to do, curse Allah/God, and die; or was I going to accept life for what it was; both good and bad!? Yes, life was trying to show me that I'd become what I was because of what life was; both good and bad; that in living, there'd be times when I felt like dying; that such would be life, as long as life lasted!

Finally it was time, my stuff was already out front; administration had just been waiting for the van to come. There were brothers from all over the prison, in the main hall to see me off! Had I been told that I'd had made such an impression on the men, I would have called someone a liar; but like it had been said: A picture is worth a thousand words! Yes, I felt like I'd been carried to the door leading to the draft room; men from general population were even there; it was amazing, simply amazing! I don't think anyone in prison would have believed how the men reacted to me leaving Arthur Kill; especially after I'd said some of everything to them [both Muslim and non-Muslim], about their treatment of each other; lack of love of self, having no feeling of self-worth, et cetera!!! There were Muslims crying, some men asking me why I was leaving; men saying the administration was getting rid of me because I had too much power; and other men were just there with no verbal comments! Kidding [at least I thought I was kidding]; I recall saying: Y'all know you're glad to see me leave; that you're here just to make sure I leave; (ha-ha-ha-ha)! I didn't think they were hearing me or that they were listening to me; I guess it's more a matter of being willing and able to act in accord with what's being said, than simply hearing it! Perhaps that was why everyone accepted me being in the positions I was in with the Jaycees; because I didn't only talk-the-talk; but I walked-the-walk! Perhaps they saw someone who wasn't just doing time; someone who had a bid, and found a way to get through it! Of course I'm only speculating; but these are men; most of them who've been up north; have seen much; have survived the madness, and made it to Arthur Kill! I said; maybe, just maybe others in the positions which I had, had tried to play the men; got busted again, and were forced out! The attitude on the part of those guys made me think about what it was like leaving Clinton, and Woodbourne; though I had different details at each of those prisons, the men/prisoners seemed to react in a similar way! No, I did not have open run of Clinton; but I don't think it was a secret that I was the "first black" clinic and sick-call aid! I didn't give in to either the police or the prisoners; my attitude was the same in the yard, the clinic, the mosque or in the cell-block! As a Muslim, it was not something I ever tried to hide; Mrs. Johnston knew it; the police knew it from day one, as did all the prisoners; they all knew I was Muslim! What they saw, they eventually knew that that's what they were going to get! They came to know and realize that I was not just another jailhouse Muslim; one of those: I'll do my bid with this; but when I get to the street; I'll do me, prisoners! Like I'd said before; I'd been told on a number of occasions, that I didn't belong there and had no business in prison! The individuals who'd said those things to me, I'm sure they knew I was a Muslim. No question I am black/African-American!

Through the years I've made sure not to let what I'd learned in prison, escape me. The life of this world has a way of letting you beat yourself down; if you're not careful; and few are! You will not only beat yourself down; you'll beat yourself up! Knowing I was headed to Fulton, I was sure to continue trying to recall the ups and downs of days gone by. Again, prison life had given me eons of knowledge. Having it was one thing, using that knowledge to help make me wise, was another! You've heard me say time and time again that the institutions of learning, in so-called free-society never would have succeeded in teaching me what "prison life" had taught me. In a very short while I was going to have to put up! I was about to get a taste of so-called free-society. How was I going to handle it; what was I going to do? I looked back, there were quite a few guys waving; others just standing there! Though I was still in Arthur Kill, I knew it was definitely on me now; whatever I didn't know about Fulton, I'd have to wait until I got there, put my feet in the water, and feel the temperature for myself!

I don't know where my head was; but before I realized it, we were at Fulton! Getting in the van, riding away from the prison; going across the bridge, through the Bronx, is all a serious blank! I don't remember any of it; before I knew it I was in Fulton; on my way to my room! It having only taken about an hour, lunch had not been served and there was nothing for us to eat when we arrived. My bags followed me; and it would be an understatement to say: it was as different as night and day (Arthur Kill and Fulton). One of the first things I paid attention to was: there were "no fences;" not a single fence or retaining wall anywhere around the facility. Fulton could in the literal sense of the word, be called "a facility!" You had to have a great amount of self control in Fulton. That holds true in any joint; but if you made it to Fulton, self control was an absolute must! The windows to the street were right there. To open them and have drugs thrown to you was simply a matter of arranging to have it done! Why would someone who's made "work release," want to have drugs thrown in to them? Work Release didn't mean you've made the parole board; you can be hit at the board, with more time [a year or less]; and still have work release! You can have work release and not go out to work; because you haven't yet gotten a job. The street is still there for those who still want to play the fool! Whatever the reason, there were those who chose to use a window to take care of some kind of business. More often than not, people playing games were able to get over. There were unannounced occasions when people were called to give urine! Being suspect was not a thing to be; because you got busted [caught]. No one could tell me it wasn't a set-up; but people didn't seem to care! Most of the men in Fulton went out for work five days per week; they were going to do whatever they did.

Did I know who'd be looking to see whether or not I'd prove to be just another "jail house" Muslim?? Again, it was not my desire to proselytize; but trying to talk to some inmates seemed like such a waste of time! All of a sudden I didn't have time. Having dealt with people, both free and incarcerated years before I became an inmate, I was well aware that the street was going to be a challenge. Nor was it a secret that Islam meant different things to different people! I'd seen in prisons all across the state; Islam meant one thing to Tom, it meant another thing to Dick, and something else to Harry. Later, working for the NYSDOCS, I came to understand that Islam also had its cultures. The Book of Allah/God (al Qur'an), and the traditions, practices and sayings (al Sunnah and Ahadith) of Prophet Muhammad; meant something to the individual when it fit what he might be doing! Me too, having the background I had as an African-American; a former FOI and follower of Elijah; and a former devout follower/supporter of Wallace [a son of Elijah], with each prospective Islam had a certain meaning for me; right or wrong. I took it; picked up the different balls, and ran with them. It didn't hit me until years later that it took time; the element of time to bring me up from where I was and am now. What was it that kept me from realizing; that whatever will be, will be? Though I didn't have then what I have now; what I had been telling the general population was true. Though I had not openly used Qur'an and/or Sunnah unless I was talking to Muslim prisoners, the only thing that should have mattered was the facts. We will all give up; submit, surrender to our Lord regardless; some of us willingly and others unwillingly. Yes, there were different runs for me as a Muslim; each of them gave me valuable insight!

Believe or not, it had only been three years that I spent in prison. Upon getting work release, I went to a program that I was involved with prior to my incarceration; it dealt with minorities and the construction trade. They were quite willing to have me put to work. They got me a job with a company in Port Chester doing carpentry. Before going to prison, I was working also doing carpentry. At that time, the Union Representative tried again and again to get me to join the union, but I refused! See, as long as I was a trainee with the program, I didn't have to worry about getting laid off! In the program, I was making pretty good money; though I wasn't making "journeyman wages," I made more than a third year apprentice in the union; what sense would it have made to join the union as a journeyman, only to get laid off? Thanks, but no-thanks. I had not yet gone to the Parole Board, but I'd found work. I'd gotten myself a job, so I wasn't stuck in Fulton all day. Watching television all day would not become a thing which before Fulton, hadn't been for me. When I left out in the morning many of the guys were asleep; but when I came back in the evening, even those who'd been out all day were in front of the television. Even with the loose weights and weight machine right there, TV was their preference. Time came and went. I went to work, went to see my mother, spent time at home during the week, and returned to Fulton in the evening. Nothing changed; those who hadn't found jobs, sat in front of the television all day; those who'd been out working during the day, found their places in front of the television after they came in. As far as weights were concerned, I was on my own. No one bothered to join me the entire time I was in Fulton. Time came and I went to the parole board. It all went well, though I could not simply allow the commissioners to ask, and I not tell them a word or two about what was on my mind! Here is a bit of what I said during my hearing: Giving someone open sway over what I do and when I do it, will never happen again! No, I will never come back to prison. All of you commissioners will be on a bean soup line, before I come back to prison. Yes, you'll be waiting for a bowl of bean soup and a piece of whole wheat bread before anyone sees as a prisoner again! Ask whomever you want to ask, they will tell you the same; I am direct and to the point. To lie would only mean one thing; it would be saying I'm afraid of you, afraid of what you think! That would be absolutely untrue; either you accept what I am saying, or you stop asking me questions…There were a few more comments, but the truth is; these things did not have to be said. Maybe I just had to unwind. But I was still a convict; they still had the power to deny my parole. Fortunately, they gave me a favorable decision and told me they really believed I would never be back! A couple weeks later, I was out of Fulton, and on parole in Mt. Vernon. My construction work as a carpenter continued, and eventually I joined the carpenters union in Port Chester. Had my life made a 180 degree turn!? Time reveals all. The next time I stepped into a prison cell, it was <u>not</u> as a prisoner.

Afterword

AS FAR AS my different stays, there is much that I could have continued to say about them all; but when would I have finished? I will say again that Sing Sing served as a boot camp for me; and Clinton was as such that if I had a worst enemy, I would not have wished it upon him! Clinton was not a place to be; especially with the work details that I had! The "Last Strong Hold" was a fraternity; killing was the "order of the day;" and done with what seemed to be immunity! Many things that I did were done, and not talked about to this very day! What you have read hopefully will open your mind to imagine. But, you'll never really know what all I did to keep my chest going up and down! I smiled my way through this educational period. I still manage to come to grips with many truths of which many are not aware. With that, I will close; hoping that I will have time to write my other books! Each of them will give you much food for thought. My second book, which is actually a continuation of "Always Know Where You're At", will definitely allow you to see the NYSDOCS from a prospective unlike anything you'd probably imagine. Like I said earlier in this book; It is said: "Power corrupts, and absolute power corrupts absolutely!" Perhaps had I not been on the other side of the fence at one time, I'd think like many of you. I'd see the correctional system as a system that is rehabilitating offenders as it says it is doing. If you've never been in prison; if you've never been a Muslim in prison; the best you could have done is speculate! May this writing help many to better understand. AMEN!

CPSIA information can be obtained at www.ICGtesting.com
Printed in the USA
BVOW03s0555070714

358228BV00001B/5/P